3000 Miles in the Great Smokies

William A. Hart Jr.

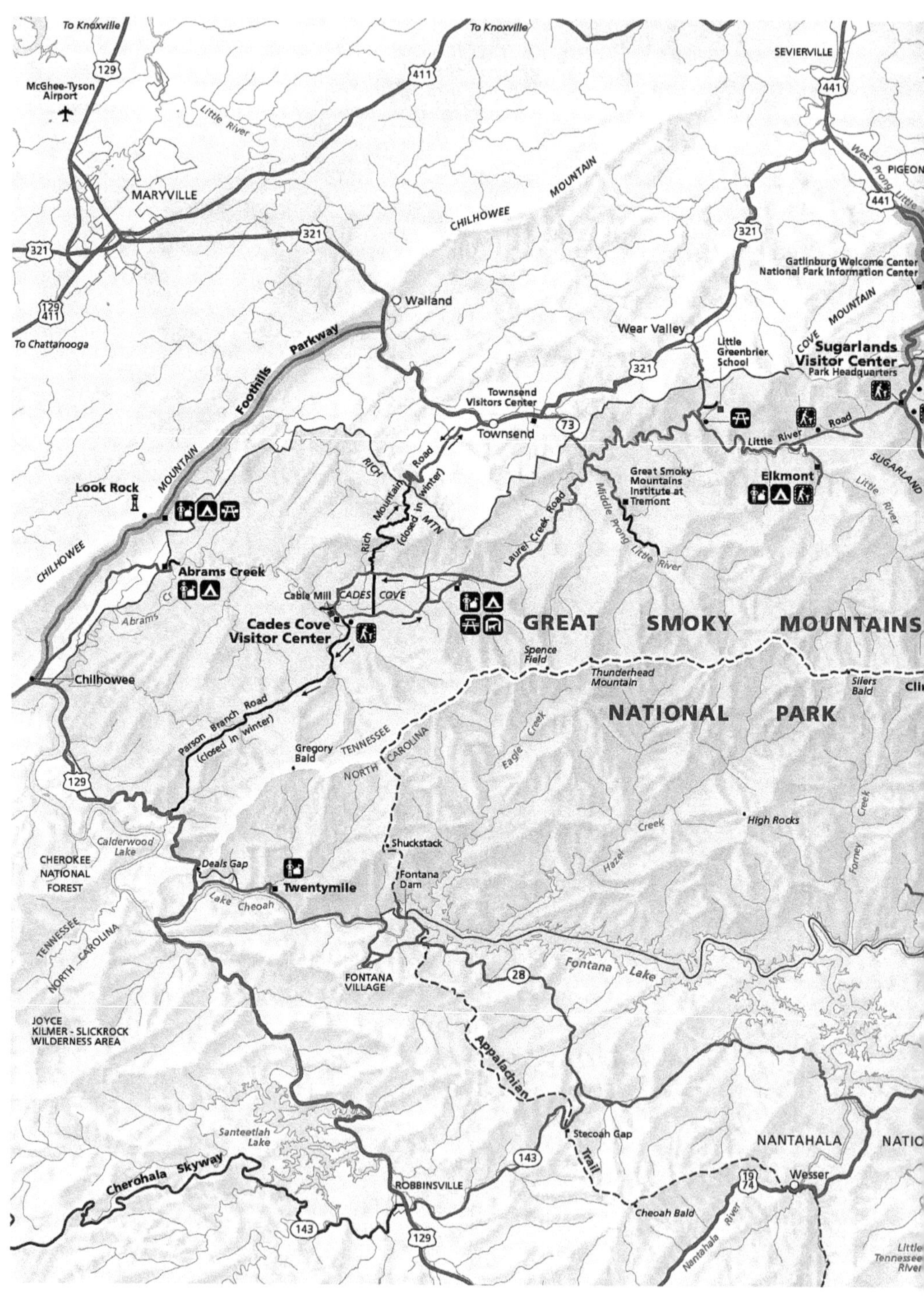

To Knoxville
To Knoxville
SEVIERVILLE
McGhee-Tyson Airport
Little River
MARYVILLE
CHILHOWEE
MOUNTAIN
PIGEON
West Prong Little
Gatlinburg Welcome Center
National Park Information Center
Walland
To Chattanooga
Foothills Parkway
Wear Valley
Little Greenbrier School
COVE MOUNTAIN
Sugarlands Visitor Center
Park Headquarters
Townsend Visitors Center
Townsend
Little River Road
SUGARLANDS
Elkmont
Great Smoky Mountains Institute at Tremont
Middle Prong Little River
Little River
RICH
Rich Mountain Road
(closed in winter)
MTN
Laurel Creek Road
Look Rock
MOUNTAIN
CHILHOWEE
Abrams Creek
Abrams
Cable Mill
CADES COVE
Cades Cove Visitor Center
GREAT SMOKY MOUNTAINS
Spence Field
Thunderhead Mountain
Silers Bald
Chilhowee
NATIONAL PARK
Parson Branch Road
(closed in winter)
Gregory Bald
TENNESSEE
NORTH CAROLINA
Eagle Creek
High Rocks
Creek
Hazel Creek
Forney
Calderwood Lake
CHEROKEE NATIONAL FOREST
Shuckstack
Deals Gap
Twentymile
Fontana Dam
Lake Cheoah
TENNESSEE
NORTH CAROLINA
FONTANA VILLAGE
Fontana Lake
JOYCE KILMER - SLICKROCK WILDERNESS AREA
Appalachian Trail
Stecoah Gap
Santeetlah Lake
NANTAHALA
Cherohala Skyway
ROBBINSVILLE
Wesser
Cheoah Bald
Nantahala River
Little Tennessee River

To Newport
Exit 443
CHEROKEE NATIONAL FOREST
Foothills Parkway (closed in winter)
Cosby
Little Pigeon River
Pigeon River
Exit 451
TENNESSEE
NORTH CAROLINA
Pittman Center
Mount Cammerer
Cosby Creek
Big Creek
Greenbrier
Middle Prong
Mount Guyot
Mount Sterling
Waterville Lake
Roaring Fork Motor Nature Trail (closed in winter)
Appalachian Trail
BALSAM MOUNTAIN
Mount Le Conte 6593ft 2009m
Charlies Bunion
Chimney Tops
Cataloochee
Cataloochee Creek
PISGAH NATIONAL FOREST
Cove Creek Rd
Newfound Gap 5046ft 1538m
Balsam Mtn Rd
Exit 20
Appalachian Highlands Science Learning Center
Newfound Gap Road
Oconaluftee River
Bradley Fork
Raven Fork
Smokemont
Balsam Mountain
Heintooga Ridge Road (closed in winter)
Big Cove Road
Black Camp Gap
Blue Ridge Parkway
Mingus Mill
Maggie Valley
Dellwood
Oconaluftee Visitor Center
Mountain Farm Museum
To Asheville
Soco Gap
CHEROKEE INDIAN RESERVATION (QUALLA BOUNDARY)
Deep Creek
CHEROKEE
Soco Creek
Waterrock Knob
WAYNESVILLE
BRYSON CITY
PLOTT BALSAMS
Tuckasegee River
ALARKA MOUNTAINS
SYLVA
Dillsboro
Blue Ridge Parkway
North
Roads in park are closed to commercial vehicles.
Unpaved road
One-way road
Historic structure(s)
Ranger station
Developed Campground
Picnic area
Self-guiding trail
Horseback riding (rental)
Observation tower
0 1 Kilometer 5
0 1 Mile 5
To Atlanta

Published by The History Press
Charleston, SC 29403
www.historypress.net

Copyright © 2009 by William A. Hart Jr.
All rights reserved

All images courtesy of the author unless otherwise noted.

First published 2009
Second printing 2010

ISBN 978.1.540229359

Library of Congress Cataloging-in-Publication Data
Hart, William A.
Three thousand miles in the Great Smokies / William A. Hart, Jr.
p. cm.

1. Great Smoky Mountains National Park (N.C. and Tenn.)--Description and travel--Anecdotes. 2. Hart, William A.--Travel--Great Smoky Mountains National Park (N.C. and Tenn.)--Anecdotes. 3. Hiking--Great Smoky Mountains National Park (N.C. and Tenn.)--Anecdotes. 4. Natural history--Great Smoky Mountains National Park (N.C. and Tenn.)--Anecdotes. I. Title.
F443.G7H37 2009
976.8'89053092--dc22
[B]
2009021534

Notice: The information in this book is true and complete to the best of our knowledge. It is offered without guarantee on the part of the author or The History Press. The author and The History Press disclaim all liability in connection with the use of this book.

All rights reserved. No part of this book may be reproduced or transmitted in any form whatsoever without prior written permission from the publisher except in the case of brief quotations embodied in critical articles and reviews.

Contents

Acknowledgements

I owe special thanks to my father and mother for introducing my sister and me to the Great Smoky Mountains National Park on family camping trips. These outings provided an opportunity for my first walks in the Smokies and instilled in me an everlasting love for the park.

I am also particularly indebted to my wife, Alice, with whom I have shared some of my most memorable outings. Her understanding of my urge to "go to the mountains" and encouragement to create a permanent record of my trips has made both my outings and this book possible. She has been an invaluable resource in creating *Three Thousand Miles in the Great Smokies*. I owe everything to her.

Special thanks go to my daughter, Sara Hart Stewart, and son, Bill, for joining me on many trips from their earliest years to the present. My time with them is treasured. Many friends have contributed to my enjoyment of the Smokies. I have warm memories of all of them. Likewise, I have fond memories of my Boy Scouting days and the Scouts who journeyed to the Smokies with me. The names of both groups follow. I extend my apology to any persons whose names I have inadvertently omitted.

Outing Companions

Bert Abrams
Darlene Abrams
Gene Baldwin
Don Barrow
Woody Brinegar
Anne Broome
Joan Cabe
Jim Campbell
Karen Campbell
Bud Cantrell
Geoff Cantrell
Mark Cantrell
Patricia Cabe Cantrell
Kim Carter
Larry Carter
Unal Cetindre
Al Coggins
Tom Downs
Bob Foxx
Chan Gordon
Miegan Gordon
Mike Harrington
Alice Hart
Lisa Hart
William (Bill) A. Hart III
William (Will) Houston Hart
Susie Heinmiller
Elizabeth Hill
Robert Hill
Ed Hina
Jay Hohmann
Alan Householder
Marv Hyatt
Claudia Konker
Rob Kranich
Keith Lasater
Lynne Lasater
Dan Lawson
Jerry Ledford
Tom Lucas
Mel Nerby
Carol Newsome
David Newsome
John Palmer
Jerome Parker
Johnny Phillips
Phil Pritchard
Tim Randall
Danny Ray
Jack Reynolds
Wayne Shepherd
Emily Spears
Jim Spears
Parker Spears
Sara Hart Stewart
Scott Stewart
Marilyn Sullivan
Ron Sullivan
Eric Tamler
Dot Titcomb
Al Watson
Evelyn Watson
Bob Weinkle
Ronald Welch
Jim Westall
Richard Wilson

Boy Scouting Companions

Bruce Adams
Bruce Abbott
Mark Ashley
David Baldwin
Curt Brown
Randy Bumgarner
Russ Campbell
David Coggins
Paul Coggins
David Crawford
Al Dunn
Bryan Fuller
Patrick Hoover
Keith Lindberg
Alton Malbon
David Plott
Jonathan Plott
G. Pressley
Monty Reagan
David Reynolds
Joey Reynolds
Doug Sams
Jamie Westal
Bobby Weinkle
Andy Young

I want to express special thanks to the following: Robert Hill, the best camping companion one could ask for. I have walked more miles in the Smokies with Robert than with any other person and enjoyed every mile. I also want to thank Al Watson, who is always a willing and adventurous off-trail explorer and with whom I have taken many arduous and interesting trips; Ed Hina, for his off-trail prowess and for the wonderful outings we shared; Bob Foxx, for many pleasant fishing trips in the Smokies and for the many fun-filled evenings before a campfire; Ron and Marilyn Sullivan, for our time together exploring forgotten logging rail grades and for imparting their knowledge about the history and technical aspects of Smoky Mountain logging; writer Geoff Cantrell and his father, Bud Cantrell, a former Great

Smoky Mountains National Park ranger, for communicating their special Smoky Mountains knowledge and experiences; and to Bob Weinkle, a delightful and trusted companion with whom I shared many memorable Boy Scout outings. Finally, I want to thank Chan and Miegan Gordon, special friends, who have encouraged my writing and who read poetry on a wonderful outing in the Smokies.

I also want to express appreciation to the following for helping make this book a reality. Unending gratitude goes to my wife, Alice, for her tireless efforts throughout the publication effort. And special thanks to daughter Sara, son-in-law Scott Stewart, son Bill and daughter-in-law Lisa for reading and commenting on the manuscript and providing technical assistance. Also, thanks go to Geoff Cantrell for reading and commenting on the book and to Kathy Noyes for technical assistance in a time of special need. And a special word of appreciation is due Laura All, Ryan Finn and their colleagues at The History Press for their guidance and support in the completion of *Three Thousand Miles in the Great Smokies.*

Through the years, I have met many dedicated employees of the National Park Service while in the Smokies. All have been friendly, courteous and helpful. My thanks go to all these persons, with a special acknowledgement to Tom Robbins and Pam Boaz, former employees, and to Kent Cave, supervisory park ranger, for their friendship and for generously sharing their knowledge of the Smokies. My pipe, "Old Danger," crafted in 1968 from a rhododendron burl, traveled the length and breadth of the Smokies with me and provided much pleasure before I gave up pipe smoking a number of years ago. Old Danger figures into some of my accounts and thus deserves mention here.

Finally, I wish to express gratitude to those persons whose early efforts resulted in the establishment of the Great Smoky Mountains National Park. My thanks and appreciation go to all those who continue the work of protecting, preserving, maintaining and sustaining the park in countless other ways. The unique attributes of this significant global resource would be lost forever without the continuing efforts of these dedicated men and women.

Introduction

My introduction to the Great Smoky Mountains National Park occurred during boyhood camping trips with my family. During these outings, my father and I took occasional day hikes along park trails. Through such walks I first learned of the mystery and grandeur of the Smokies.

Two hikes stand out in my memory because of the impression they made. The first was a walk from Hientooga Overlook toward Pin Oak Gap. Endless ranges of blue mountains spread into the distance, creating the perception that the Smokies were boundless. The second hike was to magnificent Alum Cave Bluffs. Upon reaching this awesome landmark, I noticed that the trail continued upward past a trail sign indicating the distance to Mount Le Conte and Mount Guyot. These landmarks seemed remote and mysterious, and thoughts of them created lingering curiosity about their location.

The passage of years did not erase the memories of these early trips. Time only served to magnify my curiosity and to evoke a deep yearning to visit the seemingly mystical Mount Le Conte, Mount Guyot and Pin Oak Gap. My yearning to visit the Smokies intensified over the years, and following college I began to make increasingly frequent trips intent on establishing more than a casual acquaintance with this vast boundary.

As the frequency of my walks in the Smokies increased, each visit began to take on a different meaning. I could not pass flowers and shrubs without having questions about their identities. Remains of old homesteads, outlines of old fields and rustic cemeteries led to wonderment about patterns of settlement and early life in the Smokies. Old roads, faint paths and abandoned rail grades caused me to wonder where they led and what secrets they held. Mountain peaks and place names bespoke of people and events of the past. In an effort to gain a layman's knowledge about the Smokies, I began to read about the history, flora, fauna, lore and music of the area and satisfied some of my curiosity.

However, each visit resulted in new questions and more reading and study. What began as a mere curiosity evolved into a desire to visit all parts of the Great Smoky Mountains National Park to become thoroughly familiar with the many facets of these majestic mountains. Thus, I pursued my desire to become thoroughly acquainted with the Smokies with regular visits for over forty years.

Walking three thousand miles in the great Smokies has not been my goal. These miles are a byproduct of a quest that has provided many pleasant outings and varied experiences, often shared with family and friends. I have created a record of most of these trips to document my experiences, observations and reflections. This record of backpacking trips, day hikes and fishing excursions is the source for this book.

The purpose of *Three Thousand Miles in the Great Smokies* is to recount my experiences in the hope that others who share similar interests may find enjoyment in these accounts. Also, I hope that this book will have some value in future years as a commentary on "how things were" and answer questions for others that Harvey Broome's *Out Under the Sky of the Great Smokies*, Paul Fink's *Backpacking Was the Only Way*, Horace Kephart's *Our Southern Highlanders* and George Masa's photographs and pioneering hiking information answered for me.

A Note Regarding Entries

Three Thousand Miles in the Great Smokies is organized to describe the location of many entries; however, in certain instances only general information is provided, reflected by "Somewhere in the Smokies" to protect sensitive places. Most accounts include some or all of the following, as appropriate: date, descriptive title, location and trail. In a number of cases, the same date and location appear in different sections of the book to allow me to record multiple experiences on a single outing.

I have recognized companions who shared my outings by referring to them by first name. In cases where two or more people share the same first name, I have included the first initial of their last name the first time the name is mentioned to distinguish between them. All of these persons are recognized in my acknowledgements.

For those interested in learning more about the trails of the Smokies, I encourage the reader to purchase *Hiking Trails of the Smokies*, published by the Great Smoky Mountains Association.

The Human Element

Some of my fondest memories of my trips to the Great Smoky Mountains National Park relate to those who shared outings with me or to people I met during these outings. Every experience was different, reflecting dimensions of fellowship, humor, requirements for assistance and even sadness. Regardless of the nature of these encounters, all were interesting and added to my enjoyment of the Smokies.

Interesting Encounters

A Man with a Pan

Deep Creek Trail

August 26, 1965

Bob F. and I walked along the upper reaches of the Deep Creek Trail through a virgin forest of hemlock, tulip poplar and mixed hardwood trees and marveled at the beauty that surrounded us. Masses of rhododendron covered the mountain slopes bordering the headwaters of Deep Creek, which meandered at their base. This beautiful scene seemed cloaked in a perpetual dusk, created by tall trees that allowed only a few shafts of light to penetrate the leafy canopy. The day was windless, and this wild forest was quiet except for occasional bird songs and the whispering of the stream.

As we descended along the trail near the stream, we observed a small man in his late sixties working his way along the edge of the stream, intently angling for trout. He was dressed in faded blue overalls and a gray work shirt. A worn felt hat rounded out his attire. The most unusual aspect about the man was the fact that a rusty steel frying pan was tied to his overalls by a short piece of cord.

When we drew near, we clambered down the bank and hailed the gentleman with the common mountain query, "Doing any good?" In response, he opened his canvas creel and displayed several trout approximately eight inches in length. As Bob and I planned to fish later in the day, I was interested in the lure that led to the man's success and asked what he was using. I expected him to reply with the name of a common fly pattern; however, instead of the expected response, the man replied without hesitation, "red worms." Although the use of natural bait is prohibited by park regulations, our acquaintance was determined to take a few trout home for supper as a reward for his eight-mile round trip. Thus, red worms, a guaranteed source of success, were chosen despite the prohibitions to the contrary.

Further discussion determined that the man was from "Haywood" (Haywood County, North Carolina); however, he made no mention of the frying pan, as if it was a customary part of his dress. Eventually, our curiosity motivated us to inquire why he carried the rusty pan, and the answer was revealed. Five years earlier, our acquaintance told us, he had camped at the Poke Patch Campsite and fished the upper reaches of Deep Creek. Rather than carry all of his gear up the steep trail to Thomas Divide, he had hidden some of it, including the frying pan, in a hollow tree. He had reclaimed his pan on this trip. He told us that this was the only item remaining from his cache. "Reckon the bears got the rest," he commented tersely.

A Man without a Cap

Poke Patch Campsite; Deep Creek Trail

August 26, 1965

Bob F. and I left the man with a pan and continued on to Poke Patch, a small clearing in the midst of the forest with the comforts of one primitive log table. The moment we entered the campsite, two horsemen arrived from the opposite direction. We exchanged greetings, and the two immediately departed, only to return twenty minutes later. This time, they dismounted and commenced to search through the rubble in the trash pit below the campsite. Such trash pits existed before the days of "Leave No Trace Camping." After fifteen minutes, they gave up their rummaging and approached us with concerned looks on their faces. Finally, one of the horsemen asked, "Do you have a bottle cap?"

Admiring the view from Silers Bald, July 1967.

Bob and I might have expected a request for matches, a piece of rope or some common camping item but not a bottle cap! This request was beyond our imagination. But his puzzling request was solved quickly when one of the riders produced a pint bottle of white liquor and explained his plight. The previous year, he had hidden the moonshine in a tree while camping at Poke Patch. Upon retrieving his bottle on this trip, he found that the cap had rusted entirely through. This created the need for a replacement. To prove that the contents were the real thing, he gave us a whiff before mounting and riding away without the required bottle cap. Now, I have heard of "rot gut liquor"; however, this was the first time that I had encountered "rot bottle liquor," obviously a very potent brew. We suspected that if the liquor had been left another year the bottle would have been completely destroyed.

Swallowed What?

Ice Water Springs; Appalachian Trail

September 12, 1969

Larry, his son, Kim, and I left Newfound Gap late in the afternoon and walked the Appalachian Trail to Icewater Spring, arriving there after dark. The upper shelter was occupied, so we moved to the old log shelter below, now removed, laid out our gear, gathered wood, built a fire and prepared supper.

While we relaxed about the fire after supper, one of the men camped at the upper shelter joined us around the fire. "Excuse me," he said in a shaky voice. "My wife just swallowed some kerosene. She drank two quarts of powdered milk and vomited. What else should we do?" he implored. After this introduction, the man explained that the party's water and kerosene were in similar bottles and stated that his wife had taken a swallow, mistaking the one for the other.

I pondered the situation and recalled hearing of livestock being treated with kerosene, but particulars escaped me. I assumed that kerosene had medicinal value in small doses; however, this hardly seemed an appropriate time to mention this bit of arcane information to the concerned husband.

Kim carried a first aid reference with him, and Larry consulted this source for an appropriate treatment. At length, Larry began to read from the section on poisons. After reading one paragraph aloud, he began reading silently without explanation. Finally, Larry spoke with the aplomb of a doctor and said, "I believe your wife will be all right." The young man gave a sigh of relief and departed.

When he left, I asked Larry why he had stopped reading aloud. He responded by reading the remainder of the instructions from the first aid guide. The instructions advised against inducing vomiting. Because the amount of kerosene ingested was small, we concluded that significant ill effects were unlikely.

The next morning, we visited with the woman and found her well. We parted company with our neighboring campers, relieved that no lasting harm had resulted from this mishap.

The Human Element

A Love for the Area

Hazel Creek Trail Between Proctor and Sawdust Pile

September 1, 1978

Robert and I arranged to be transported from Fontana Marina across the mirror-smooth waters of Fontana Lake to the mouth of Hazel Creek. As we gazed toward the Smokies, wispy white clouds lifted, revealing dark blue slopes on the north shore of the lake. I had been intrigued by the romance of Hazel Creek for years, and this was my maiden trip to become acquainted with this historic part of the Great Smokies.

After embarking, we followed an old road that led in half a mile to the site of the town of Proctor, a logging town that had once boasted one thousand residents at the peak of the logging era. The center of activity at Proctor was a large band mill operated by the Ritter Lumber Company that was capable of producing many thousands of board feet of lumber per day. Stores, a theatre, a school, many residences and other buildings associated with logging operations made up the town. The forest was reclaiming the town, and only a few traces remained of Proctor's past glory.

The Granville Calhoun House, now used as quarters for the National Park Service personnel, sat adjacent to a beautiful section of Hazel Creek. Mr. Calhoun, a friend of Horace Kephart's, must have cherished the fine setting when Proctor was a thriving town. Beyond the Calhoun House were the skeletal remains of the sawmill's brick kiln building and a depression that had been the mill's log holding pond. Both were choked with touch-me-nots, briars and weeds. There was little to remind us of the logging era, when struggling steam engines moved large logs from the very crest of the Smokies to this location to be cut into lumber.

Robert and I had not gone more than a mile beyond the old mill site when we stopped to talk with two trout fishermen who we met on the trail. The older of the two men told us that he was a former resident of Hazel Creek. He shared how his love for the area brought him back year after year to visit his home territory and to angle for trout. During our discussion, he recounted how he had helped his father move the last residents from Hazel Creek after Fontana Dam began to back up the waters of the lake and how "the water came up to the running boards" of his father's truck as they moved friends and family away from the land they loved. He also pointed out the bridge near where we stood and told us that the bridges were so unstable when he was a youth that the school bus stopped before crossing the creek and the passengers walked across the bridge and reboarded the bus on the other side.

Passing through Proctor confirmed for Robert and me that it is only a vanished memory of another time. However, in the minds of those who once lived there, Proctor and Hazel Creek are alive with the treasured memories of family and friends and of life lived in a thriving and vital community.

A Beautiful Language

Sugar Fork Campsite; Hazel Creek Trail

September 1, 1978

Robert and I enjoyed a leisurely walk along the Hazel Creek, stopping frequently to admire stretches of rushing water and pools such as the Brown Hole, with its slow swirls and eddies. This relaxed pattern of travel brought us eventually to the Sugar Fork Campsite, where we made camp on a small flat area bordered on one side by Hazel Creek and Sugar Fork on the other.

During the afternoon, we walked the old road along Bone Valley Creek and eventually reached the gray weathered Hall Cabin, the last remaining cabin on Hazel Creek, where we rested in the September warmth and gazed at the verdant mountains beyond. Afterward, we returned to camp, prepared supper and enjoyed the evening cool.

Two other campers joined us about dusk, and in time the four of us gathered for conversation around a small campfire. One of the men looked familiar to me, but he obviously did not recognize me. After searching my memory, I remembered meeting him on Raven Fork years before and even recalled his first name, although his last name escaped me. I addressed him by his first name, and his face reflected amazement with a "how did you know that?" look. When I reminded him of our first meeting, our friendship was rekindled.

My acquaintance, who was a member of the Eastern Band of the Cherokee, told about his childhood as we sat around the flickering fire. He said that he had been permitted to speak only the Cherokee language at home when he was growing up. As a result, he spoke Cherokee fluently, and at our request, he spoke this beautiful language for us, allowing us to appreciate the soft sound and cadence of his words as the glow of the fire faded.

Although Robert and I were inept at duplicating Cherokee words, we fully appreciated the significance of a language that had been spoken long before the land was taken from the Cherokee, and we hoped it would live forever.

Robert and I savored our time with these men, who were strangers at first but friends by the close of the evening. Day ended as the soft murmurs of the nearby stream lulled us to sleep, a language we understood and appreciated.

The Human Element

The Pipe Looks Familiar

Fontana Dam

September 4, 1978

Robert and I completed a four-day walk in the Smokies that ended at the Fontana Dam Visitor Center, where we paused to rest and to enjoy a cold drink. While we relaxed, I decided to have a smoke and lit up my pipe, Old Danger.

Now Old Danger is not just any pipe. He began his life growing up as a rhododendron shrub in Frying Pan Gap near Mount Pisgah on the Blue Ridge Parkway. He grew there for many years, forming a woody burl the size of a softball. Unfortunately, bulldozer work left him uprooted and discarded to weather away the remainder of his life. I met him in 1968 while on a picnic in the gap in which he grew up, carried him home and converted his burl into a wonderful pipe.

In time, the family christened my new pipe Old Danger because of his tendency to cast off his coals, burning holes in my clothing, car seats and furniture. Ultimately, Old Danger was banished from the house. Nevertheless, before his retirement he was a constant companion for many years on my outings in the Smokies.

In any event, a man walked up to Robert and me and said, "I know you fellows." We had to admit that he had the advantage, because neither of us recognized him. It took some discussion to establish a connection. In so doing, the man reminded us that we had camped together two years earlier at Tricorner Knob Shelter. He told me that he recognized me by my pipe, which I had smoked at the time of our first meeting.

Could he have been saying, "I don't recognize your face, but the pipe looks familiar"? Needless to say, Old Danger did not let me forget who made the most lasting impression.

What Did She Say?

Oconaluftee Visitor Center; Mountain Farm Museum

October 14, 1978

Bill and I spent our morning trout fishing in the Oconaluftee River. Our efforts proved nonproductive; however, the spectrum of autumn colors along the stream border was spectacular, and we enjoyed watching fallen red and yellow leaves slowly drifting in the current, swirling and moving in aimless patterns that cast fleeting shadows on the stream bottom.

In the afternoon, we visited the Mountain Farm Museum and joined the throng of visitors who were observing molasses making. We all watched as the green cane juice flowed slowly around the baffles of a wood-fired evaporator and turned into rich amber as it became syrup. The process was supervised by a mountain man and woman who attended to all duties associated with the process.

The woman stood at the end of the evaporator, where the molasses flowed into a kettle. When she deemed the molasses to be of proper color and consistency, she dipped her index finger into the sticky liquid and lifted a thread of molasses toward the sun. After critically examining the wisp of syrup she said, "Them's larruping."

I had never heard the term "larruping" and did not know the definition of the word. Under the circumstances, I presumed that she meant that the molasses met her criteria for acceptable quality. Upon reaching home, I researched all my resources on mountain terminology but could not find a definition for larruping. The word remained in memory, however, and ultimately, with the publication in 2004 of the *Dictionary of Smoky Mountain English*, I found a definition at last! In simplest terms, "larruping" can be defined as being "very tasty."

Thinking back on that autumn day more than twenty-five years ago, I have no doubt that the woman was correct. The molasses were larruping.

Among the Greats

Cherokee Fairground; Cherokee, North Carolina

April 14, 1979

Bob F. and I met in Cherokee and enjoyed a morning drive into the Great Smoky Mountains National Park. Afterward, we returned to the Cherokee Fairground, where a ramp festival was being held. The ramp—sometimes called wild leek—was our primary reason for getting together. We planned to enjoy this mountain delicacy later in the day; however, we had time to spare before lunch so we strolled about the fairground and visited craft and other displays in the interim.

During our ramble over the grounds, we met a number of Bob's friends from Cherokee, including Chief John Crowe, the distinguished leader of the Eastern Band of the Cherokee Indians. And we observed three Indians participating in a blowgun contest, one of whom was Goingback Chiltosky, a famed artisan, whose carvings are widely admired and preserved in collections, including that of the Smithsonian Museum. Later, I saw Mary Ulmer Chiltosky, Mr. Chiltosky's wife, who was famous in her own right as a civic leader and author and who preserved Cherokee history and lore. Her contributions are many.

Another person who was present was Amoneeta Sequoyah, a great Cherokee medicine man. He wore a broad-brimmed western-style hat with a colorful beaded band that gave him a certain flair that was most appealing. He possessed the knowledge of the use of natural plants and was known to create medicines from plants, herbs, bark, leaves and berries.

The meal that Bob and I had come to sample was served at noon. It consisted of ramps fried with eggs, ramps fried with potatoes, Indian bean bread—thick corn meal with beans cooked in it—hominy and a ten-inch fried trout. The meal was well worth the $2.50 that it cost. Bob and I ate our fill and enjoyed every bite of this delicious fare.

At the end of the day, I felt fortunate to have been among people whom I considered to be Cherokee greats. These respected Native Americans had descended from a proud and mighty people with a rich historical and cultural heritage. Their history, though significant, contains many episodes of great sorrow. The gravest of these periods was the travesty leading to their removal to Oklahoma, chronicled as the Trail of Tears.

Words of Wisdom

Mount Le Conte Shelter; Boulevard Trail

October 15, 1981

Robert and I had embarked on a four-day trip and were spending our first night in the trail shelter on Mount Le Conte. We arrived with plenty of time in which to arrange our gear, and then we visited Cliff Top to admire the majesty of the mountains from this vista. Finally, we ambled among the rustic and historic log buildings of the Le Conte Lodge complex and then visited the lodge itself to admire its simple but pleasant decor.

While visiting the lodge, we learned that ninety-year-old Gracie McNicol was a guest. Miss McNicol was the subject of a book titled *Gracie and the Mountain*, which described her experiences during many trips to Mount Le Conte. I was familiar with Miss McNicol from reading about her and hoped to meet her later. As it turned out, this opportunity occurred.

Miss McNicol, accompanied by a friend, paid a visit to the shelter after dark, much to my delight. She was a handsome woman with pleasant features, silver hair and a broad smile. She wore a bright red jacket and blue jeans, and a bright plaid scarf was wrapped around her head to stave off the October chill.

Miss McNicol seated herself on a shelter bunk, and in a gentle, friendly manner she began to tell of her experiences. I enjoyed her accounts and was most impressed by the fact that she was celebrating her 230th trip to Mount Le Conte, although she went on to complete 244 trips before her death. She completed 174 of these on foot, and the remainder had involved a combination of horseback travel and hiking; in more recent times, her trips were all by horse. What an accomplishment!

After our pleasant visit, Miss McNicol rose and made preparations for her departure. Before leaving, however, she shared with us words of wisdom, words that I have never forgotten and have tried to emulate in my own life. After all, she was a living role model who brought her advice into perfect focus. In the sincere hope that you will benefit as well, I share her words with you: "Keep walking and you'll stay young."

A Cold Stare

Straight Fork

May 22, 1982

Bill and I walked up Straight Fork and fished appealing stretches of stream, casting dry flys into runs, pools and quiet riffles. Male Adams, Adams Variants and Royal Wulff patterns were productive and lured trout to strike, sometimes cautiously and at other times with furious abandon. Rainbow trout with bright red stripes and speckled trout with their milk-white fin tips and pink-red spots succumbed to our lures. Most were small and were quickly released to dart back to their sanctuary in the depths of the stream. Thus we moved up stream, catching and releasing trout without retaining a single fish.

A short distance below the confluence of Straight Fork and Balsam Corner Creek, I thought I detected the faint smell of wood smoke. The smell grew stronger as we ascended, leaving no doubt that a fire burned nearby. While Bill remained behind to fish, I moved quietly ahead and located the source. As I stepped through a screen of rhododendron, I saw a man standing in the shelter of a rocky bluff on the opposite side of the creek. Before him was a freshly made fire, which produced gray smoke that swirled upward into the trees.

I walked to the edge of the stream and raised my hand in greeting but only received a cold stare in response. This lack of acknowledgement struck me as strange and certainly not customary when encountering someone in the mountains. My puzzlement at the man's behavior lasted only a few moments, however. As I surveyed the setting, I spied a small pile of speckled trout on a rock, perhaps ten, not four feet from where I stood. These had been cleaned and were ready to cook. All was now clear! The man was a poacher who had violated park fishing regulations by retaining speckled trout and by catching more than the legal limit. I felt sure that my appearance had surprised him and contributed to his unresponsiveness. Furthermore, I suspected that he was not alone and that his partner was probably hidden in the nearby rhododendron thicket.

Without further effort to communicate, I made several casts in the run that lay between us and turned back through the rhododendron. Although park regulations had been violated, I had no doubt that the evidence was consumed without delay after my departure.

A Veritable Whirlwind

Derrick Knob Shelter; Appalachian Trail

October 5, 1982

Ed and I began our day intent on locating and following a forgotten trail that was depicted on an old map. After battling rhododendron thickets and working our way steeply upward to a small gap on a long ridge, we reached the faint trace that would serve as our trail for the remainder of the day.

Our afternoon was spent following this path. The sourwood, tulip poplar, oak and maple trees along the crest and on the slopes below us were splashed with brilliant fall colors that radiated under the autumn sun that shone from a cloudless sky. A gentle wind rustled the trees, and leaves floating toward the forest floor created a dry rattle as they brushed against lower branches. Beyond the sounds of the season, all was peaceful.

Eventually, we made our final ascent and walked from the forest into the grassy clearing above the Derrick Knob Trail Shelter. As we approached, we saw a plume of smoke and someone burning trash in front of the shelter. My first reaction at seeing this scene was one of disappointment after a day spent in the quiet of the mountains.

Upon reaching the shelter, we met the occupants, Tom and Amyjohn, and their friend, Bill. In sizing up the situation, it was Amyjohn who burned the trash. As Ed and I chatted with them, we learned the full story. When they arrived, they found the shelter in poor condition as a result of other campers who had left trash inside. Amyjohn couldn't stand the mess, so she carried the cans and papers outside and burned them. While we watched, Amyjohn stamped the cans flat with her heavy hiking boots. Next she dug a hole with a heavy piece of metal and buried the cans. As if this was not enough, she swept the inside of the shelter with a makeshift broom made of small tree branches, greatly improving the appearance of the shelter area. When the shelter was clean, Amyjohn built a fire and cooked supper.

Ed and I were tremendously impressed—awed might be a better term—by Amyjohn's good deed and the energy and dispatch with which she completed her chores. She was a veritable whirlwind of energy.

Ed and I spent a most pleasant evening chatting with Tom, Amyjohn and Bill. They were thoughtful and conscientious campers. And our time with them contributed meaningfully to the enjoyment of our outing.

This story should end here; however, there is more. On October 25, 1983, when Al W., Ed and I were camped at Cabin Flats, Al shared an interesting event. Earlier in the month, while he was hiking a portion of the Appalachian Trail east of Camel Gap, he stopped to visit with a man and woman he encountered along the trail. The young woman told Al that he reminded her of someone she had met and asked him if he had hiked the western Smokies in October 1982. He told her he hadn't but that he knew two people who had, Ed and Bill. Then Al asked, "Are you Amyjohn?" And indeed it was Amyjohn! She was startled and surprised at Al's out-of-the-blue identification, an identification made by a complete stranger. Al was able to identify Amyjohn because I had shared with him the details of our meeting with Tom and her.

There is even more. On January 12, 1992, while climbing the Anthony Creek Trail on the way to Spence Field, Woody and I were overtaken by Tom and Amyjohn, who were enjoying a winter outing in the Smokies. We walked to a snowy Spence Field together. It was delightful to see this pleasant couple after almost ten years and to obtain an update about their lives since our first meeting.

Regretfully, I have not encountered Amyjohn and Tom on the trail again since our last meeting; however, I cherish fond memories of both.

Alone?

Wild Cherry Branch

February 12, 1984

My goal on this bleak February day was to locate and follow an abandoned trail that once ascended Wild Cherry Branch from Highway 441 to Burl Gap on Thomas Divide. I relished a solitary winter day in the mountains and was excited by the possibility of discovering one of the forgotten trails of the Smokies.

My travel was unhurried. I took time to enjoy the beauty of the stark winter forest, which offered the extremes of steep rhododendron-covered bluffs and nearly open, almost level areas timbered with straight tulip poplar trees. The tracks of fox and deer were evident along my path, attesting to wildlife activity in the forest wilds. And I noticed snow and ice formations along the branch, reminding me that winter was dominant in the mountains.

The old trace I followed did not appear to have been used, and I felt totally alone. In fact, I could not imagine a logical reason for anyone to visit this cove, especially in midwinter. Needless to say, I was quite surprised when I observed movement below me. While I watched, a human form appeared! It was a young Cherokee man, who appeared to be in his late teens, moving slowly and looking intently at the snow-covered earth immediately in front of him. I remained motionless and unnoticed. Indeed, the young man might have walked right by me had I not spoken to him and broken his concentration.

I was certainly curious as to why anyone else would be tramping the slopes along Wild Cherry Branch. It didn't take me long to learn that the young man was hunting ramps, a wild leek that is a gourmet treat when properly prepared. I was mystified, however, as to how he found ramps in the snow and did not hesitate to ask this question. He explained that he looked for the dried ramp stems left from the previous year. Once discovered, the tender new ramps could be dug from the dark, rich earth at the base of the stem.

After a few minutes, the man's parents joined us. All three were engaged in the search for ramps. I walked and talked with them for a few hundred yards until they turned into a hollow where ramps had been plentiful the previous year. I bid them farewell here and continued along Wild Cherry Branch in an unsuccessful effort to locate the trail.

Alone? I had thought I wanted to have a day to myself! I concluded, however, that my meeting with this friendly Cherokee family was an excellent trade for solitude. And, in addition, I learned the secret for finding ramps in winter.

Excellent Candy

Pole Road Campsite; Deep Creek Trail

July 5, 1985

Alice and I set aside two days to walk the Deep Creek Trail, making this our Fourth of July celebration. We began on Thomas Divide and descended into the valley of Deep Creek, where we viewed a majestic forest and later savored the beauty of Deep Creek as it tumbled between verdant slopes. We traveled slowly and stopped often to admire the ever-changing scenery, to listen to the trilling of the winter wren and to admire the graceful form of a garter snake that lay beside the trail.

We ate lunch at the Poke Patch Campsite and during the afternoon counted off Cherry Creek, Bee Tree Creek and Nettle Creek as we crossed each one on our way to the Pole Road Campsite. We pitched camp there and adjourned to Deep Creek, where we spent an hour talking and skipping small flat stones across the surface of a pool just as we had as children.

Following supper, we joined a family of three from Cherokee who were also camped at the site and shared their fire. They expressed a deep appreciation for the Smokies and told us that they camped in the park whenever their schedule permitted. While we enjoyed their fire, we were treated to their excellent peanut brittle, which they generously shared with us. This was a welcomed treat after the filling but unexceptional meal that I had prepared.

The woman who had prepared the peanut brittle was kind enough to write the recipe on a cardboard box lid and share it with us. I include it here for those interested in trying it.

Deep Creek Peanut Brittle

1 cup sugar
1 dash salt
½ cup Karo syrup
1 to 1½ cups of raw peanuts
1 tablespoon butter
1 top vanilla (cap full)
1½ teaspoon baking soda

Cook sugar, salt and syrup for two minutes (stirring continuously); add peanuts; stir and cook six and a half to seven minutes until light brown in color. Add butter and vanilla; stir and add soda. Pour onto a pan and cool.

Our day had been perfect. We had enjoyed the beauty of the Deep Creek Valley, met and spent time with a delightful family and toasted the day with excellent peanut brittle. What more could we ask?

Alice Hart at Caldwell Fork on a New Year's Day walk, January 1, 1991.

Bill and Alice at Clingmans Dome, October 2, 2004.

Humorous Experiences

A Strange Honeymoon

Enloe Creek Campsite; Enloe Creek Trail

September 8, 1973

After several years of camping and fishing on Eagle Creek, Bob F. and I decided to spend a portion of our vacations in the eastern end of the Great Smokies. After making this decision, Bob arranged with a friend, Jerome Parker, to transport us by horse to Enloe Creek. On the chosen day for our trip, we met Jerome at his home in the Tow String community and were treated to an excellent and bountiful breakfast prepared by Mrs. Parker on a large iron wood stove. Afterward, Mr. Parker saddled three horses, secured our packs on a fourth and led us up Hughes Ridge. Although not a horse person, I managed to stay astraddle of my mount and reveled in the luxury of surveying the forest without having to keep my eyes on the trail. As an added bonus, we enjoyed listening to Jerome's accounts of herding on Becks Bald in pre-park days.

Eventually, we left Hughes Ridge and descended to Raven Fork along the Enloe Creek Trail. Upon reaching the Enloe Creek Campsite, Bob and I unloaded our packs while Jerome made preparations to continue across Hyatt Ridge to Straight Fork, where he was scheduled to meet John Crowe, chief of the Eastern Band of the Cherokee Indians, and several of his friends, who he planned to transport back to Raven Fork for several days of camping and fishing. A young man and woman were already camped at the site when we arrived, and after our chores were completed, we visited with them. During our conversation, Jerome told the couple, "I am going to cross the ridge and return with the chief of the Cherokee and five of his braves." He then embellished this fact by telling them that the chief and his party were going to camp on the opposite bank of Raven Fork and "dance war dances all night long."

Afterward, Jerome mounted his horse and rode across Raven Fork leading all his horses. As he ascended the bank beyond the ford, now spanned by a bridge, he waved his gray Stetson hat in the air with a flourish straight from an old western movie and disappeared from sight.

The young couple had distressed looks on their faces after Jerome's departure, and I sensed that they were really concerned by the unfolding events. I tried to console them by telling them that they had nothing to fear when the Indians returned. Despite my best efforts, it was apparent by the looks on the couple's faces that my comments brought no comfort. Finally, the young man looked at me dejectedly and commented, "This is a hell of a way to spend a honeymoon."

Later in the week, Bob and I joined Chief Crowe and his party and spent a pleasant evening around their campfire. The Indians laughed about the couple, now departed, who had seemed strange and aloof. During their discussion, the young man's comments occupied my thoughts—"This is a hell of a way to spend a honeymoon"—and I wondered how they responded after they returned home when asked, "How was your honeymoon?"

Moo Bears

Hemphill Bald; Hemphill Bald Trail

April 25, 1976

Sara and I parked at Polls Gap and stepped into a gray, fog-shrouded morning with heavy wind gusts providing our welcome. A foggy mist immediately condensed on our skin and clothing. Nevertheless, we began following an old rail grade that was our route for a while, intent on completing a thirteen-mile loop that entailed crossing a number of peaks of five thousand feet or more. We were immediately captivated by the beauty of fringed phacelia that grew in lush patches near the trail and by trillium that dotted the forest floor by the hundreds, the first of many wildflowers enjoyed during our outing.

We paused at Sugartree Licks, so named to denote a place where herdsmen once salted their livestock when the high tops of Cataloochee Divide were used for pasture prior to the formation of the national park. Other picturesquely named landmarks that lay along our route were Strawberry Knob, Buck Knob, Maggot Springs Gap and Little Bald Knob. Each of these had a story to tell; however, we could only speculate about the derivation of these names.

The wind howled constantly and swept gray fog in ghostly patterns through gaps in the divide. I felt a sense of unfathomable mystery, which I had experienced before on such days. The blurred shapes of trees, drifting fog and wild sounds of the wind contributed to this sensation, which was heightened by the hoarse croaking of a raven that flew unseen overhead. There was a certain charm in the feel of the day, and I recognized it as part of the mystique of the Great Smokies.

By the time we reached Hemphill Bald, the air had cleared and the grassy expanse of the bald lay ahead. Sara walked in front of me, and when she first sighted the bald she shouted, "Look, a bear!" Indeed, there in front of us was a dark form with the coloration of a bear. Upon closer examination, however, the form was not that of a bear. It was a Black Angus steer that grazed on private property adjacent to the park boundary.

As we climbed Hemphill Bald, I chided Sara about the dangers of "moo bears."

And she responded with a sheepish grin and a defensive "Daddy!"

A Tragedy Narrowly Averted

Raven Fork

July 2, 1977

Bill and I began climbing at daybreak from Straight Fork toward Low Gap through beautiful forest filled with the sounds of tumbling water and the singing of birds. Our hearts were light as we contemplated a successful day of fishing on Raven Fork.

In time, we passed through Low Gap on Hyatt Ridge, and some distance below Low Gap we exited the graded trail and followed a faint trace kept open by those who fish upper Raven Fork. Our route led through wet undergrowth, patches of stinging nettle and beautiful wild touch-me-nots. Eventually, we reached the clear stream and began our day of angling.

We both experienced success, catching both rainbow and speckled trout on various dry fly patterns. Most were below the nine-inch size limit; however, we were able to retain a few rainbows over nine inches. Despite our mixed success, our fisherman's optimism prevailed and we expected to catch a "keeper" in every run and pool.

At one point during our morning, I almost experienced a serious tragedy. While bending to drink from a small stream at its confluence with Raven Fork, my pipe slipped from my overalls pocket, fell into the rushing waters of the creek and quickly washed into Raven Fork's currents. I stood frozen as Old Danger gained momentum and began to float away. In a few seconds it would be too late. Old Danger would be lost forever! Something had to be done. I made a frantic dash, threw myself prone at streamside, stretched over the water and grasped the pipe at the very last moment. Although soaked and somewhat the worse for wear, Old Danger fortunately recovered and survives until this day.

Eventually our day ended and we recrossed Low Gap, arriving at our vehicle at 7:30 p.m., more than thirteen hours after our start. Because of the lateness of our return, I called Alice to report that we were on our way home. During our conversation, I told her that we had experienced some anxious moments and faced a time of great peril. In her mind, I'm sure she envisioned some harm befalling our beloved son. Finally, I explained, "Old Danger almost drowned." There was a moment of silence. Then Alice responded and uttered one word, a word that I will leave to your imagination.

"Yes, I Was Her Pupil"

Lost Cove Campsite; Eagle Creek Trail

September 3, 1978

Robert and I left Spence Field Shelter, where we had spent the night, and descended the steep trail leading down Eagle Creek. I looked forward to seeing this watershed again and to visiting familiar Gunna Flats, Big Walnuts and Eagle Creek Island, locations along a trail with more than a dozen fords.

We reached the Lost Cove Campsite near Fontana Lake in early afternoon, where a contingent of campers from Sylva, North Carolina, had set up a substantial camp. It consisted of a large sheet of black plastic supported by ropes and was sufficient to shelter the five or six members of the party under one "roof." Heavy sleeping bags provided bedding. Likewise, they had heavy black iron frying pans to fry potatoes and onions, a traditional mountain camping meal, and, of course, to fry tender trout rolled in a thick layer of cornmeal. I had seen such camps before employed by natives who visit the park and have to admit that they have a certain practicality that sets them apart from backpackers caught up in the latest fads in gear and food. These men used the gear they had, a practice familiar to me also. And they came to camp, fish and share time together, and from all appearances they were well prepared to accomplish their objectives.

After a walk of approximately nine miles, Robert and I were ready for a rest, so we shed our packs and visited at length with these hospitable campers. During our visit, I learned from one of the men that my mother-in-law, who lived in Sylva, had been his teacher many years before. This led to a discussion about his school recollections. I had expected him to express warm reflections about school and my mother-in-law. Instead, he paused and said reflectively, "Yes, I was her pupil. Boy, she sure could burn a little fellow's ass." Well, this wasn't the response I had expected; however, I could certainly identify with his experience when I recalled my own encounters with the paddle as a youth.

The Human Element

Coping with a Blazing Inferno

Little Bottoms Campsite; Little Bottoms Trail

April 12, 1980

Sara and I spent several days backpacking in the southwestern end of the Great Smokies. After a rainy night at Cane Creek Campsite, we set off for Little Bottoms following the Cooper Road, Hatcher Mountain and Little Bottoms Trails to reach our destination. These trails were pleasant to walk and afforded a variety of woodland scenery. Particularly pleasing was the trail crossing of Oak Flats Branch. Here a small, serene stream flowed through a hemlock grove. These large trees contributed subtle shading and filtering of the light, intensifying the beauty and appeal of this glade.

Upon reaching Little Bottoms, Sara and I surveyed the area about the campsite and concluded that it was situated on an isolated mountain farmstead. The remains of a chimney, an old apple tree, stone piles from past field-clearing efforts and the second-growth forest that dominated the bottoms attested to earlier occupancy here. Later we were joined by another couple, a young man and woman, and overheard the young man tell his companion that the stone piles, which were several feet high, had been placed there to fill in an old pit toilet. Upon hearing these comments, Sara and I thought we heard the ghosts of those who once lived here laughing uproariously, caused by the fact that their field-clearing efforts had been misunderstood.

Our supper preparations began in the usual manner with the lighting of my much-used and faithful Svea stove. This time, however, problems developed with a worn fuel cap gasket that allowed pressurized fuel to escape and ignite. Repeated efforts to correct this problem were unsuccessful, and each time I relit the stove it flamed up again, growing worse with each lighting.

Sara, who had seated herself on a log across from me, observed my efforts and began scolding me for continuing to relight the stove after it had flashed up several times. Despite her rebukes, I resolved to make one last attempt to repair and restart the stove. This time the stove burst into a large glowing ball of flame, totally engulfing it.

The flames reached a height of two feet, and the situation that had been troublesome at first now became a serious problem. At this point a number of things happened suddenly. First, Sara somersaulted rapidly backward away from the flames from her perch on the log and tumbled into the dirt. Next, the frayed cuffs of my overalls caught fire. Not a major fire, mind you, just simmering, slow burning circles of small orange flames around each frayed cuff. Finally, the stove was consumed with ever-increasing flames.

Now, this was not a situation that called for a lengthy discussion to address the problems at hand. Direct and immediate action was essential. I grasped a pot of water with one hand and dashed it on the stove, extinguishing the inferno. Next, I removed my hat with the other hand and began to beat out the glowing flames on my cuffs. The greatest damage that occurred, however, was to my pride and ego. This was the result of a severe tongue lashing that I received from Sara, which began even before she had recovered from her ungainly tumble into the dirt. Now that Sara is an adult, she still berates me for this episode whenever her childhood outings with me are discussed. She just can't let it go!

Gallantry Lives

Steeltrap Creek Campsite; Forney Creek Trail

August 27, 1980

Robert and I reached the Steeltrap Creek Campsite in early afternoon. This was our last day of a multi-day trip, and we relished spending our final afternoon in leisurely pursuits. In Robert's case, he caught and released several speckled trout. I was not as ambitious. I dozed in the sun and enjoyed the whispers of the nearby stream.

We had concluded that we would have the site to ourselves as no campers had arrived by dark. We were wrong, however, because four other people arrived within the hour. We visited with these newcomers and enjoyed a time of getting acquainted and shared fellowship.

Robert, always the gentleman, counseled these campers about the importance of suspending their food bags away from bears. In fact, with a great show of gallantry, he offered to perform the task of safely securing their food, sharing knowledge that he had gained after many years of hiking and camping in the Smokies. When I retired, Robert was three or four feet above the ground as he shimmied his way up a spindly sapling a few inches in diameter to properly hang their food. I knew they were in good hands and that my assistance was not needed.

I awoke before the others the next morning. And when I surveyed the campsite, I had a good laugh. After all of Robert's efforts to suspend the food bags, I found that one food bag was suspended a mere four feet above the ground on the spindly arching sapling and that the other rested on the ground, unmoved from the previous night. Both were easy prey for any bear that happened by. Fortunately, we were lucky and had no woolly visitors.

When Robert arose, I complimented him for his gallantry and for the way he had carefully secured the food of our neighboring campers. There wasn't much he could say! In fact, he didn't utter a single word. His only response was a sheepish grin. Yes, there may have been a bit of carelessness, but gallantry lives.

Without a Kiss

Alum Cave Trail

October 15, 1981

Robert and I walked along the Alum Cave Trail through a beautiful cove hardwood forest. The trees were largely bare except for scatted clusters of gold, red and yellow leaves. Eventually, we climbed upward through the eroded opening of Arch Rock and entered a forest of fir trees. In time we trudged across the dusty soil beneath Alum Cave, where we paused to admire the impressive overhang of this spectacular bluff.

Well above this landmark, as Robert and I rested for a few minutes, we were approached by a young man wearing a broad-brimmed western hat bedecked with a grand display of feathers. He paused to visit with us and related that this was his second trip to Mount Le Conte. He told us that on his first trip he had been accompanied by a young woman who had packed all her gear in a suitcase, which he had carried to the crest. After telling us this, he expressed the opinion that he was probably the only person who had ever carried a suitcase to Mount Le Conte.

After the young man's story ended, he was quiet for a few moments. Then he said reflectively, "You know, I didn't even get to kiss her once." In parting, the young man said that his lady friend had asked to join him on his second trip. The fact that he was alone told the rest of the story. Carrying a suitcase to Le Conte was not a feat he wished to duplicate, kiss or no kiss.

Boy Scout Outings

The Magic Hat and P7

Mount Sterling Campsite; Baxter Creek Trail

August 12, 1974

The troop and I left Laurel Gap Shelter, where we had spent the night, and headed for Silers Bald along the Mount Sterling Ridge Trail. This relatively level grassy trail was too pleasant to pass in haste, so our pace was leisurely.

We drank cold water from splashing sources and enjoyed the fragrant smell of bee balm and bergamot that surrounded them. At other times, we stopped, rested against our packs and relished the sense of outdoor freedom that we enjoyed.

Beyond Pretty Hollow Gap, we began our climb toward Mount Sterling as the distant sounds of thunder warned of impending rain. The thunder moved closer and the dramatic rumbles grew in intensity. Large, lush drops of rain began to pelt down, and in a short time, the rain fell in torrents, which turned the trail into a muddy stream. This continued with fury when we reached the crest of Mount Sterling. The Mount Sterling fire tower occupied the highest point of the crest. A fire warden's cabin, now removed, sat a few yards west of the tower. I crowded ten Scouts and their gear under the small porch of the cabin and settled down to wait out the rain, which showed no sign of abatement. The breeze chilled damp bodies and spirits deteriorated noticeably.

As we all huddled together, I told the Scouts that I wore a magic hat—an ancient Duxbak hunting cap. I turned the cap backward and explained that when I turned my cap around again the rain would stop. My fabrication created a good deal of disbelief, but it turned the thoughts of anxious minds to something other than their discomfort. In time, I turned my cap around and pronounced that the rain would cease in twenty minutes. True to my word, the skies cleared, the sun appeared and we spent a pleasant afternoon on the crest of Mount Sterling.

When evening arrived, we gathered around a small fire and told stories. One was related to a feature on the crest. At the base of Mount Sterling fire tower were rectangular cement slabs about four feet long arranged to form the figure "P7." Several of the Scouts asked what P7 represented. I presumed, although I was uncertain, that this marking helped to identify the fire tower from the air; however, I used the question to create a story about a notorious spy who carried the code name P7.

With great elaboration, I explained that P7's airplane had been on a secret mission to bomb the atomic energy plant at Oak Ridge, Tennessee, and explained that he had crashed on the crest after a hard-fought air battle over Mount Sterling. I told them finally that the cement slabs had been placed on the crest to mark the spy's grave.

As I spun my yarn, I looked at the circle of young men gathered around our small fire that popped, hissed and crackled in the stillness of the night. Their faces reflected touches of orange from the glow of the fire, and these same faces uniformly bore expressions of rapt attention as my story unfolded. These young men, whose spirits had ebbed in the chill of a summer rain in the high Smokies, reflected a certain happiness that comes with a bit of hardship. They were now warm, well fed and experiencing the joys of shared friendship. Such are the rewards of Scouting.

Tell Us That's Not True

Cataloochee Group Camping Area

February 22, 1975

The Scout troop pitched camp in the Cataloochee Group Camping Area situated on the site of an old farm. A beautiful old springhouse fashioned with smooth, fist-sized, round creek stones was the only reminder of earlier settlement here. Tents were pitched on a bed of soft golden pine needles beneath a grove of white pines, and an adjacent grassy field provided a place for games. Campfires cast a golden glow on moving figures, whose shouts of laughter punctuated the quiet of evening.

After supper, we gathered around a campfire and told ghost stories. As was customary on our outings, I fabricated a story about a gruesome murder that had occurred at our campsite years before. I built the story around the landmarks and features at the site to add credibility and reality to my tale. The hissing and cracking of the fire, the dancing golden flames and the magic of the night captured the imaginations of my wide-eyed audience, who listened intently. The older Scouts feigned fright, and the younger Scouts' faces grew serious as the story progressed.

When the story ended, the boys retired to their tents, taking with them the image of a grisly dismembered hand resting in the round basin of the springhouse. Many hoped against hope that the story was not true.

They Conducted Themselves with Grace

Laurel Gap Shelter; Balsam Mountain Trail

June 10, 1975

Bob W. and I were leading a group of Scouts on a fifty-mile hike in the Smokies, one that began at Mount Sterling Gap and ended at Highway 441 at the Kephart Prong trailhead. On this particular day, our walk began at Walnut Bottom, and we were destined for Laurel Gap Shelter via the exquisite Gunter Fork Trail. This entailed fording Big Creek and crisscrossing Gunter Fork several times on our ascent. We enjoyed a leisurely pace during the day because our walk was only six miles and we had no requirement to hurry.

We ate a simple lunch at the base of a high trailside cascade and admired a film of water that glided over the sloping face of rugged stone. A light rain began to fall after lunch, necessitating the use of rain gear, and a steady breeze chilled us when we paused to rest. The rain and fog obliterated the grand views that are normally available on upper reaches of this trail.

We slogged into Laurel Gap at 2:30 p.m. wet and cold. Bob and I gathered damp wood and built a fire to warm our charges while they spread out their sleeping bags and other gear in the shelter. The fire and a change into dry clothing soon put an end to chattering teeth and flagging spirits.

We were joined later in the afternoon by a young man and woman. The woman was soaked from the continuing rain and appeared to be on the verge of hypothermia. Her companion expressed concern for her welfare and urged her to change into dry clothing.

Boy Scouts filled the shelter and were perched on bunks like vultures. I wondered how the change of clothing was to be accomplished in view of the lack of privacy. The answer was simple enough, however. The young man held up his poncho to shield his companion, and she stepped behind it, only to emerge a minute or two later in a dry outfit. During this exercise, Bob and I were standing in front of the shelter. We immediately turned our backs to the impromptu screen in a display of courtesy. We now faced the Scouts. We were amused to observe the expressions of the boys during this exercise. They recognized the delicacy of the moment and knew they shouldn't look, but an occasional pair of darting eyed betrayed their curiously.

The couple's food supply was limited to two cans of tuna, a container of peanut butter and a jar of jelly, yet they had several more days of travel—travel that they were ill prepared to undertake. We shared our supper with them and offered to lead them the next day to a road along which they could secure a ride. In view of their limited provisions, they accepted our offer and indeed followed us the next day to Straight Fork Road at Round Bottom. In parting, I loaned the couple twenty dollars when I learned that their finances were as meager as their food supply.

A few days later, after our trip had ended, I received a letter of thanks and the repayment of my loan. The note indicated that the couple had secured a ride five minutes after we separated and that their trip had ended without further hardships. Particularly gratifying to me was a statement in the letter that read, "We enjoyed the boys. They conducted themselves with grace."

The Human Element

Be on Your Best Behavior

Hyatt Ridge Trail

June 11–12, 1975

After leaving the young couple who had accompanied us to Round Bottom, the troop climbed a segment of the Beech Gap Trail on our way to McGee Spring. Approximately one mile from our destination, I heard the distant sound of a vehicle. (Authorized vehicles were allowed on certain park trails during this era.) The sound grew closer, and finally a jeep lurched into sight and ground past us. As it passed, I caught a brief glimpse of the driver, who wore a gray Stetson hat.

We reached McGee Spring at 4:30 p.m. and busied ourselves in pitching our camp. Our neighbor and his companions who had arrived in the jeep were doing the same, led by the man in the hat. When our preparations were complete, I walked to their campsite to introduce myself. As I drew closer, I recognized Jerome Parker as being the one who wore the familiar gray Stetson.

I was glad to see Jerome again and visited with him and his companions at length. Jerome related that he was preparing camp for John Crowe, chief of the Eastern Band of the Cherokee Indians, and his party, which included a judge from a nearby county. The chief's party was scheduled to arrive the next day by horseback.

The skies darkened while I spoke with Jerome, and I returned to camp to expedite supper preparations. Given the impending threat of rain, we decided to have our simplest meal, soup, in order to beat the rain. This decision was a wise one, because the rain began falling vigorously just as supper ended. This circumstance forced us to retire to the protection of our tents for the remainder of the evening.

The next morning, we parted company with Jerome and began walking the Hyatt Ridge Trail toward Low Gap. Bob and I urged the Scouts to look and act their best in order to make a favorable impression in the event that we met Chief Crowe and his party.

We had just crested a small knoll and begun a steep descent on a segment of trail that was muddy and slick from the previous evening's rain when we encountered the chief, the judge and their companions approaching on horseback. The young men were indeed on their best behavior, and Bob and I were proud of their orderly appearance. However, just as I started to greet the chief, my feet lost traction on the slick trail. One moment I was standing. The next I was performing an uncoordinated dance, complete with several shuffles and a kick step. My ungainly dance ended with me plopping into the mud with a mushy thud. I arose, greatly embarrassed, with several millimeters of mud on the seat of my pants.

I gathered my composure and dignity the best I could after my tumble and introduced Bob and the Scouts to the chief and his party. I had previously met Chief Crowe and welcomed the opportunity to meet him again. We continued our walk after our meeting, and I was pleased that all had been on their best behavior. Well, perhaps all but one!

GOOD DEEDS RECEIVED AND REPAID

Trail Magic

Tricorner Knob Shelter; Appalachian Trail

July 3–4, 1976

The holiday weekend provided Robert and me with an opportunity for an outing in the Smokies, so we embarked on a three-day trip that began at Round Bottom. We spent our first night at Laurel Gap Shelter and our second at Tricorner Knob Shelter, which we reached in early afternoon. With time to spare, we left our gear in the shelter and followed the Appalachian Trail around Mount Guyot to Mount Guyot Spring. From this point, we picked our way through dense fir trees and over blowdowns on a circuitous route that led to the top of Mount Guyot, the second highest mountain in the Smokies.

Upon our return to the shelter, which had been vacant when we left, we found that an interesting assortment of hikers had begun to assemble. There were two couples who seemed suspicious of the others and kept to themselves. Both of the young men wore giant knives on their belts that were fully eighteen inches in length, and one of their female companions had hiked in medium-heel ladies' dress shoes in vogue at the time. Later, two college students arrived. One of these retired at 4:00 p.m. and only rose for a brief supper. Next came two young hikers from Florida. One of these had a large battery-powered radio that probably weighed two or three pounds suspended from his pack by a long cord. The radio swung awkwardly as he walked. In addition to these there were two backpackers from Birmingham, Alabama, a pump salesman from New Orleans and an eighteen-year-old woman named Lisa, who limped into the shelter. She told us she was walking the Appalachian Trail, having begun her walk at Springer Mountain, Georgia.

Robert and I talked well into the evening with the two men from Birmingham, the pump salesman and Lisa, who entertained us by playing her recorder while perched on an upper bunk. We learned that Lisa had injured her ankle a few days earlier and had decided to leave the trail and seek medical attention for her injury.

Lisa's plight concerned Robert and me. We were nine trail miles from the nearest road, a remote one at that, and a source of medical attention involved a further trip of many miles. Given these circumstances, we offered to assist her in obtaining medical attention the next day.

During the final day of our outing, we added the heaviest items from Lisa's pack to our own to lessen her load. When this was completed, we began our nine-mile tramp on a portion of the Hyatt Ridge Trail that led to McGee Springs, a segment that has been abandoned for many years. Torrential rains began to fall not long after we began our walk, turning the horse trail to a muddy stream and wetting us from head to foot despite the fact that we were wearing ponchos.

We reached Round Bottom at 1:00 p.m., loaded our soaked gear and drove Lisa to the C.J. Harris Hospital in Sylva, North Carolina, where she was able to obtain medical attention in the emergency room. The physician who treated her diagnosed her ankle as being bruised and sprained.

Although the physician instructed Lisa to remain off her foot for two days and return for a further examination, she ignored this advice and asked to be driven to an Appalachian Trail hiker hostel in Hot Springs, North Carolina. We complied with her request and said our farewells to Lisa in Hot Springs after seeing her safely to the hostel. She promised to write and report on her trip. Unfortunately, we never heard from her again so the outcome of her trip remains a mystery.

Many years later, I hiked the Appalachian Trail in sections. On numerous occasions, complete strangers provided friendship and voluntary acts of kindness. Hikers refer to these generous gestures as "trail magic." This term had probably not been coined when Robert and I assisted Lisa. However, I now know that we performed "trail magic" for Lisa.

I Don't Care What People Say about Fruitcake

CCC Campsite; Forney Creek Trail

August 27, 1980

Robert and I spent a relaxed morning at the CCC Campsite, marked by its large chimney, a reminder of the Civilian Conservation Corps camp that once occupied the site. And I enjoyed a long smoke with Old Danger sitting beside the swirling waters of Forney Creek while Robert meandered downstream to revel in the sounds of stream and forest.

Afterward, we visited with two other backpackers, a man and his son, who shared the site with us. Both were cordial campers, and we enjoyed their company. As we were preparing to begin our day's walk, these two men insisted on giving us a gift of a one-pound Claxton fruitcake. What a welcomed surprise! We thanked them profusely and accepted this gift without hesitation.

Although I have heard fruitcake jokes for years, one does not make such jokes after eating backpacking food for four days. This fruitcake was wonderfully delicious. In fact, at every stop we ate a few slices of this treat, grateful to the givers. By midmorning, the cake was gone!

Time has not diminished my appreciation of this kindness, nor have I forgotten how good that fruitcake tasted.

The Cheese Sandwich, the Trail Mix and the Rice

Mount Le Conte Shelter; Boulevard Trail

October 15-18, 1981

Many have heard the Biblical account of the fishes and the loaves. However, few have heard the Smoky Mountain story of the cheese sandwich, the trail mix and the rice. This story follows.

Robert and I ascended to the crest of Mount Le Conte, where we planned to spend the first night of our four-day outing. Upon reaching the Mount Le Conte Shelter, we claimed bunks, laid out our gear and afterward climbed to the vista at Cliff Top, where we surveyed a breathtaking panorama of blue mountain ranges spreading westerly under silver-gray skies.

As we lounged on the rocky outcrop, several of the overnight guests at Mount Le Conte Lodge joined us and casually announced that a bear had entered the shelter and destroyed some gear. This hardly seemed possible! I had been the last person to leave the shelter, and I was sure that I had closed and latched the metal-framed, wire-covered shelter door, one that was designed to resist bears. This made no difference at that point—the damage had already occurred. Therefore, we continued to enjoy the scenery without undue alarm.

In time, we returned to the shelter. When we arrived, we found six or eight lodge guests with somber looks on their faces standing in a semicircle in front of the shelter. They confirmed that a bear had indeed entered the shelter. I felt responsible for this and examined the door to determine the bear's means of entry. I found that the bear had given the door a mighty pull with its paw, causing the latch to pivot, allowing the door to open. A safety chain was available but, alas, I had not used it to secure the door.

Robert and I made a quick assessment and realized that the bear had stolen one of our food sacks, punctured Robert's aluminum fuel bottle and crunched his cooking kit. A trail of paper led from the shelter into the brambles behind the shelter, indicating the route that the bear had taken with our food. We followed this trail and found the torn remnants of what had been our food, now only empty wrappers that were randomly strewn about. The bear had consumed almost all of our dehydrated food, and all we could salvage were two packages of biscuit mix, my pipe tobacco and a package of soup mix. It was obvious from the debris left by the bear that others had experienced the same fate at its paws and teeth.

The guests were still present when we returned to the shelter with the salvaged remains of our torn food sack. They seemed more concerned about our plight than we were. We concluded, however, that although our rations were severely reduced we could still make our planned walk, one that entailed nights at Pecks Corner and Cosby Knob Shelters and an exit at Big Creek on the fourth day.

The next day we shared a five-ounce can of pork and beans for lunch, a much smaller lunch than originally planned. Along the way, however, hikers who learned of our plight shared a cheese sandwich, two handfuls of trail mix and a hearty helping of hot rice served at one of the shelters. It was through the kindness of strangers that Robert and I enjoyed fairly decent meals despite the bear's vandalism.

Although a cheese sandwich, trail mix and rice did not feed the multitudes, it certainly helped satisfy the appetites of two hungry backpackers.

"I Know the Maker"

Bone Valley Campsite; Hazel Creek Trail

October 4, 1982

Ed and I had passed the previous evening with a cordial horse party from Haywood County at the beautiful Bone Valley Campsite. All of us had gathered around a glowing campfire and engaged in quiet conversation and storytelling, punctuated by laughter at the more humorous stories that were shared during the evening. This was a special time of fellowship, no doubt duplicated many times here by others who had sought the beauty and solitude of Hazel Creek.

Ed and I arose early in order to devote our day to off-trail exploration. As we were making final preparations to depart, the leader of the horse party walked over and gave me a gift and in so doing said, "I know the maker."

In other circumstances, this pronouncement might have been interpreted as a religious proclamation. In this case, however, the words had an entirely different meaning. You see, the gift he gave me was a plastic soft drink bottle filled with white liquor! Thus, the man's statement, "I know the maker," was his assurance that this was not just any white liquor, but liquor that was safe to drink because he was familiar with and trusted the man who made it.

This was a kind gesture from a mountain man that was motivated by the fellowship that developed the previous evening. I accepted his gift and expressed my appreciation to a man who had been a stranger when we met but a friend when we parted. How could I have done otherwise? After all, he knew the maker.

"How Are You Going to Get There?"

Indian Camp Creek to Timothy Creek

July 20, 1985

Before the Old Settlers Trail was marked and designated, a friend who was an employee of the park service told me that some of her colleagues had "gotten through" a sequence of trails between Greenbrier Cove and the Cosby section of the Great Smoky Mountains National Park. This knowledge motivated me to see if I could duplicate their feat and led to several trips, of which this was the last, to unravel the old pathways.

I followed the Maddron Bald Trail to a point that was an estimated half-mile beyond the Willis Baxter Cabin, where I bore right on a path that evidenced some clearing in the past three or four years. The path passed through a formerly settled area and led to Dunn Creek, which I descended to Snag Branch and to the next part of my puzzle of trails.

I began an ascent along a small branch and passed through fern-covered glades. In one of these, a movement caught my attention and brought me to a halt. Above me on the slopes was a large black bear that had been startled by my approach. I watched as the bear fled and proceeded cautiously in the direction of the vanished bear in the hopes of again glimpsing this majestic animal. The bear was not to be seen again, although I could hear the sounds of twigs breaking in the distance as it made its escape.

After this sighting, I crossed Snag Mountain to Webb Creek and followed a series of trails familiar from previous walks to Texas Creek, Noisy Creek, Redwine Creek and ultimately to an old chimney on Timothy Creek, a point at which I had lost the trail on an earlier outing. Upon reaching this junction, the puzzle of how all the paths, trails and old roads between Greenbrier Cove and Cosby fit together. I had finally "gotten through" the maze.

Earlier in the day, I experienced extreme pain in my left knee. At times I could hardly move it, but by favoring it, I could travel slowly and had walked most of the day in this condition. Now, with the cross-country portion of my walk complete, I contemplated the miles of road walking that would be required to return to my vehicle and anticipated a long, uncomfortable trip with a painful knee. Nevertheless, this was my only option.

Exiting the park involved following an old road near Timothy Creek to the park boundary. My exit led immediately in front of a home where a woman was talking to a man seated in a pickup truck. I felt distinctly uncomfortable in walking out of the forest so close to a dwelling, and to dispel any doubts about my intentions, I tipped my hat and spoke to the couple as I approached. In response to my greeting, the man asked me if I'd been hiking. I responded affirmatively and described both the motive for my walk and the route I'd taken. When the man learned that my vehicle was parked miles away, he asked, "How are you going to get there?" Upon learning that I planned to walk, he insisted on driving me there.

Needless to say, I was most gratified by the offer from this friendly stranger. I had not anticipated such kindness. The man introduced himself as we traveled and told me he was the pastor of a small church in the area. Also, he told me that he had walked many of the old trails with his grandfather and expressed his love for the Smokies.

I greatly enjoyed my visit with this Samaritan and reflected on the open, honest manner of a man who was a descendant of the hardy people who had settled the nearby slopes that were included in the national park. His act of kindness had special meaning for me and added immensely to my enjoyment of this day in the Smokies.

Mishaps and Tragedies

Unimaginable Loss

Spence Field; Appalachian Trail

April 4, 1970

I joined Larry, Larry's son, Kim and two of their companions for an overnight trip to Spence Field. This was my first visit to this historic landmark, and I was especially pleased to have the opportunity to explore a place where livestock was herded for many years before the coming of the Great Smoky Mountains National Park and where early Smoky Mountain hikers described experiences of camping while on their mountain jaunts.

We climbed the Anthony Creek and Bote Mountain Trails to reach our high-elevation destination. When we reached the crest, I found Spence Field to be a nearly open expanse of yellow-brown grass that I estimated to be ten to fifteen acres in size. It was interspersed with serviceberry, rhododendron, laurel and briers, and the growth along the borders of the field seemed to be encroaching into the once-open area. As we tramped across the expanse of this mountaintop meadow, I tried to envision what it looked like in previous years, when the lush grass was manicured like a well-kept lawn by livestock in the hundreds.

Our path led northeasterly along the Appalachian Trail toward Rocky Top and ended at a log shelter, now removed, in a small, sloping grassy clearing on the North Carolina side near the trailhead of the Jenkins Ridge Trail. The open side of the shelter was covered with chain-link fencing to keep out the bears, and a crude stone fireplace was situated in front. Above it was a cover of soft grass that invited a nap in the sun.

Following camp preparation and a nap in the sun, we returned to Spence Field, where we met a man who identified himself as the grandfather of six-year-old Dennis Martin, who disappeared from the crest of Spence Field the previous June. He told us that his grandson had become lost while playing near the new shelter on the west end of the field, and he said that the boy's father and he had begun a search for the missing boy almost at once; sadly, they were unsuccessful in locating Dennis.

An intensive search followed with over 1,400 searchers at its peak. Unfortunately, no trace of the lost child was ever found despite the best efforts of the many searchers. Now, many months after the disappearance and with no clue as to the boy's fate, the grandfather and two companions continued searching in the hope of bringing closure to the tragedy.

I had great respect and sympathy for the grandfather and admired the dedication and perseverance that caused him and his friends to search week after week for some clue that would help solve the mysterious disappearance. I felt a sense of great sadness for the family who experienced the unimaginable loss of their son. An excellent account of the search for Dennis Martin is described in *Lost! A Ranger's Journal of Search and Rescue* by Dwight McCarter and Ronald Schmidt.

The Human Element

Unplanned Trip to Cades Cove and Points Beyond

Upper Eagle Creek; Eagle Creek Trail

September 13–14, 1972

Bob F. and I began this trip with the expectation of spending a pleasant week camping and trout fishing on Eagle Creek. Although these expectations were partially met, an unexpected event in the middle of the week abruptly shortened our outing and denied us the full vacation we planned.

The fourth day of our outing—September 13—followed the same pattern as all the others. We fished near camp and returned about 3:00 p.m. with fish for supper. We cleaned our catch and enjoyed a smoke in the bright afternoon sunshine. While we relaxed, Bob suggested that we gather additional firewood to replenish our supply. It was this suggestion that precipitated the end of our trip.

When we finished smoking, we searched above camp for fallen wood suitable for our fire. Bob located a downed poplar and cut it in two. I then proceeded to drag a section some five inches in diameter and ten feet long back to camp.

My progress was halted suddenly when the log became entangled in some weeds and I twisted and jerked it to work it free. As I did this, I inadvertently shoved the butt end forcefully against a tree immediately in front of my face. The rebounding log struck me a severe blow in the mouth, leaving me dazed and in pain.

At first, I didn't know what had happened. I touched my mouth and found it bloody. Then I spat out a mouthful of blood and initially thought I had cut my lip. We returned to camp immediately, and I used a small mirror to examine the injury. This examination revealed that I had a gaping laceration in the center of my tongue!

Bob and I discussed my injury and decided that it was too severe to delay medical attention until our planned departure several days away. We weighed the alternatives for seeking help. We could walk to Fontana Dam, a day's walk, or we could proceed to Cades Cove, which was closer. Cades Cove was the obvious choice.

I made a compress out of a clean handkerchief to control the bleeding. Next, Bob and I packed light packs, secured our camp and began climbing the rugged trail toward Spence Field, which entailed an elevation gain of approximately two thousand feet.

Bob and I made good progress in reaching Spence Field, where we paused at the spring for a drink of cold water before crossing into Tennessee. We paused again for a rest before descending the Anthony Creek Trail to Cades

Cove. During this pause, I told Bob that I regretted that my accident would shorten our trip. Bob seemed sympathetic, and I felt he appreciated my concern; however, these thoughts were shattered when Bob replied, "Oh, don't worry, Man Who Speaks with Forked Tongue." Fortunately, his sense of humor was not damaged by our change of plans.

We reached the entrance to Cades Cove Campground at 8:00 p.m., where we were fortunate to encounter Ranger Mike Moyer. Bob, acting as our spokesperson, explained the events of the last several hours and asked the ranger if he could assist us in obtaining medical attention. Ranger Moyer readily consented and drove us to the hospital in Maryville, Tennessee. Before leaving us, he insisted on loaning us twenty dollars, all the money he had with him, when he ascertained that Bob and I had only nine dollars between us.

Bob and I were dressed in work shirts, overalls and work boots. We each had a five-day growth of beard, little money and no identification other than our fishing licenses when walked into the Maryville Hospital and explained our plight to the emergency room nurse. To our surprise, she showed no concern and asked us to wait while she called a doctor.

The doctor arrived in due course, and at 11:00 p.m. I was lying on the emergency room table while my tongue was being sutured. As I lay under the bright lights, I reflected on the irony of the day. During the morning I had played trout on the end of a nylon leader; now at day's end I was at the end of a leader.

When the doctor completed his work, he told me that I had bitten completely through the center of my tongue and that seven stitches had been required on the top of my tongue and three on the bottom to close the wound. The doctor assured me that my tongue would heal without problems, but he said that it would be sore for a while. He was correct on both accounts.

The doctor was kind enough to drive Bob and me to an inexpensive motel, and we bedded down about 1:00 a.m. after a long day. On September 14, we walked to the bus station in Maryville and purchased tickets to Waynesville, North Carolina, with our few remaining dollars. Bob's wife met us there, and Bob and she delivered me to my doorstep, where I was greeted by a surprised wife, who had not expected to see me for several days.

I repaid Ranger Moyer's loan with interest on returning home, and I have always been grateful to him for his kindness to Bob and me. Likewise, the nurse and doctor in Maryville were most courteous to two strangers who emerged from the Smokies when others might have treated us with suspicion.

One final responsibility remained for Bob and me to wrap up the details associated with this trip. We returned to Eagle Creek the following Saturday to recover the camping and fishing gear that we had left in our haste to reach Cades Cove. With this done, all that remained was for my tongue to heal.

Courting Danger

Oconaluftee River

July 4, 1975

Bill and I were angling for trout near the confluence of Raven Fork and the Oconaluftee River when our efforts were interrupted by a family of four who floated toward us on large inner tubes with plywood seats lashed to them. The father occupied one of the tubes, the mother and a preschool daughter occupied the second and another daughter, approximately eight years old, occupied the third.

The father floated past us and washed slowly downstream; however, the tube with mother and daughter lodged on a rock in front of us, and they were unable to move. Seeing their predicament, Bill and I waded out and dislodged them. When we did this, I cautioned the mother about the dangers of swift waters ahead and asked if they had life preservers. She responded that they did but had left them in their vehicle.

We waded downstream after this encounter and stood by as the three tubes swept through a swift chute where the Oconaluftee River and Raven Fork meet. I was relieved that they made it safely; however, another run waited at the end of this pool, where the waters flowed swift and deep. The father passed through the small rapids at the head of this pool and moved safely beyond. However, the mother and daughter lodged a second time in a very precarious place just above the rapids leading into the pool, bringing her tube and that of the oldest daughter to a halt. Bill and I observed this whole affair and realized that the situation was too dangerous for them to proceed farther.

Given this state of affairs, I waded into the water, picked up the oldest daughter from her tube and carried her across the current to the opposite bank. I then turned back for the second daughter. By this time, however, the father had realized the seriousness of the situation and had waded into chest-deep water below his wife's tube. He then gathered the youngest daughter in his arms, apparently intending to carry her to safety. The combination of swift current and the slippery stream bottom caused the man to lose his footing and fall backward while clutching his daughter. When his wife realized what was happening, she became hysterical and jumped into the current to save both her husband and her daughter. Finally, the father regained his footing, and he and his wife and daughter clung together in the pool. I inched forward again, removed the second daughter and carried her to safety with her sister. In the meantime, the man was able to extricate himself and his wife from the current and ultimately reach the security of the bank.

When this episode ended, Bill and I departed, hoping that the family would call off their venture in the interest of safety. Certainly, the possibility of a drowning was very real in this instance. We concluded that we did not need fireworks for our Fourth of July celebration. Four strangers on inner tubes had provided all the excitement we needed for one day.

A Sad Story

Silers Bald Shelter; Appalachian Trail

August 30, 1979

Silers Bald Shelter was a welcome sight after Robert's and my long climb out of the Hazel Creek Valley. Dropping heavy packs and resting in the vacant shelter on a warm August afternoon was pure joy. We didn't have the shelter to ourselves long, however, because three backpackers joined us within the hour. They seemed a somber bunch, but when one of them told us their story, one that I later verified as being true, we could understand their sadness.

As the three young men climbed Clingmans Dome along the Appalachian Trail earlier in the day they came upon a man sitting near the trail propped against a tree with eyes closed and his hands in his pockets. They spoke to the man but received no response. After repeating their greeting and again receiving no response, they received a shock: the man was dead! They told Robert and me that evidence at the scene gave the appearance that the man had taken his own life.

Faced with these unexpected circumstances, they had responded properly. They walked to the Clingmans Dome parking area, where they contacted park service personnel, who returned with them to the scene. After the park service representatives conducted an investigation and took their statements, the men were allowed to continue their walk.

The story was a sad one, and the young man who told it still appeared shaken by his experience, and understandably so. In time, the three backpackers busied themselves with camp activities; however, these chores could not remove the sadness they had experienced during their outing in the Smokies.

A Whisper in the Trees

Balsam Mountain Trail

September 10, 1992

I climbed from Walnut Bottom to the crest of Balsam Mountain and began walking the Balsam Mountain Trail toward Pin Oak Gap, my destination and the end of a pleasant three-day outing. Although I had enjoyed sunny, ideal backpacking weather throughout my journey, rain began to fall when I was within two miles of Pin Oak Gap. I heard it before I felt it. It began as a whisper in the trees as drops of water created a soft cadence as they pattered on the leaves overhead. Eventually, I donned my rain gear for protection against the rain that continued until I reached Pin Oak Gap about 3:30 p.m.

The rain increased in intensity as I drove along the one-way winding road to Round Bottom, where I forded Straight Fork on the auto ford (now replaced by a bridge). I continued through Big Cove, driving beside the beautiful Raven Fork, and arrived home with no further thought of the weather. However, as it turned out, my departure from the area was most timely.

The next morning, when I opened the September 11 issue of the *Asheville Citizen-Times*, I read the following:

> *Cherokee—Emergency workers evacuated homes and campgrounds in Swain County's Big Cove community near Cherokee Thursday after a cloudburst swelled creeks and rivers.*
>
> *Several bridges were washed out by the 7:30 p.m. rain that sent a 12-foot wall of water tumbling down the Raven Fork River, county emergency management coordinator David Hyatt said.*
>
> *Several people were trapped in their homes and calls were being put out for helicopters to evacuate them, Hyatt said.*
>
> *"They're having a tough time of it now," he said an hour into rescue operations.*
>
> *Emergency officials reported about a 20-foot wall of water rushing down the Oconaluftee River. Extensive damage was reported to bridges and roads along U.S. 441.*

Sara and Bill Hart in Cades Cove at the beginning of a backpacking outing, April 7, 1979.

> *Cherokee police said they had evacuated about 500 people as of 10:00 p.m. along the banks of the Oconaluftee River. A few businesses in town had opened up evacuation centers, dispatchers said.*

As I read about this disaster, one that I escaped by a few hours, I realized that I had witnessed the beginning of this storm while walking on Balsam Mountain. It had begun as a whisper in the trees.

Smoky Mountain Stories

During my years of rambling I have collected a number of stories and anecdotes related to the Smokies. I heard some of these while camping in backcountry campsites, while others were shared on hikes and others still were relayed to me miles from the Smokies by persons with firsthand knowledge of their subject. Some of these describe true events, others are probably complete fabrications and some may be based on fragments of truth. All have been, I suspect, subject to embellishment. Regardless, I have treasured these stories because they have added another dimension to my enjoyment of the Smokies.

A Treasure-trove of Stories

Fontana Marina

September 15, 1970

After four days on Eagle Creek, Bob F. and I walked to Fontana Lake, where we were met by Alvin Jenkins, an employee at the Fontana marina, who ferried us back across the lake. We were reluctant for our trip to end and chose to visit with Mr. Jenkins at the marina before returning home. Unbeknownst to us, Mr. Jenkins was a natural storyteller with a treasure-trove of colorful stories that he willingly shared. Most of these were about Quill Rose, one was about Will Orr and one was about himself. I listened intently, spellbound by his narratives. I have added my own titles to these accounts but, otherwise, have included these as I recall them.

Quill Rose and the Revenuers

Quill lived well up Eagle Creek in an isolated location, accessible by a rough trail that led upstream from the Little Tennessee River. Quill's remote homestead was an ideal place to manufacture illegal white liquor, and Quill periodically occupied himself in this craft.

It was known to a revenue agent named Worley that Quill made liquor, and Worley and a companion journeyed to the area on horseback for the purpose of raiding Quill's still. They arrived late in the evening and were greeted by Quill, who suspected that they were revenue agents, with a question as to what their business was. Mr. Worley replied that they were travelers bound for Tennessee. Because it was late in the day, Quill invited the two men to lodge with him for the night. He stabled and attended to their horses, fed the men supper and afterward served them his home brew.

When morning came, the men arose and told Quill that they had changed their minds and would not be going to Tennessee after all. With this pronouncement, they returned the way they had come, and Quill continued his illicit trade.

In a later meeting between Rose and Worley, Rose asked Worley why he had not made an effort to raid his still on his earlier visit. Worley told Quill that he had treated him and his friend so kindly that it would not have been fair to raid his still in view of his gracious hospitality. Thus, Quill's hospitality and Mr. Worley's sense of fair play averted a planned confrontation.

The Sham Battle

There were few inns in remote mountain areas in earlier times. Because of this circumstance, it was customary for travelers to request lodging at cabins along their route. Usually, they were accommodated for a small fee.

Quill Rose and a companion were traveling together. When night approached, they requested and were granted permission to spend the night at a cabin along the trail. There were several young men at this particular household who made a practice of engaging in sham battles before their guests as a form of mischievous entertainment. While their unsuspecting guests sat before the fire, the boys would pretend to fight and revel in the surprise and alarm that their antics caused.

Quill and his companion sat by the fire after supper, and as was customary, the boys started to fight. Chairs toppled and noise levels increased with the commotion as the fighters slyly watched for their guests' reactions.

Quill Rose was a fighter in his own right and not easily shaken by any threat. After the sham battle had raged for a few moments, Quill pulled out his long-barreled pistol and called to his friend: "John, pull your gun and come over here. Let's kill these SOBs before they hurt themselves."

The sight of Quill's weapon and his rough pronouncement caused the fighting to cease immediately. The room became silent and order was restored. Quill and his friend had abruptly turned the tables, and they spent a peaceful evening without further outbursts from their surprised hosts.

The Attempted Suicide

During his travels, Quill encountered a doleful man who had thrown a rope over the limb of a large oak tree and was attempting to hang himself. Quill dismounted and asked the man for an explanation of his actions. The man explained that his wife had died recently and that his life had become unbearable without her.

After hearing the man's explanation, Quill said, "Well, let's not waste time. I'll help and get done with it."

With the prospect of a successful hanging now at hand, the bereaved man began to make excuses and eventually changed his mind about the hanging altogether. Quill's bluff had been successful.

Will Orr and the River Crossing

An old man by the name of Will Orr and a casual acquaintance of his were traveling together along the banks of the Little Tennessee River when they came to a ford. A flat-bottomed boat was available at the crossing, but it was moored on the opposite side of the stream.

Old man Orr, armed and cantankerous, pointed his pistol at his acquaintance, who was also armed, and took his weapon. He then ordered the man to wade into the cold river and bring the boat back across, keeping his pistol trained on him all the while.

The companion was in no position to argue. He retrieved the boat and transported Mr. Orr to the opposite side warm and dry. When they landed, a brief struggle ensued, and the wet, angry companion reclaimed his weapon and aimed it at Mr. Orr.

He took Orr's weapon and ordered the old man to "take the boat across the river and leave it." Orr did as he was commanded and waded across the river, this time at gunpoint himself. Both men were now cold and wet, and their score was settled. They continued their journey without further difficulty.

The Fisherman and the Ranger

Mr. Jenkins told us that he fished Hazel Creek on occasion when he was not working. He said that his favorite lure was a spinner and a nymph called a "yellow hammer." He showed us this combination and told us emphatically that it was a "sure-fire fish getter." Then he went on to relay an encounter with a park ranger on one of his Hazel Creek trips when he had caught several fish on this lure. On this day a ranger had inspected his catch, which consisted of several large trout, and implied that they had been caught using red worms for bait, a violation of park fishing regulations.

On a later fishing trip, Mr. Jenkins experienced great success using his favorite spinner and fly. He caught and released several small trout; however, he kept two trout that were fourteen and seventeen inches in length. Just as he emerged from the stream, the ranger approached him. Our acquaintance told the ranger, "You've catched me now." The ranger, who had watched every cast from a concealed position along the bank, said, "I saw you catch the first fish and the last one, and I know you caught them honestly."

This exchange enhanced the mutual respect between the fisherman and the ranger. Their friendship was cemented by their encounter this day.

Visiting with Paul Fink

Johnson City, Tennessee

May 21, 1977

Paul Fink is one of my Smoky Mountain heroes. He was an early Smoky Mountain hiker, author and historian and an important influence during the formative period leading to the establishment of the Great Smoky Mountains National Park and the Appalachian Trail. I have always admired him for his many contributions.

I communicated with Mr. Fink for a few years near the end of his life, often sending him copies of photographs that I had taken while visiting places in the Smokies familiar to him in the hope that he would vicariously enjoy his beloved Smokies. When I learned that Mr. Fink had not seen the 1976 edition of Horace Kephart's *Our Southern Highlanders*—with George Ellison's introduction, one that credited and thanked him for sharing material—I resolved to take him a copy.

I drove to Strong Memorial Hospital in Johnson City, Tennessee, and arrived at his door at 9:45 a.m. His door was partly open, and I knocked lightly and faced Mr. Fink, who was sitting at a table working over a pile of old photographs. I then stepped into the room and timidly said, "Pardon me." Mr. Fink looked up and boomed, "Pardon you, hell. What are you here for? Make it short, I'm busy!" Stammering and off guard, I quickly told him who I was and was prepared to give him the book and leave immediately.

Mr. Fink, who would be eighty-five at his next birthday, gradually warmed when he recalled our previous correspondence and the photos I had sent. He then asked me to pull up a chair and spoke with me for the next two hours, although I made several attempts to leave to avoid tiring him. But he began another story and I remained. He had a keen mind and spoke of his past recollections in an interesting, enjoyable and sometimes humorous way. I cherish those hours in his presence.

The following are some of the less serious aspects of our conversation, beginning with my favorite story.

The Bear Tooth

Mr. Fink had once been asked to come to Gatlinburg to escort a number of distinguished northerners, as well as a few locals, to visit a local peak. Mr. Fink referred to one woman in the party as "having diarrhea of the mouth" because of her comments regarding mountain people. On the way to the landmark, Mr. Fink found a boar tusk and plotted with Wiley Oakley, a noted mountain man, guide and personality in his own right, to have a bit of fun at the woman's expense.

Upon reaching their destination, Mr. Fink dropped the boar tusk in the dirt and then "rediscovered" it. Then the following exchange ensued. Fink, holding up the tusk, said to Oakley, "Aren't there bears in this area?"

Oakley: "Mought be."

Fink: "Don't bears shed their teeth this time of year?"

Oakley: "They mought do that."

Fink: "Doesn't this look like a bear tooth?"

Oakley: "Yep! Mought be."

Mr. Fink said the woman was completely taken in by this act. He thereupon presented the boar tusk to her, one that was passed off as being a bear tooth. The woman was enthralled.

Mr. Fink, with a gleam in his eye, said he wondered if someone eventually told her she was the victim of a joke. And he wondered how she reacted when she learned that she had been given a boar tusk instead of a bear tooth.

Crown Fire

Mr. Fink asked me if I had ever seen a crown fire. When I told him I had not, he explained that a crown fire is a fire that spreads rapidly through the tops of trees. He said he observed this terrifying sight once with a friend. The friend had observed, "The scriptures say the earth will be consumed by fire. Don't you guess we ought to step back?"

"What Did You Do Then?"

Sugar Fork Campsite; Hazel Creek Trail

June 17, 1981

Bill and I walked the familiar trail beside Hazel Creek to the Sugar Fork Campsite, arriving there in the early afternoon. We spent the balance of the day fishing before returning to camp to prepare supper. Following our meal, we visited around the fire with some Haywood County natives who shared the site with us.

One of our new acquaintances, with his face illuminated by the orange glow of the campfire, grinned and told the following story.

A man who was camping on Hazel Creek some time in the past stored his firewood in his tent to ensure a supply of dry wood for his fire. One night after the man had retired, a bear came into his camp and rubbed itself against the side of his tent. In an effort to scare the bear away, the man grabbed a stick of firewood and struck the bear soundly on the rump through the thin tent wall. Instead of running, the bear wheeled about and ripped the side out of the tent with one swipe of its mighty paw, leaving the man and the bear face to face. When the man later recounted this story and reached the part where he and the bear were facing each other, his listener asked, "What did you do then?" In response, the teller of the tale replied, "Why son, I apologized!"

Dead Man's Boots

Bone Valley Campsite; Hazel Creek Trail

October 3, 1982

Ed and I walked toward the Bone Valley Campsite, where we planned to camp for two days, exercising muscles used to a sedentary pattern of activity. When we arrived at the site, we found already there a party of five horseback riders from Haywood County, North Carolina. As a matter of coincidence, we had camped with the leader and two members of this party the previous year, and we were pleased to renew our acquaintance with these congenial campers.

We shared a cheery fire with members of the party after supper. Conversation dealt initially with Smoky Mountain camping experiences and then moved to accounts of mountain happenings. It was at this point that the leader of the horse party told a story that had been passed down in his family for years. It is repeated here as I recall it.

Many years before, the leader's great-grandfather was traveling on a mountain trail and happened on the scene of a murder just after it had occurred. The killer had robbed a man returning from South Carolina with money received from the sale of horses and hidden the body in a hollow tulip poplar tree. When the killer discovered that his crime had been witnessed, he turned his gun on our storyteller's great-grandfather and forced him to remove his boots and to put on the boots of the dead man, thus implicating him in the crime. After the killer had ordered the change of boots, he sent the hapless witness on his way wearing the dead man's boots. The great-grandfather carried the burden of his knowledge about this brutal crime throughout his lifetime. He finally related the story to family members on his deathbed and assured them that he had no part in the murder.

A Place Name That's Not on the Map

Leicester, North Carolina

Circa 1984

Will Crisp lived in Leicester, North Carolina, for many years; however, he was born along Chambers Creek in the Great Smokies before the formation of the national park. Will told me that when he was a young man he herded cattle on Welch Ridge and stated that there were two springs on the side of Welch Ridge that the herders called "Cow Shit Springs." When I asked Will how these springs earned this name, he indicated that the two springs were so close together that a cow could lie down between the springs and drink from one and shit in the other.

Needless to say, the North Carolina nomenclature committee that verified and assigned place names following the founding of the park did not include this landmark on the map.

Scenes and Reflections

The Great Smoky Mountains National Park is unsurpassed in its grandeur and beauty. The mood of the mountains can change from minute to minute and from season to season, offering a never-ending variety of sights, sounds, colors and sensations. I have often felt a sense of deep reverence while in the Smokies and given thanks for the moment as I marveled at a grand vista, paused to enjoy a small setting of exquisite beauty, witnessed a sunrise or sunset, absorbed the sounds of nature or appreciated the vast variety of flora and fauna found in the park. It is difficult to adequately capture these experiences and sensations in words or photographs. I will attempt, however, to describe particular scenes and reflections as a means of recalling special moments.

Scenes

The Unveiling of the Smokies

Cliff Top; Mount Le Conte

June 1971

Skies darkened and rain began to fall after supper, cloaking the crest of Mount Le Conte in somber gray. Robert and I donned rain gear, climbed to Cliff Top, huddled on this stone outcrop and watched the wind-driven fog swirl about the crest, occasionally revealing brief glimpses of dark green fir trees below. While we observed this scene, the fog began to lift and we witnessed the gradual and magical unveiling of the western mountains.

The rain-washed skies became crystal clear and peaks were outlined starkly against the golden backdrop of the setting sun.

The impact of these few minutes was dramatic. We gazed at this quiet mountain panorama until dark caused our reluctant return to Mount Le Conte Lodge.

Cold Smoke

The Chimneys

January 2, 1978

In time, Robert and I gazed down at the sharp promontories that are aptly named the Chimneys. Holding to rhododendron with leaves tightly curled in response to the cold, we half walked and half skidded along frozen earth to their base and climbed steeply upward over a stony spine to the highest promontory, employing considerable care to avoid a misstep and a fall from this popular landmark.

When viewed from far below, these peaks might give one the impression of chimneys. Once we were on the crest, we experienced the sensation of being on a roof, the roof of the mountains. The Chimney on which we stood had another feature resembling an actual chimney. This one had a natural opening in the stone, one that provided a view of the dense heath growth below. An updraft of cold air rushed through this "chimney" and created an interesting display of frozen ice embroidery around the opening.

The cold smoke provided no warmth, yet we huddled about the opening as if it did and gazed at the grandeur before us. Far below was a deep valley, where the West Prong of Little Pigeon River gradually flowed to the northwest. Mount Le Conte was above us on the opposite side of the valley, its crest covered by a mantle of white. Le Conte's spectacular beauty was breathtaking. We lingered, transfixed by the view of the mountain's white mass framed by the bluest of blue skies.

Breathtaking Beauty

Mountain Farm Museum

October 14, 1978

Bill and I approached the Great Smoky Mountains National Park from Cherokee, North Carolina. Upon entering the park, we were greeted by a scene of breathtaking beauty. The green expanse of the Enloe-Floyd

Bottom lay before us, bordered by a weathered split-rail fence. A plume of blue-gray smoke curled from the stone chimney of the handsome log cabin at the Mountain Farm Museum and floated in the still air. Behind the farmstead, with its assemblage of old farm buildings, was a backdrop of mountains tinted with autumn's pastel colors that merged into white clouds that diffused the sun's rays and bathed this panorama in soft light.

The pristine beauty of this scene made us feel that we had been transported back in time to the previous century. Little seemed changed from a long-vanished era. Although I always experience a sense of inner peace when I enter the park, this moment seemed especially magical.

Scenes of Present and Past

Rabbit Creek Trail

April 11, 1980

After a night at Scott Gap, Sara and I climbed across Pine Mountain, following an old road that ran toward Abrams Creek. A vista along our route allowed us a distant view of picturesque Happy Valley, which is adjacent to the park boundary. A white church, houses, farms and fields, all miniature in the distance, portrayed a rural scene untouched by expanding development in the region. Had we been here fifty years earlier, I expect that this picture would have been little different.

When we were within earshot of Abrams Creek, we came upon an old homesite situated in a nearly open grassy glade. A carefully laid chimney constructed of fieldstone marked the location of a long-vanished home. Yellow daffodils and jonquils with crisp almost-white blooms grew about the chimney, reminding us of a family's love for their home and desire to enjoy the beauty of these flowers each spring.

These scenes—the distant views of Happy Valley and the old homeplace near Abrams Creek—were some of the special rewards of this day in the Smokies. These experiences allowed us for a short interval to savor another era.

Sara making a cold fording of Abrams Creek, April 11, 1980.

Sun on Ice

Greenbrier Pinnacle

November 29, 1980

I climbed snow-covered Greenbrier Pinnacle on a cold, windy morning. When I ascended to the slopes below the crest, I reached a vantage point from which I could view the main Smoky Mountain divide. Particularly notable was the distant Sawteeth section, so named because its irregular profile reminded early hikers of the teeth of a saw.

The clouds above the Sawteeth were dark and threatening, yet the sun's slanting rays glowed beneath them, creating radiant, almost translucent, silver and gold cloud borders. These bright rays also reflected on the rime that coated the distant crest with an effect that was quite beautiful. Darker hues of blue on lower slopes mixed with the brilliant white rime above to create an exceptional and appealing winter landscape.

Unsurpassed Views

Hughes Ridge Trail

January 16, 2006

Ron, Marilyn, Jerry and I climbed along Hughes Ridge in ever-deepening snow. The world through which we walked was a palette of muted colors—grays, browns and blacks—displayed against a backdrop of white. In shaded coves the shadows gave a cold, blue cast to the bleak forest, while the slopes of Mine Ridge well above us reflected the sun with a white intensity.

As we ascended, the skies became overcast, and dark clouds replaced the blue that we had enjoyed earlier. From high vistas we looked back on Thomas Divide, which lay across the valley, and found that the divide had taken on shades of purest purple under the prevailing charcoal-gray skies. I marveled at the fact that I had never before enjoyed this particular combination of colors and contrasts, and I recognized that the Smokies are never without their special surprises and rewards.

SUNRISES

Moon Shadows

Little Dudley Creek

January 25, 1981

I began walking an old road along Little Dudley Creek in the predawn darkness. The temperature was twenty-five degrees, and a heavy frost covered the ground. A three-quarter moon cast a silver glow on the forest, creating subtle patterns of light and delicate shadows. Where the moon's full light fell on frost-coated grass, the delicate ice crystals on the grass glinted with diamondlike sparkles.

With only the moonlight to guide me, I carefully picked my way along in the shadowy road trace as the darkness began to fade imperceptibly. I found it necessary to light a match to read the graying trail sign that provided directions at my first junction.

My new route climbed away from Dudley Creek at this point and ascended through open woods, affording a fine view of the eastern mountains. I stopped and admired the silhouetted outlines of these dark forms, forms that were enhanced by the silver and gold rays of the rising sun. These rays gradually increased, brightening the sky with fresh color that spilled over the mountains and flowed into the forest about me. The intensity grew, and it was day.

Streams of Sunshine

Meigs Creek Trail

November 25, 1981

The sounds of the stream flowing through the Sinks faded behind me as I climbed the Meigs Creek Trail, walking briskly to build up warmth against the chill of early morning. After cresting a low ridge, I followed my path gently downward to Meigs Creek and an easy ford, one of many along the trail. A thin cloud layer floated overhead. The rays of the rising sun pierced these clouds through infrequent openings, and shafts of golden sunshine glowed with such substance and body that I felt that I could almost grasp them in my hands. The clouds themselves glowed with luminosity, adding a soft light to the mist in the air. This vision often caused me to pause in admiration.

Dawn

Deep Creek Trail

September 6, 1982

Bill and I walked along Deep Creek in the semi-light of early morning in a world that seemed devoid of color except for shadows of gray, black and white. This was a temporary state, however, as the promise of day was at hand.

Day dawned over mist-shrouded mountains. At first, a faint pink tint was noticeable. Then, the whole sky was transformed by degrees to a golden pink. Ever-increasing rays of the sun caused the sky to glow with breathtaking translucence until the whole was radiant with gold and pink hues. This spellbinding transformation from night to day was accomplished with the symphonic sounds of Deep Creek serenading us while we made our way through Deep Creek Valley. The dramatic sunrise was so enthralling that I almost regretted the fact that full daylight had gradually erased the colors of sunrise.

Beauty Spots

A Mountain Jewel

Somewhere in the Smokies

June 30, 1984

Al W. and I reached an abandoned trail after a morning of slow off-trail travel, most of it accomplished in a steady, light rain. After a brief rest at a rotting signpost with its faceless, broken sign lying on the ground, we began our ascent to a prominent peak that was approximately two miles away and 1,700 feet above us.

One and a half hours of difficult scrambling was required to cover the next mile along a route choked with briars, blowdowns and rhododendron thickets. These tangles clawed at our clothing and skin as we crept through this maze. In time, however, we moved into more open forest and travel became easier.

Excitement increased as we approached our goal. The best was yet to come, however. Our path led through a nearly open glade, where the forest thinned and lush grass spread beneath scattered trees. The rain had now stopped, and the sky became brighter as clouds drifted away to reveal glimpses of blue overhead. This small green meadow with its rain-washed freshness on the wild slopes seemed like a gleaming jewel set in the midst of the mountains. This beauty spot possessed a compelling charm that caused us to pause in wonder.

The Highlight of My Day

Somewhere in the Smokies

September 2, 1989

I was engaged in an off-trail walk and had followed an old logging rail grade to its end. After completing this portion of my outing, I planned to ascend 1,400 feet to an abandoned trail and incorporate it in my return to my starting point.

My ascent began pleasantly enough. I walked along a small branch through a sun-dappled forest decorated with beautiful turtlehead with its exquisite pink blooms. This led me to the base of an unnamed cascade with a film of frothy water that seemed to glide for an estimated 100 to 150 feet over solid stone that sloped upward at a forty-five-degree angle, although I could not view it in its entirety from the base.

The ascent around the cascade required considerable time. Part of the time was consumed in selecting a route, and the balance entailed a physically difficult ascent, well away from the cascade. I was completely unaware as I climbed that the highlight of my day awaited me above the cascade.

Once I reached the bluff-like crest, I beheld an almost level glade that was formed like an imperfect circle with a diameter of perhaps fifty or sixty feet in a forest of hemlock trees interspersed by a few tall hardwoods. A thick growth of rhododendron bordered the clearing. Although the surface appeared smooth, this was an illusion. Lush grass covered small stones on the floor of this glade, and water flowed everywhere through it with unseen whispers. The sun's rays, filtered by the forest cover, reflected silver on the shiny rhododendron leaves along the border and brightened the center of the clearing. I was moved by the awe-inspiring perfection of this remote, wild place. The recollection of this scene has remained as a singular memory.

White Lace

Mount Sterling Ridge Trail

November 8, 1992

Tom D., Jim S. and I walked the Mount Sterling Ridge Trail on the final day of a three-day outing. The weather had been cold, and a light snow had fallen, accompanied by foggy evenings. All of these elements combined to create one of the most spectacular displays of rime I had ever seen.

We had begun this day at Laurel Gap Shelter under overcast skies. By midmorning, the clouds had cleared and the sky was a deep blue. When we looked upward, we gazed into a forest of fir and hardwood trees in which every limb, branch and twig was covered in a thick coating of frosty white rime. The slanting rays of the November morning sun reflected on this display, which fairly sparkled with a white brilliance that enhanced the complex lacelike tracery above that was framed by blue sky.

Although we took photographs in an attempt to capture this breathtaking scene, our efforts fell short. The most lasting and complete images were those in our minds.

A Geometric Pattern

Bradley Fork Trail

January 16, 2006

One after the other, Ron, Marilyn, Jerry and I descended the snow-covered Bradley Fork Trail along Taywa Creek as the setting sun cast long shadows in this narrow valley. While we trudged along, I gazed at the passing landscape and was attracted by a jumble of chair-sized boulders that seemed frozen in a static cascade on the steep slope across the creek. The tops of these boulders were blanketed with snow; however, their sides were exposed to the sun, which had caused the snow to melt, exposing the rich, dark green covering of moss on each boulder.

As I focused on this scene, the whole appeared like a geometric pattern of irregular green and white shapes, all set against a backdrop of stark winter woods. This artistic structure of stone, moss and earth was compelling in its simplicity. There was special beauty here, beauty that compelled me to stop in admiration.

Sounds

Reflections in the Sun

Scott Mountain Trail

October 19, 1980

My route entailed a climb of approximately 1,700 feet along the Scott Mountain Trail. I walked the narrow footpath that wound along shaded slopes, crooked through the head of small coves and led across the crests of side ridges. It was a pleasant afternoon, one without the necessity of meeting any schedule but my own.

On one of these ridges, I chose a sunny place, reclined against a log in the warmth of the autumn sun and concentrated on the sounds of the forest. I listened as dry leaves rustled gently in the breeze and occasionally released their hold on delicate twigs to drift downward, making dry clicking sounds as they brushed against other leaves on their gliding path to the forest floor. The occasional bird scolded me from the treetops. At times gentle breezes stirred the air in patterns like random notes played on a scale. All was quiet save the natural sounds of the forest, creating a period of peaceful relaxation. I relished the pleasant time that I spent here, a time when no human sounds intruded on my ears.

Thunder and Lightning

Newfound Gap

March 21, 1982

I arose at 4:30 a.m. and enjoyed a quiet drive toward the Smokies, anticipating a pleasant day on the trail. By the time I reached Cherokee, North Carolina, heavy raindrops had begun to fall, accompanied by thunder and flashes of lightning.

This storm continued until I reached Newfound Gap. I parked there in the predawn darkness to watch while the lightning played over Thomas Divide and the valley of the Oconaluftee River. Long flashes of lightning arched through the black sky in irregular yet graceful patterns. Some of these almost seemed to duplicate themselves and seemed to refute the old saying that "lightning never strikes twice." With each radiant burst, the mountains were visible for brief seconds in a pale and ghostly yet beautiful display of fleeting light.

The storm was accompanied by loud bursts of thunder that reverberated across the mountains like a continuous drumroll, one magnified a thousand times over. My vehicle shook as the storm swept over the gap with tremendous intensity, accompanied by sheets of rain that came in wind-blown waves. These sounds—the thunder, the pelting rain and the wind—were just as dramatic as the lightning that danced in the sky with vivid intensity.

What an excellent beginning to a day in the Smokies!

If a Tree Falls

Balsam Mountain Trail

July 25, 2005

We were not far from Pin Oak Gap, Ron and I, when we were distracted by a noise. This was not one of the common sounds one expects to hear while on a Smoky Mountain outing. The sound we heard was that of a falling tree in the nearby forest. It began with the distant brushing of limbs being struck as the tree began its fall. The brushing sound reached a crescendo as the falling tree crashed into the larger limbs of neighboring trees, and then there was a moment of silence followed by a muffled thud as the heavy rotten trunk of a forest giant struck the soft earth. It was an eerie sound, one that I had heard on a few other occasions. It was a sound that marked the cycle of life and death in the forest, and we had been privileged to savor the moment.

Trees and Flowers

An Array of Blooms

Gregory Ridge Trail

June 14, 1980

Alice and I passed the prostrate body of the "the Big Poplar" and eventually made a switchback to reach the main crest of Gregory Ridge. Once on the ridge, we were treated to the spectacular beauty of a prolific growth of flame azaleas, with blooms ranging in color from pale yellow to the deepest orange-red colors imaginable. Each bush seemed to possess a color variation of its own, and we stopped frequently to admire the variety and beauty of these graceful blooms that brightened the forest. Time was ours, and no schedule dictated that we hurry on before paying tribute to nature's handiwork; thus, many blooms were examined and admired on our way to Gregory Bald.

Cheaper by the Dozen

Brushy Mountain Trail

July 27, 1980

My climb led me through beautiful terrain. A miniature oasis of green plants grew in a moist seepage at the base of a gray boulder not far from the former Great Smoky Mountains Hiking Club Cabin. Farther along, I passed through a thick stand of laurel and rhododendron that scarcely allowed the sun's penetration. At another point, I counted two dozen yellow-fringed orchids growing in profusion along a short segment of my path. These beautiful yellow orchids with their clusters of delicate yellow blooms were dazzling, and I inspected many of them as I passed. When I gazed beyond my immediate surroundings, I looked upward at Greenbrier Pinnacle across the valley to the east. Trillium Gap appeared as a small wooded depression to the west, while the lower slopes of grand Mount Le Conte lay to the south.

Of all these scenes, it is the yellow-fringed orchids that I remember most vividly. Never again have I viewed as many of these beautiful wildflowers in one location.

Breathtaking Displays

Roundtop Trail

May 17, 1981

We began a gentle ascent around the slopes of Roundtop and Joint Ridge and crossed the headwaters of Big Branch before descending gently to Little Roundtop. All along this portion of our walk, Robert and I were rewarded by breathtaking displays of laurel blooms. Every bush was adorned with showy clusters of pink-white blooms, all made brilliant by the bright sun. The appearance of the forest here was unlike any scene I had observed before, with hundreds of laurel bushes fully cloaked in delicate displays of color, almost as if coated by a thick layer of snow. Robert and I paused frequently to absorb this unique woodland scene and to savor occasional distant views of beautiful Tuckaleechee Cove.

Rain-dampened laurel blooms beside the Gunter Fork Trail, May 25, 1997.

White Corridors

Bote Mountain Trail

July 17, 1981

Alice and I climbed steeply upward on the Bote Mountain Trail, drawing ever closer to our destination—Spence Field. The rhododendrons lining our path were adorned with abundant white blooms that were beautiful to view. These blooms were in the last phase of their grandeur, however, and many had fallen. As we ascended, we walked in a virtual corridor of white with blooms overhead and afoot. It was quite remarkable!

A Sense of Timelessness

Laurel Falls Trail

January 2, 1982

We walked along the paved portion of the Laurel Falls Trail—Al W., Robert and I—in the early morning light. This popular trail, often crowded during the tourist season, was quiet, lonely and gray under a misty fog that cloaked the mountains. When we reached Laurel Falls, we found that recent rains

Robert Hill and Bill Hart in a forest of large trees, January 2, 1982. *Al Watson photograph.*

and melting snow had expanded the volume of water cascading over the two levels of this famous landmark, providing a study of white against a backdrop of gray, green and brown as water, stone and forest combined in a winter collage. After admiring the beauty of the falls, we climbed beyond, ascended Chinquapin Ridge and walked through virgin forest filled with hemlock and tulip poplar trees of massive proportions. When we looked upward at the uppermost branches of these giants, they seemed to disappear into the gray mist that clung to the slopes. The dark trunks on the slopes above and below us stood like silent ghosts. This open forest with its ancient trees evoked feelings of reverence and awe and a sense of timelessness. I was grateful that this wonderful forest had escaped the logger's axe and saw.

A Window to the Past

Albright Grove; Albright Grove Loop Trail

February 26, 1984

Jim C., Karen, Alice and I climbed upward on the Maddron Bald Trail in chilly, invigorating morning air, fresh with the chill of winter. In time, our trail led along the perimeter of Albright Grove, a small stand of virgin timber that had somehow survived the logging era. We rested near the entrance to the grove on a weathered chestnut log and ate crisp apples while we surveyed the winter forest, decorated with patches of snow, moss, lichens and ferns.

The Albright Grove inspired a sense of reverence. We looked on a forest that had remained unchanged for hundreds of years. It provided a window through which we could view the past and created an emotional experience like that in viewing a treasure of incomprehensible value. Giant trees grew all about, and our eyes were drawn upward by the straight lines of massive trunks to limbs that spread overhead like the arches of a grand cathedral. Words seemed inadequate to express our awe at the majesty about us.

As Far as the Eye Could See

Chasteen Creek Trail

April 24, 1988

Spring had arrived, and the Smokies were experiencing a transformation. New growth was emerging from beneath the bleached gray leaves of autumn that covered the forest floor. Trees were alive with the unfolding of leaves, fresh and green with new life. Wildflowers were arrayed in natural displays that contrasted artistically with the decaying boles of fallen trees with their mossy coverings.

It was amidst this setting that I began climbing the slopes of Hughes Ridge following the old road along Chasteen Creek, one that I had often traveled. My familiarity with the route caused me to look forward to landmarks and details that I had mentally recorded from past visits. Traces of old rail grades, old fields, abandoned homesites, a prominent waterfall and the climbs and switchbacks were all anticipated in turn.

Upon reaching an elevation of three thousand feet, I passed through pleasant open woods on my right, populated by straight tulip poplar trees. The sparse foliage allowed the bright sun to flood the forest, which was blanketed with trillium as far as I could see. The display of pink-white three-petaled flowers stood above the blanket of green on the forest floor like suspended snowflakes, each one reflecting the brightness of the sun with white radiance.

The land here sloped into a gentle depression. A small stream flowed between moss-covered borders and dashed over level after level of jumbled stones in a frothy white strand that was divided and rechanneled again and again by the stream's stony course. The myriad trillium and the small stream was a picture of natural symmetry. The beauty of this scene was captivating.

A Surprising Discovery
Indian Creek Motor Trail
November 23, 1990

As I climbed the Indian Creek Motor Trail, I made a surprising discovery. I found several brown, spiny burrs nestled among the drab leaves in the trail. I examined one of these and concluded that it was too large to be a chinquapin burr. Subsequently, I was left with only one other conclusion. I had discovered chestnut burrs! The chestnuts from these burrs were not present, however. They had already been harvested by the forest creatures.

These burrs are a rare find, indeed, although the nuts are coveted by the wild inhabitants of the forest. As I held one of the burrs, I reflected on the value of the chestnut tree before it fell victim to the blight that killed most of these trees by the 1930s. The wood of the chestnut tree was used for cabin and barn construction and made durable fence posts; men earned income by stripping and selling its bark for use in creating tannic acid; the nuts were eaten by mountain families and gathered and sold for extra income; and livestock was fattened on this natural bounty, to say nothing of its benefit to wild birds and animals.

Before long, the blight would claim the small tree that furnished the burrs I admired. However, I had been allowed the opportunity to witness the tenacity of the chestnut tree. It continues to attempt to reclaim its former stature as one of the important trees of the forest. Perhaps those who labor to find a blight-resistant chestnut will one day be successful.

She Loves Me, She Loves Me Not
Mount Sterling Trail
August 23, 1992

As I climbed the Mount Sterling Trail, I noticed a thick covering of dodder draped across the low foliage beside my path. Dodder is an attractive parasite that takes its nourishment from the host plant on which it grows. It is easily identified. It looks like fine, smooth orange strings with small white flowers. It twines over and around low weeds, grasses and shrubs and can sometimes form into heavy tangles.

My father identified this plant for me when I was quite young, perhaps in response to one of my many "what" questions, and I immediately thought of him when I saw the matted orange tangle. My father called the plant "dodder," as well as "love vine." His explained that when he was a boy he was told that if one placed a strand of dodder on another plant and it continued to grow, it meant that your sweetheart loved you.

I can never pass dodder without thinking of my father's name for it, love vine, a much more charming name than dodder.

A View of Hell

Gunter Fork Trail

May 25, 1997

Bill and I planned a walk of approximately nineteen miles beginning at Mount Sterling Gap and ending at the Big Creek Trailhead. The Mount Sterling, Mount Sterling Ridge, Gunter Fork and Big Creek Trails constituted our route, one that provided a sampler of the high country as well as the beauty of the Big Creek Valley.

By the time we reached the Gunter Fork Trail, it was raining lightly, and the mountains were shrouded in gray clouds. As we descended below the clouds, we were treated to distant views of laurel slicks or "hells," which appeared as smooth green openings in the dense forest that surrounded them. The smooth appearance of these hells is deceptive, however. These patches are so called because they are composed of dense tangles of rhododendron and laurel that are virtually impenetrable.

As Bill and I viewed the multiple hells, we were glad that we were not faced with the prospect of fighting our way through them. Notwithstanding the unflattering name for these places, they were quite beautiful when viewed through wisps of lifting fog, made so by the distinct trace of pink that overspread them, the effects of early pink blooms that adorned the distant rhododendron. We paused to take in this view, one that would be even more dramatic in June when the rhododendron reached full bloom.

Growing against Logic

Chasteen Creek Trail

December 19, 2005

Ron, Marilyn and I spent a day on Chasteen Creek in exploration. We enjoyed bright sun, blue skies and winter woods. Bare trunks of trees reached skyward, drawing our eyes upward. We noted wildlife signs along our route. These included the rootings of wild boar in search of food, trees horned by deer and scat that may have been that of a coyote. Also, we viewed streams that ran clear in which an occasional trout darted in blue-green pools.

Although the woods were bare and the forest floor drab with a covering of bleached leaves, we found fresh green growth that defied the logic that says that green plants should not appear until spring. These exceptions to the rule were the crane-fly orchid and puttyroot orchid, both of which we found growing near the trail. They are winter favorites of mine and easily spotted and identified. However, their delicate, subtle flowers that appear later in the year when the leaves have withered are much more difficult to locate. I was glad that these plants defied logic and gave us the opportunity to enjoy a reminder of spring on this winter day.

STREAMS

Timeless Gifts

Bradley Fork Trail

October 17, 1970

I walked for an hour on the Bradley Fork Trail and, with no particular reason to rush my trip, left the old road to select a streamside vantage for a brief period of relaxation. Several rainbow trout were feeding near the surface, and I observed their effortless movements. One eleven-inch trout would rise, select an unseen morsel and return to the depths, exposing a flash of red on its silver side in its quick forays in search of food. This pattern was repeated over and over, much to my enjoyment.

My focus shifted from the trout to colorful red and yellow autumn leaves that slowly drifted past, swirling and sinking into emerald waters and resurfacing again to drift downstream in the slow current. This kaleidoscope had endless variations, complemented by the sun's rays that played on the water, creating tiny flashes of brilliant silver.

Bradley Fork in winter, December 19, 2005.

These random scenes caused me to reflect on how infrequently we stop to observe the patterns of life about us. The rapid pace of our modern world too often causes us to overlook the small gifts in our daily lives, yet these timeless gifts offer pleasure, as they did for me on this October day. My experience beside the stream reminded me that I was often too busy to appreciate the small blessings in my life.

Deep Creek in Winter

Deep Creek Trail

February 26, 1977

Deep Creek displayed the effects of the severe cold weather of the previous week. Large, irregular sheets of ice shaped like jigsaw puzzle pieces filled the creek. Trickles of water flowing into the creek were frozen into miniature static waterfalls that sparkled like gemstones in the sunlight. Twigs in or near the water were encased in a delicate coating of ice. The ice patterns and formations seemed endless and could not be passed without marveling at their winter splendor.

Morning after a Rain

Eakaneeltee Campsite; Eagle Creek Trail

October 8, 1982

Ed and I arose on the last day of our six-day outing in the Smokies. We had been lulled to sleep the previous evening by a gentle rain. The rain ended sometime during the night, and we arose to a misty gray dawn. As there was no reason for an early start, I walked along Eagle Creek after breakfast and admired the beauty about me. Green rhododendron contrasted with the silver surface of the creek, which reflected the fog-filtered rays of the sun. A damp coating of rich moss along the stream banks further enhanced the contrast. The trees above were covered in bright red, yellow, maroon and fading green leaves that fluttered in the morning breeze. I was captivated by the moment.

Stream Vistas

Deep Creek

May 30, 1988

Bill and I walked several miles up the Deep Creek Trail to trout fish; however, our real excitement was Deep Creek itself, with its ever-changing vistas. Random gray stones of all sizes shaped the course and flow of the stream. These stones were variously encrusted by lichen or covered by rich green moss. Likewise, the appearance of the stones beneath the surface of the water was just as unique. Some were covered by dark green moss that provided secure footing for wading. Others were clean and frequently slippery. Here and there pockets of yellow-white sand were tinged pink with miniscule pieces of red garnet, adding an unusual touch of color to the stream bottom. Deep Creek's waters flowed beneath overhanging leafy tree branches. Rich grass grew on small islands in the stream, gaining a meager foothold in the thin layer of damp earth between the stones. The stream was open in places and closely sheltered by the forest in others. The effects of this growth produced a mixture of lighting effects ranging from full illumination to the depths of shadows.

Scenes and Reflections

A Unique Cascade

Gunter Fork Trail

September 10, 1992

I forded Big Creek's cold waters and began my climb up the Gunter Fork Trail to one of the many beautiful cascades in the Smokies. After about two miles, I reached a cascade some 150 feet high. The water at the top fell free for a few feet until striking a wall of Thunderhead sandstone. From there it glided down the face of the stone, expanding in a filmy glaze of liquid that glinted in the sun. On its journey downward, the water passed over a band of gray-brown conglomerate near the bottom, adding another interesting feature to this landmark. The water's journey ended in a small, shallow pool beside the trail. In retrospect, I realize that I have always anticipated with pleasure each visit to this beautiful place.

Big Creek below Walnut Bottom, May 25, 1997.

Azure Stones

Bradley Fork Trail

January 16, 2006

We were on the final segment of a sixteen-mile hike—Ron, Marilyn, Jerry and I—when we reached at 4:30 p.m. the segment of trail that paralleled Bradley Fork. As we descended this stream, we were entertained by a variety of pools, runs and small cascades. In one pool immediately beside the trail, the watercourse divided. On the far side of the pool, the water rushed away, following the main stream channel. On the trail side, the water flowed out in a shallow eight-foot-wide channel immediately below me. When I gazed down into this pool, I gazed at a stream bottom paved with silver dollar–sized flat stones deposited there by the natural force of the water with such perfection that they were mosaic-like in appearance. They were azure colored beneath the clear, glinting water that was flecked with silver highlights reflected from the sky above. Perfection!

Sensations and Reflections

Star Light, Star Bright

Russell Field Shelter; Appalachian Trail

October 23, 1975

Al C. and I were walking the Appalachian Trail from Clingmans Dome to Fontana Dam and stopped for the night at Russell Field Shelter. Supper chores were over, and I left Al visiting with other backpackers while I walked into the overgrown field above the shelter. The stars overhead appeared as sparkling silver-golden pinpoints framed in a black sky. I looked at this panorama for long minutes examining the intriguing star patters overhead. In time, I lowered my gaze and focused on the distant land that lay west of the Smokies, where the lights of faraway settlements appeared as a reflection of the stars. It was perfectly quiet and serene, and the chill of autumn served as a foretaste of the winter that lay ahead. This experience was a perfect ending to my day.

A Debt of Gratitude

The Bryson Place; Deep Creek Trail

February 26, 1977

Johnny, Bill and I embarked on a twelve-mile circuit that entailed walking all or a portion of the Deep Creek Trail and all of the Indian Creek and Martins Gap Trails. After descending the latter, we reached the historic Bryson Place, so named for the owners in former times of the last homestead on Deep Creek, and the approximate halfway point in our outing. The old house that for years had served as a base for campers and rangers had vanished. However, we did locate the marker that commemorates Horace Kephart's last permanent camp in the Smokies not far from the Bryson Place Campsite in a small level area by Deep Creek.

This marker consisted of a small millstone, partially buried in the earth, to which was affixed a plaque that bore the following legend:

On this Spot
Horace Kephart—Dean of American Campers
And One of the Principal Founders of the
Great Smoky Mountains National Park
Pitched His Last Permanent Camp
Erected May 30, 1931 by Horace Kephart Troop
Boy Scouts of America—Bryson City, N.C.

I reflected on Horace Kephart's contributions. Through his efforts and the efforts of many like-minded citizens, the Great Smokies were preserved and protected as a national park. That we could stand at the Bryson Place beside the fast-flowing waters of Deep Creek in the midst of a magnificent forest made me realize that I owed a debt of gratitude to all those who had the foresight to preserve this vast resource.

Signs of Life

Low Gap Trail II

February 11, 1978

Weeks of indoor activity provided motivation to break this sedentary pattern and return to the Smokies for a long walk. Subsequently, I tramped along the gated road leading to Cosby Campground in the cold before dawn and questioned the wisdom of my early morning venture, realizing that I could be home in a warm bed and not shivering in the darkness. I knew that this emotion would pass, however, because I knew that the rewards of my outing would outweigh the perceived advantages of remaining home.

Ultimately, I reached and ascended the Low Gap Trail toward the main crest of the Smokies. As I neared Low Gap, the grade was completely snow covered, and I studied the telltale tracks of fox, mice, deer and birds. These provided tangible evidence of life in a forest that otherwise seemed cold and sterile. These tracks appeared to be only aimless patterns, but in reality, they reflected the purposeful search for food and shelter, essentials for survival. It was interesting to study these tracks and trails to determine the identity and purpose of the creatures that left them—signs of the drama of their lives.

Unexpected Brightness

Derrick Knob Shelter; Appalachian Trail

May 27, 1979

I awoke at 3:30 a.m. with a case of indigestion and arose to secure a remedy from my pack. Following treatment, I stood in the shelter doorway admiring a starry sky. Suddenly, a bright flash of white light streaked overhead. At first, I thought the flaming object was a shooting star; however, it was much closer and brighter than other shooting stars I had seen. In fact, it reminded me of an exploding Roman candle. The object creating the brilliant light arcked overhead, with the arc ending southeast of Clingmans Dome, where it burst into several flaming pieces that hurtled toward the earth. It was so close that I fully expected to see the pieces strike the earth and listened to hear subsequent explosions. There were none, however, and in seconds the light disappeared.

This sight left a mysterious and somewhat disconcerting impression on me, and I pondered this sighting trying to determine what I had just witnessed. Later, when I recounted this experience to friend, he speculated that I had seen a bolide—a bright, exploding meteor—which was probably the case. This unusual sighting was indeed spectacular and is etched forever in my memory.

A Rainbow Over the Smokies

Silers Bald; Appalachian Trail

August 30, 1979

A brief afternoon shower swept the Smokies as Robert and I enjoyed the patter of the rain from the protection of Silers Bald Shelter. When the skies cleared, I climbed to the crest of Silers Bald, or Silers Meadow as it was sometimes called by early herders and hunters, to admire the always visually pleasing mountain panorama. Little did I know that a surprise awaited me. In addition to the views, a most marvelous rainbow composed of a spectrum of soft pastel colors arched high over the mountains ending directly above Mount Le Conte. I was captivated by the beauty of the rainbow and considered myself especially fortunate to have observed its colorful arc.

A Mystical Forest

Mount Collins; Appalachian Trail

October 26, 1979

I awoke at Mount Collins Shelter to a world that was immersed in thick fog. The gray mist softened the outlines of the forest and created a sense of intimacy. I was surrounded by a mystical forest with shapes softened and distorted by the fog, which limited my views to perhaps one hundred feet. When I reached the Appalachian Trail and began ascending toward Clingmans Dome, I was still surrounded by fog that had frozen on the upper branches of fir trees, creating lacelike patterns of white that contrasted markedly with the dark green of protected lower boughs. The gusting wind caused fine frozen particles of ice to drift down about me like snow, coating the trail with a dusting of fine icy powder. This was a pleasant way to begin a day in the high country of the Smokies.

Memories of My Father

Alum Cave Bluffs; Alum Cave Trail

October 15, 1981

Robert and I climbed to Alum Cave Bluffs and stood in the powdery dust beneath this grand wonder. While I rested, I recalled my first visit to this site with my father more than thirty years before and was grateful to him for leading me on my first walks in the Smokies. As I thought about that day long ago, I remembered the mixture of wonderment and awe that I experienced on that occasion. It was this experience more than any other that created in me a lingering curiosity that motivated me to seek out and explore the Smokies as an adult. Now, many trips later, as I stood at one of my Smoky Mountain shrines, I knew that my curiosity was insatiable and that the Smokies would always hold for me a spell that could not be broken.

The Meaning of Preservation

Gatlinburg Trail

January 29, 1984

Alice and I began a short walk along the Gatlinburg Trail, a trail leading from the town limit to the Sugarlands Visitors Center. As we stepped across the boundary line between Gatlinburg and the Great Smoky Mountains National Park, we noted a dramatic contrast. Commercial endeavors occupied one side; nature's handiworks occupied the other. On one side the sounds of traffic predominated; the sound of the river serenaded us on the other. We were thankful that the Great Smoky Mountains are preserved because of these extremes. Only through preservation can one fully appreciate the developed and undeveloped and keep both in perspective.

What Did It All Mean?

Newfound Gap

June 15, 1984

I seated myself in a wooden chair in the eastern end of the Newfound Gap Overlook facing the impressive Laura Spellman Rockefeller Memorial. There were hundreds of other people there who, like me, had gathered to celebrate the golden anniversary of the Great Smoky Mountains National Park.

The formal ceremony began at noon with the playing of the national anthem, while the nation's flag fluttered in the breeze that caressed the crest. Dignitaries from North Carolina and Tennessee presented messages, and Mr. Robert Bushyhead, a member of the Eastern Band of the Cherokee, delivered a benediction in English, repeated in the beautiful Cherokee language.

I wondered what it all meant—all the words and ceremony. Perhaps the meaning was not in the spoken word but rather in the act of celebrating

The grassy expanse of Spence Field, October 4, 2004.

Autumn on Eagle Creek, November 18, 2007.

the fiftieth year of the existence of the Great Smoky Mountains National Park itself. Certainly, this was a celebration of the contributions of the many people, past and present, who worked to establish, protect and preserve the Great Smokies. Also, in celebrating the milestone of the fiftieth year, it seemed to me that there was an implicit charge to maintain the national park for the enjoyment and education of future generations. Finally, I recognized that I owe a debt of gratitude to those who made the Great Smoky Mountains National Park a reality and to those today who continue to maintain the original dream and vision.

ANIMAL OBSERVATIONS

I have always enjoyed seeing, hearing and discovering the signs of animals during my outings in the Great Smoky Mountains National Park. These experiences have added an extra element of pleasure to my hikes and fishing trips. Additionally, they reinforce the importance of the national park as a vast resource for protection of a full range of flora and fauna. Although this chapter is ostensibly about experiences with wild animals, I have included one dog story here, because of an encounter in the wild environment of the Smokies.

MICE AND THEIR KIN

When the Campers Are Away

Derrick Knob Shelter; Appalachian Trail

October 28, 1977

Bill and I prepared supper and enjoyed the companionship of the other campers in the shelter. In time, we all retreated to our sleeping bags, and the shelter grew quiet. With all the campers out of the way, the mice came out to play. With great speed and agility, they scaled the cords from which packs were suspended and entered the packs, rummaging at will through their dark recesses in search of food. Their tiny claws and teeth made a variety of distinct sounds as they clawed, munched and chewed canvas, foil and paper while on their way to a furtive feast. They climbed along the chain-link fence that stretched across the front of the shelter. When illuminated by an occasional flashlight beam, the mice reminded me of high-wire walkers in a circus. Also, they scampered along log bunk frames and across sleeping campers with abandon. The patter of little feet and chewing of little teeth continued into evening until sleep dulled my hearing of their nocturnal ramblings.

A Bowl of Mice

Shuckstack Fire Tower; Appalachian Trail

September 4, 1978

From our camp at Cove Creek, Robert and I climbed to the Appalachian Trail on our way to Fontana Dam. When we reached the trail to Shuckstack Fire Tower, we made the short climb to the tower, where we enjoyed hazy views of the Smokies. While there, we paid a visit to the fire warden's cabin. We found that the porch was open, and we had a look around. The main feature there was a cabinet filled with heavy white ceramic dishes for use by those manning the tower during fire season. This in itself was unremarkable; however, the unusual feature was the fact that a mouse's nest had been carefully constructed in a cereal bowl. The builder of this nest—probably a white-footed mouse—was in residence. She possessed golden fur, round ears and dark brown-black eyes. She was not alone, however; other smaller mice shared the bowl with her, a cozy abode indeed. The mouse peered at us curiously, apparently wondering what creature had disturbed her happy home. We admired the mouse briefly. However, a look was sufficient, and we quickly moved away to avoid creating a tempest in a cereal bowl.

Our Entertainment for the Day

Somewhere in the Great Smokies

October 27, 1983

It was late in the afternoon when Ed and I reached our campsite after a day that entailed miles of strenuous off-trail walking. We quickly made camp, prepared a simple supper and relaxed after our rigorous day, intent on enjoying the charm of our wild setting. Although we had not expected to be entertained beyond this, a tiny shrew made its appearance at our feet and moved quickly past in its frantic search for food. Needless to say, we were intrigued by the appearance of this miniscule animal because such sightings are unusual.

Good Luck Charm

Derrick Knob Shelter; Appalachian Trail

October 4, 2004

Sara and I awoke to clear sky and bright sun, ideal weather for our walk to Spence Field. As I contemplated the day ahead, I welcomed sharing one of my favorite sections of the Appalachian Trail with Sara. I looked forward to climbing Thunderhead and Rocky Top, as well as visiting other interesting points along the way.

I donned my clothing, sat on the edge of the sleeping platform and began putting on my boots. I placed my foot in the first boot and tightened and tied the lace. Then I put on the other boot. There was something hard in it, however. I pulled it off and tipped it over, and out dropped a small buckeye that had been partially gnawed by a mouse. Unfortunately for the mouse, it had lost its treasure, or perhaps its booty, in my boot.

I grew up listening to mountain lore that taught that carrying a buckeye brought good luck. Hence, I preferred to think that the buckeye was the mouse's gift to me and intended to serve as my good luck charm. In any event, I accepted it in this spirit. You know what? It worked. Sara and I enjoyed good luck and an excellent trip!

Squirrels

"Robbing Hood" Strikes Again

Sheep Pen Gap; Gregory Bald Trail

August 28, 1977

We spent the first night of our multi-day trip at Sheep Pen Gap. During our first evening at this pleasant campsite, a flying squirrel (or at least that's what we suspected), while searching for food, gnawed several holes in Robert's pack while it was suspended by a rope from a high limb. I hung my pack from the same tree on the last night of our outing and found several holes in it the next morning when I lowered it. We concluded that the "Robbing Hood" of squirreldom had taken its revenge a second time; however, we could not blame our nocturnal robber for doing what came naturally.

Like a Circus

Rainbow Falls Trail

November 9, 1980

The crispness of the morning was pleasant, and Bill and I anticipated the pleasures of walking to Mount Le Conte by the Rainbow Falls Trail—the first time on this trail for both of us. As we climbed, we observed tumbling Le Conte Creek and heard its voice, which filled the air with a continuous refrain that was at times a whisper and at others a roar. We also observed the remains of rock walls and a few rotting timbers along the lower reaches, evidence of a time when the stream's margins had been settled and farmed.

Signs of human presence vanished as we climbed higher, and we invaded the territory of the red squirrel, or boomer, as it is called by mountain folk. These beautiful rusty-red creatures scolded us severely from high above and spread the alarm throughout their treetop domain, an alarm picked up by their brothers and sisters, that strangers were approaching.

We paused and watched the boomers as they traveled from tree to tree on limber branches that bent precariously under their weight. We felt like circus spectators, and as such marveled at their feats of agility and daring that were for our benefit only.

A Christmas Feast

Smokemont Campground

December 26, 1986

I donned a warm jacket, pulled on my day pack and walked through the unoccupied portion of Smokemont Campground, heading for Bradley Fork and a day in the Smokies. The trees were drab and bare, except for the dogwood trees, which were adorned with clusters of bright red berries that appeared like decorations on a Christmas tree. These beautiful clusters had not gone unnoticed by the gray squirrels. They seemed to be everywhere. They climbed trees, worked their way along branches or just deftly sat holding the fruit in their agile paws while they gnawed off the red covering to reach the delicious seeds. I counted twelve squirrels engaged in a Christmas feast of grand proportions. This sighting was a delightful preface to my day in the mountains.

Rabbits

I'm Glad You're Hare

Mount Le Conte Shelter; Boulevard Trail

May 24, 1970

Starting at Newfound Gap, I walked to Mount Le Conte via the Appalachian and Boulevard Trails and arrived at the shelter with time to spare, the first arrival of the day. As I stepped into the shelter clearing, I was greeted by a large rabbit, probably an eastern cottontail, which nibbled contentedly in a patch of rich green grass fifteen feet from the shelter. The rabbit paused when I arrived and studied me briefly through large dark eyes before returning to its meal. Eventually, the rabbit retreated into a thick patch of blackberry canes behind the shelter, where I suspected there was a snug nest with awaiting young.

How Did the Story End?

Deep Creek Trail

May 30, 1988

After a pleasant day of trout fishing several miles up Deep Creek, Bill and I reluctantly reeled in our lines and began the long walk to our vehicle. As we neared Bumgarner Branch, Bill, who led the way, halted abruptly, brought to a stop by a large blacksnake that lay beside the trail. The snake was perfectly motionless and seemed oblivious to our presence, demonstrating no inclination to flee. The reason for the snake's reluctance to move became apparent to us in a few moments. A small rabbit scarcely bigger than my fist sat nearby. The rabbit's small ears were flattened against its gray back, and its dark eyes glistened with fear as it sat frozen no more than three feet from the snake.

While we viewed this scene, we heard voices behind us. Given the fact that people were approaching, we felt that we had to act in haste to prevent potential harm to these creatures, particularly because snakes are subject to mindless killings. Bill quickly picked up a stout, straight stick and lifted and moved the blacksnake out of sight of the trail and away from the frightened rabbit. Once this was done, we walked on ahead of the approaching party, leaving the rabbit where it sat and counting on its natural camouflage and instincts to protect it.

How did the story end? The outcome of the drama rests with the imagination. Did the rabbit flee? Did the snake return seeking to consume its prey? The end of the drama remains a mystery.

WEASELS

Dead on Arrival
Hyatt Ridge Trail
July 2, 1977

At daybreak, Bill and I began climbing the Hyatt Ridge Trail toward Low Gap through a beautiful forest filled with the sounds of tumbling water and the singing of birds. We walked steadily, admiring forest scenes in the changing light of day. Our hearts were light as we speculated about a successful day of fishing on Raven Fork. The topic of conversation changed, however, when we discovered the body of an immature weasel—I believe it was a long-tailed weasel—on the trail. On closer study, the body seemed to be unharmed, as we could discern no reason for its death. Had a fox killed it? Whatever the cause, the body symbolized the natural cycle of life and death that plays itself out largely unnoticed by the casual observer.

Hot Pursuit
Noland Creek Trail
March 17, 1984

I drove to Noland Creek accompanied by Bill and his friend, Jeff, for a trout fishing outing, my first of the year. As we assembled our fishing rods, a park ranger stopped to examine our fishing licenses. Afterward, Bill and Jeff walked on to the stream to fish while I remained to chat with the ranger.

In time, I walked down the Noland Creek Trail, noting fresh beaver signs along the way. When I rejoined Bill and Jeff, they recounted an interesting wildlife sighting they had observed earlier. Upon rounding one of the bends in the trail, they encountered a rabbit running toward them at full speed. A long-tailed weasel was several yards behind the rabbit in vigorous pursuit. When the rabbit and weasel approached Bill and Jeff, both animals fled into the forest. I regretted that I missed this unique sighting. Perhaps my day will come!

Mink

I'm Surprised to See You Here

Somewhere in the Smokies

November 22, 1986

I had spent much of my day along a remote, ascending creek, admiring a variety of views along this small stream as it tumbled down from the heights, a major chain that joins the Smokies. The sun brightened my little valley as day progressed, creating a distinct line between light and shadow on the mountains above me. I watched a grouse fly recklessly through thick rhododendron, wondering how it managed such agility in full flight. I watched the sun's rays reflecting off the gold and brown feathers of a large hawk that glided silently overhead. All of these simple joys added to the pleasure of my strenuous but enjoyable climb.

I stopped periodically during my ascent to determine my bearings. During one of these pauses at about five thousand feet, I chose a moist rock on which to rest while I studied map and altimeter, enveloped in the quiet of the forest. Suddenly, I heard a twig snap in the nearby rhododendron

Straight Fork in the spring, May 26, 2005.

and became instantly alert. I listened intently for several moments, but there were no other sounds. As I sat peering into the dense rhododendron about me, I was surprised by a small dark form, presumably the mysterious twig snapper, that came scurrying from the undergrowth and hurried by me, passing within three feet of where I sat. I knew immediately that this busy creature was a mink. It was so close, in fact, that I could see its beady eyes and small ears and even see glistening droplets of water on its heavy, dark, chocolate-colored coat. The mink appeared to think I was a natural feature of the landscape and seemingly paid me no notice as it scurried by.

This sighting was most exciting and unexpected. It is rare that one ever observes a mink and rarer still to see one at the higher elevations. However, through further research, I learned that mink have been observed at higher elevations than my sighting. Nevertheless, the mink provided me with a story to tell the family on my return home.

Groundhogs

I Spy

Oconaluftee River

October 14, 1978

Bill and I fished the Oconaluftee River under an October sky that left its reflection on the gliding waters. Maple, sycamore, beech and tulip poplar trees along the borders of the stream were arrayed in a spectrum of color representing autumn at its best. It was a great day to be out.

As I fished a favorite stretch of water, casting nymphs into the current and watching them drift downstream, I noticed a pair of dark eyes peering at me from the opposite side of the stream. I'm not even sure how I identified this animal. After all, it was cleverly concealed and not at all where I would have expected it be. Nevertheless, it was there. It was the head of a groundhog.

Seeing groundhogs is common in the Smokies. In fact, I always look for them when entering the North Carolina side of the park in the field near the Mountain Farm Museum. They may be frequently viewed here standing at attention at the entrance to their burrows. I even saw one that appeared to be an albino on more than one occasion in 2006.

What made the sighting so unusual was the location of the groundhog. It stared at me from the end of one of the entrances to its burrow. This opening, however, was located in a perpendicular bank approximately eight feet high, and the entrance, filled by the groundhog's plump body, was four feet above the edge of the stream and four feet below the surface of the earth above. In effect, the groundhog enjoyed a streamside view, a view on which I had intruded.

Once I had spotted my furry friend, the groundhog looked at me from a dozen feet away, and I looked at the groundhog in a game of I Spy. Our game continued for a full minute before the groundhog tired of playing and retreated into the depths of its home beside the river. After its departure, I regretted that our game had ended; however, I was pleased to have had this opportunity to view a groundhog in an unusual riverside environment.

Raccoons

Turning Over a New Stone

Little Cataloochee Trail

April 9, 1977

Alice, Sara, Bill and I and Tim and Susie (two of Sara's and Bill's friends) enjoyed a spring outing in the Little Cataloochee Valley. We paid a visit to the historic Hannah Cabin, walked through the vanished settlement of Ola, lunched on the grounds of the picturesque Little Cataloochee Baptist Church and ascended the old road toward Davidson Gap to visit the Messer Barn, since relocated into the Big Cataloochee Valley.

The children and their friends lagged behind while Alice and I moved ahead, talking quietly. As we approached the Messer Barn, we were surprised to see a large raccoon one hundred feet ahead of us. Although raccoons are normally nocturnal, this raccoon was working a double shift and busily turning over stones in a small branch that ran across the old road that served as our trail. The raccoon had not detected our presence and continued its search for food while we crept closer, admiring its beautiful gray-brown coloration and lush plume of a tail with alternating bands of black and gray-brown. Finally, the black-masked animal turned toward us, gazed for some seconds and then raised its head, curiously sniffing the air, as if trying to decide what action to take now that its territory had been invaded by alien intruders.

The raccoon was not long in making up its mind. It lumbered unhurriedly away and into the undergrowth, where it probably turned over a new leaf, although Alice and I would have preferred to continue watching it turn over new stones.

SKUNKS

A Strange Dance

Russell Field Shelter; Appalachian Trail

October 23, 1975

Following a pleasant day on the Appalachian Trail, Al C. and I camped at Russell Field Shelter, where we enjoyed a simple meal and the fellowship of shelter mates before eventually retiring. The shelter grew quiet as talking subsided and tired backpackers drifted off to sleep.

The shelter was not to remain quiet for long, however. After perhaps thirty minutes, we heard metallic scraping sounds on the floor. Now awakened, I shined my flashlight in the direction of the noise from my position on an upper bunk. It did not take long to find the source. My beam focused on a large, beautifully marked striped skunk that had obviously entered the shelter in search of food.

The skunk shuffled confidently about, sniffing for leftovers. After surveying the floor, it moved to the lower bunk where Al slept, raised up on its hind legs and sniffed only inches from Al's head before moving to a clear plastic bag left on the shelter floor that contained our garbage. While I watched, the skunk edged its head and shoulders into the bag and licked the residue from an empty tuna can with its pink, darting tongue. Next, the skunk, obviously sure that there was more food in the can, attempted to pull the lid from the can for better access. In doing this, the skunk's foot became wedged between the lid and the can.

When I realized the plight of the skunk, a sense of horror gripped me as I imagined the repercussions that would soon occur. While I considered what was to come, the skunk emerged from the bag, shaking its foot in an effort to remove the can, while I shuddered thinking "Here it comes!" This was followed by a strange dance, accompanied by the sounds of *klunk*, *klunk*, *klunk* as the tuna can struck the earth floor of the shelter with each step the skunk took. What next? I continued to think "Here it comes!" I knew that any moment the skunk would fill the shelter with noxious spray as the ultimate statement of displeasure. After several more *klunk*, *klunk*, *klunks*, the skunk was able to shake the can from its foot. Thankfully, it then exited the shelter. I felt a great sense of relief that the incident ended without negative consequences for the skunk, as well as for those in the shelter.

This was my first encounter with a skunk in the Smokies. Following this one and others, I know that skunks are fairly predictable around campers if left alone. I also learned from the strange dance at Russell Field Shelter to always hang everything, even if it's garbage and even if it's in a shelter.

Outstanding in His Field

Spence Field Shelter; Appalachian Trail

October 29, 1977

Bill and I descended from the crest of Rocky Top and walked over the golden grassy expanse of Spence Field, eventually arriving at the Spence Field Shelter. After claiming bunks, I returned to the field above the shelter, reclined against a lichen-encrusted stone and dozed in the warmth of the afternoon sun.

The rustling of dry grass behind me slowly brought me to my senses. Turning carefully, I sighted a beautifully marked striped skunk with its distinctive black-and-white markings and bushy tail that was cautiously but purposefully coming across the field to investigate me. Needless to say, I remained perfectly motionless as the skunk crept within a foot of my leg. The skunk paused at this point, scented the air with its shiny black nose and ambled away to other pursuits, leaving me to relax and gaze on the mountains beyond.

I Didn't Want to Say Anything

Pecks Corner Shelter; Appalachian Trail

October 27, 1983

Al W., Ed and I reached Pecks Corner Shelter late one afternoon after a strenuous off-trail walk that had consumed most of our day. Upon arrival at the shelter, we were greeted by four other men, who had arrived before us. When supper chores were completed, we visited for a while and then retired one by one, except for one night owl who remained by the fire.

I climbed to my upper bunk situated against the shelter wall and enjoyed the pleasant comfort of my down sleeping bag, drifting off to sleep in the cool autumn air. Then it happened! I felt something pressing against my sleeping bag. The pressing sensation began against the back of my legs, moved along my hips and then caressed my shoulders. Next, I heard the patter of small feet near my head. I was conscious of these movements; however, I never fully awakened and returned to deep sleep when the sensations ended.

When morning came, the night owl, who had remained by the fire, told me that a large skunk had visited the shelter and had climbed onto the platform to examine my sleeping form. The skunk was the source of the sensations I had felt as it squeezed between me and the shelter wall. The night owl said, "I didn't want to say anything" when explaining his hesitation about warning me of the presence of the skunk. He feared that a sudden motion on my part would have brought out the worst in the skunk's disposition. Needless to say, I appreciated his precaution. Silence is golden and, possibly, odor free.

BEAVERS

First Signs of Beaver

Eagle Creek Trail

September 12, 1970

This was our first visit to Eagle Creek, and Bob F. and I looked forward to the excitement of walking a new trail, enjoying the beauty of the Smokies and fishing for a few days on upper Eagle Creek. We had not ventured more than a mile from Fontana Lake when we reached an area where beavers had constructed a small dam on a side drainage feeding Eagle Creek. The industrious beavers had felled small trees near their dam, leaving in their place gnawed, sharp-topped stumps. These trees, along with small limbs and mud, had been incorporated together into the dam, evidencing the beaver's mastery of dam design and construction.

This was my first experience with beavers in the Great Smoky Mountains National Park, and it was special to me because it marked the presence of an animal thought to have been absent from the Smokies since the early part of the twentieth century, until first noted on Eagle Creek in the 1960s. In the intervening years since seeing my first signs of beaver, I have noted that they have extended their range to many of the major streams on the North Carolina side of the park. I have welcomed their return and always enjoy finding evidence that they have been as busy as beavers.

Just Swimming

Lakeshore Trail

September 10, 2005

We had just been ferried across Fontana Lake to Hazel Creek for a long weekend of camping at the Proctor Campsite. As we walked along the edge of the lake on the short segment of trail between Fontana Lake and the campsite, Sara observed an immature beaver swimming near the shore. While we watched, the beaver plunged beneath the lake's vivid green surface and resurfaced seventy-five feet away. The process of diving and resurfacing occurred twice, allowing the beaver to cross the Eagle Creek embayment before we lost sight of the graceful swimmer. Our beaver sighting was the first time I had actually viewed one in the park, although I had frequently found their signs. This sighting reminded us that when given a chance nature can reclaim the land and establish a habitat that makes it possible for wildlife to live and prosper.

Foxes

On First Impression

Double Springs Gap; Appalachian Trail

November 1966

I stepped into the chilly air that was accompanied by harsh winds that swept the Clingmans Dome parking area. Sightseers there emerged into the cold for a brief glimpse of the mountains and quickly retreated to the warmth of their vehicles. It was not my intention to seek refuge on this dreary day, however. I was bound for Silers Bald with the twofold goal of enjoying high mountain vistas and visiting a Smoky Mountain bald for the first time.

In time, I reached Silers Bald and enjoyed the expansive views from the solitude of the bald. Reluctantly, I turned back after a long rest on the crest and set a brisk pace to stave off the cold that penetrated my clothing.

A few paces north of Double Springs Gap, I was startled to see a reddish-colored animal in the trail seventy-five feet ahead of me. On first impression, I thought it was a small dog. I stopped to study the animal at the same time that the animal stopped to study me. It was at this point that I realized that the animal was not a dog at all but rather a red fox. I could clearly see its delicate head and pointed ears, look into its intelligent dark eyes, admire its glossy coat and observe its bushy tail with a white tip—all against a backdrop of a bleak forest.

After a period of mutual examination, the beautiful animal exited the trail in a single bound, leaving me to continue on. Of the fox encounters I have experienced in the Smokies, the long moment spent viewing this beautiful animal stands out in memory as my favorite.

What's That Sound?

Rich Mountain Campsite; Indian Grave Gap Trail

October 20, 1976

I reached the Rich Mountain Shelter (now a campsite) mid-afternoon after a pleasant day of walking in the mountains above Cades Cove. Shadows grew long with the approach of evening, and I began to suspect that I would have the shelter to myself. Before long, however, two hikers approached, climbing slowly beneath the burden of large backpacks. When they reached the shelter, they lowered their packs and introduced themselves. The young man said, "Call me Dome like dome light." The young woman introduced herself as Aurora. Both were from Thailand but lived in the United States. They were taking advantage of their time here to see the country. Dome told me that he was a political science major and that Aurora was an anesthesiologist. After introductions, this pleasant couple performed camp chores, conversing in the musical patterns of their native language.

When darkness descended over the high cove where we camped, we retired—I to my upper bunk, and Dome and Aurora to the lower. At 1:00 a.m. I was awakened by the sound of a heavy object striking the tin roof of the shelter. This initial noise was followed by the sound of a creature walking about on the roof just above my head, causing the tin roof to squeak with each step. Because the shelter had been constructed on a site excavated from the side of the mountain, it was a simple matter for the animal standing above me to jump from the bank behind the shelter to the roof.

Whatever was on the roof had certainly jolted me out of a sound sleep. What was it? In the fog of semiwakefulness, I assumed it was a bear.

Dome and Aurora had left their packs unprotected in front of the shelter, although I had suspended their food with my own to prevent loss in the event of a bear visit. I suggested to Dome, who was also awakened by the noise, that he move his and Aurora's packs into the shelter in the hope of protecting them if a bear appeared.

The sounds on the roof ceased as suddenly as they began, and Dome and I waited quietly for the form of a bear to loom around the wall of the shelter at any moment. While we waited, we probed the darkness with our flashlight beams, but there was no bear to be seen. After what seemed like minutes, our lights focused on a moving form fifty feet in front of the shelter—it was the mysterious roof walker! As it turned out, the animal that had disturbed our sleep was not a bear; it was a red fox that was now bounding into the darkness, white-tipped tail streaming behind. I had no doubt that the fleeing fox had a smug smile on its face, amused by its game of "alarm the backpackers." Once the game ended, we returned to warm sleeping bags and slept the remainder of the night without further excitement.

A Sign of Boredom

Cades Cove Loop Road

August 14, 1981

Sara and I had been walking in Cades Cove and were circling the cove on the Loop Road on our way back to our campsite when traffic slowed to a crawl. This, of course, is not unusual in Cades Cove; however, progress seemed slower than normal and we wondered at the cause of the delay.

Eventually, our question was answered when we reached a red fox that was sitting on a bank about the height of the passenger window, watching the parade of tourists pass. Each vehicle stopped briefly, halting all the others, to allow passengers to admire the fox before moving on. We, like the others, took our turn, pausing momentarily to view this beautiful animal.

The fox's coat was glossy and reddish in color, and its eyes were attentive, framed by a delicate, well-formed head. The fox was uninterested, however, in the seemingly endless flow of traffic. In fact, the fox confided this fact to us as we passed. Well, not in so many words; however, the fox yawned mightily, revealing a perfect set of sharp teeth, as if to say, "I'm bored by all this." Our feelings were not hurt by the fox's attitude. After all, the fox had seen a lot more humans than humans had seen foxes.

Coyotes

Echoes

Spence Field; Appalachian Trail

October 4, 2004

Sara and I were on the Appalachian Trail west of Spence Field following the crest of the Smokies. It was early morning and we were beginning another day on the trail when we first heard the sounds. There was a series of yipping barks and howls emanating from far below on the North Carolina side that echoed up and out of the valley in a musical serenade that was at the same time eerie and beautiful. We paused to listen. These were the unmistakable sounds of coyotes—a sound that I had heard once before on Hazel Creek. These howls and yips came in bursts, often separated by intervals of minutes before the next serenade began. Coyotes were not present when I first began hiking in the Smokies; however, they have moved into western North Carolina in the intervening years. Sara and I enjoyed a special music that is likely to remain in the Smokies forever.

WHITE-TAILED DEER

An Infrequent Sighting

Chasteen Creek Trail

April 24, 1971

Bill, who was five years old, and I camped at the Lower Chasteen Creek Campsite. This was Bill's first overnight camping trip in the Great Smoky Mountains National Park, and I had chosen this particular site for our outing because our walk was far enough for Bill to have a sense of adventure but not far enough for it to tire him. I carried our gear, and Bill carried a small sack filled with stuffed animals.

With Bill's assistance, I built a campfire and prepared our supper. Afterward, we roasted marshmallows, and Bill made fire sticks from burning twigs and used them to make orange circles and shapes in the darkness while I smoked Old Danger and observed him. Upon completion of this entertainment, we retired to warm sleeping bags and a comfortable night's sleep.

We arose to a bright, clear morning and prepared a nontraditional backpacking breakfast of bacon, eggs and biscuits, which we slathered with butter and jelly. This meal was sufficient to fortify us for the day ahead.

Following breakfast, exploration was the next item on our day's agenda. We followed the old road up Chasteen Creek for perhaps a mile and explored old fields and abandoned homesites looking for patterns of former habitation. As we wandered aimlessly, we sighted a deer in one of the overgrown clearings and watched while the deer bolted and fled up the hillside, displaying the white underside of its erect tail. This was significant to me because this was my first observation of a deer on the North Carolina side of the park. Little did I realize that deer observations would become one of the more common wildlife sightings that I would make in the Smokies in the years ahead.

After our rambles, I packed our gear and Bill packed his animals for our return trip home. Bill had many stories to tell his mother and sister, including his account of our deer sighting—his first in the Smokies.

Between Mother and Child

Bradley Fork

May 22, 1977

Bill and I walked three miles up the Bradley Fork Trail and began fishing Bradley Fork on our way back to Smokemont, selectively choosing pools and runs that offered the best opportunity for success. This tactic proved successful. Both of us caught and released several beautifully colored rainbow trout in repayment for our efforts.

A short distance below the confluence of Chasteen Creek and Bradley Fork, we waded across Bradley Fork and continued our descent on a long-abandoned rail grade that passed through overgrown fields. The area appeared to be an excellent deer habitat, prompting me to comment to Bill about the likelihood of seeing a deer. Almost as soon as these words were spoken, a doe stepped onto the grade sixty feet ahead of us. Then she faced us and moved skittishly, as if she wanted to flee, yet she stood her ground. Bill and I stood motionless and observed the strange behavior of the beautiful deer for a full minute.

Suddenly, a movement near the streamside drew our attention and introduced another element into the drama. A small fawn, large enough to have lost its spots, lifted its head and climbed the bank on delicate legs to join its mother. Once reunited, both moved quickly away in graceful bounding leaps with white tails raised in alarm. Bill and I realized that we had almost come between a mother and child. As a result, we had been rewarded by a demonstration of the deer's maternal instinct to protect her fawn.

An Idyllic Scene

Abrams Falls; Abrams Falls Trail

April 13, 1980

After a night at the Little Bottoms Campsite, Sara and I walked two hours at a leisurely pace to reach Abrams Falls. No others had yet arrived, and we had the area to ourselves. We dropped our packs and selected a vantage point from which to admire the crystal waters of Abrams Creek plunging in plumes of white foam into the dark and expansive pool at the base of the falls. On the opposite side of the stream, oblivious to our presence, was a doe that browsed in an effortless and relaxed manner on abundant spring foliage at the border of the pool.

It was as if the beauty of the falls, shimmering pool and graceful deer had been posed in anticipation of the appearance of a great artist who would capture the moment in a grand natural landscape. Yet all of this was ours. The setting and scene were idyllic and made the rigors of our outing worthwhile just to enjoy this one moment.

ELK

Elk in the Smokies

Caldwell Barn; Big Cataloochee Valley

June 12, 2004

Alice and I stood in the loft of the Caldwell Barn with several friends, sheltered there to avoid a hard rain that drummed mightily on the barn's tin roof. We were there to learn about the Elk Project, a project that resulted in the restocking of elk in the Great Smoky Mountains National Park, and to observe the elk for ourselves.

Late in the afternoon, six elk entered the field that spreads across the narrow valley above the barn and grazed contentedly, always remaining close to the border of the forest. They were majestic animals, and seeing them was an excellent experience.

Later, as Alice and I discussed the elk, I expressed mixed emotions about their presence in the Smokies. While tourism has received a boost from the elk, for selfish reasons I regret that they have significantly increased visitation to the Big Cataloochee Valley. I have always enjoyed the valley because it seemed like a hidden gem and regret seeing this change with the influx of visitors. The future of the Elk Project is yet undetermined, however. Time will tell whether elk will flourish in the Smokies.

Signs of Elk

Oconaluftee River

December 31, 2005

Winter trout fishing on the Oconaluftee River has its special pleasures, pleasures that Bill and I decided to enjoy on the last day of the year. We cast nymphs in the beautiful, clear water that magnified and brought out the subtle colors of the smooth stones on the stream bottom. It also magnified small, submerged, pale green sticks that had been stripped of their bark, sticks that were perhaps one-half inch in diameter and one to two feet in length. These sticks were the undeniable work of beavers that made their homes under the stream bank. Rushing water flowed against mossy banks that supported a heavy growth of rhododendron, which sported tight buds that would become pink-white flower clusters in June. The bare stems of yellow root, so named for the bright yellow color that appears when the stems are scratched, stood in ranks along the stream margin. All of these details added pleasure to our day. The missing element, however, were the trout. They proved reluctant to sample our lures, and we concluded our efforts after a couple of hours.

Upon recrossing the stream to reach our vehicle, Bill called my attention to an eight-foot-tall sapling that was scarred and torn from bottom to top, leaving strands of bark hanging loosely like ribbons. Although I had frequently seen trees horned by deer, I had not seen anything like this, nor had Bill. He quickly recognized, however, that this small tree had been horned by an elk that had ranged from the Cataloochee Valley many miles away, where they had first been stocked, to the bottoms along the Oconaluftee River. This was a significant discovery and one that gave special meaning to our day despite our lack of angling success.

European Wild Boar

Was That Laughter I Heard?

Spence Cabin Branch; Eagle Creek Trail

September 13, 1972

Bob F. and I were climbing the steep trail toward Spence Field, making good progress until we reached Spence Cabin Branch. At this point, we came face to face, or maybe face to snout, with a large, snorting European wild boar with sharp, curved, ivory-colored tusks. The animal probably weighed 200 to 250 pounds and appeared quite formidable. Now, this was my first encounter with a wild hog, and I was not sure what to expect. Stories of the hog's reputed ferocity instantly came to mind, and I fully expected the boar to charge at any moment. Certainly, the hog was standing its ground and keeping its beady eyes focused on Bob and me.

My mind raced to determine the best course of action. I finally decided that "When in doubt, climb a tree" was the best course of action and instinctively moved off the trail and into the brush in search of a suitable tree to climb. Although I do not believe that Bob had seen the boar at this point, I heard a *thump* as his pack hit the ground, and I heard his pounding feet following me into the undergrowth.

I quickly examined several trees—they were all too small—and finally selected the best of the lot to climb, all the time looking over my shoulder at the hog. Just as I selected my climbing tree, the hog gave two snorts and strolled into the forest opposite from the way Bob and I had fled. When I finally looked around, I found myself facing Bob. We both had our hands around the same tree, a sapling about three and one-half inches in diameter. How we would have both climbed this tree, had we faced this necessity, remains a mystery! We gave each other sheepish looks, returned to the trail without comment and continued our climb.

As I have thought back on this encounter, I have concluded that the hog's final noises may not have been snorts after all. I am embarrassed to admit that I believe that blasted hog was laughing at Bob and me as we attempted to climb the same small sapling.

Wild Hog in the Road

Indian Creek Trail

January 1, 1979

After walking along Thomas Divide and Sunkota Ridge, Robert and I descended from Martins Gap into the upper reaches of Indian Creek. As we walked the old road through the narrow Indian Creek Valley, our attention was drawn to the dark form of an animal standing resolutely in the middle of our path. At first glance, I thought it was a black bear, but the coarse black hair and long snout gave it away. Yes, as we drew closer there was no doubt that the animal was a European wild boar in the 150-pound range.

Notwithstanding the hog's insistence on hogging the road, pun intended, we continued walking slowly toward it. Finally, when we were within fifty feet of it, the animal bolted and climbed into an old overgrown field beside the road, displaying its thin, curly tail in its flight. Here it paused momentarily before trotting swiftly up the slopes and out of sight.

With the boar episode behind us, we walked on in the misty rain that had begun to fall. While we walked, I thought of my first hog encounter. I had taken evasive action then. After a number of sightings during the intervening years, my experiences had taught me to be wary of wild hogs but not to fear them. In later years, when I have thought of this experience, I have recalled an old ballad titled "Wild Boar in the Woods." Robert and I could have written our own song on this wet afternoon—"Wild Hog in the Road." Somehow, however, this title doesn't quite have the ring of the original.

A Warning

Eagle Creek Trail

July 17, 1980

Bill and I dismantled our camp at Ekaneetlee Creek and walked down the Eagle Creek Trail toward Fontana Lake, lamenting the end of our pleasant five-day outing in the Smokies. Without warning, our progress was halted suddenly when a dark black form darted across the trail fifteen feet ahead of us, grunting menacingly as it passed at full speed. We immediately stopped in our tracks, startled by this surprise encounter, and observed the fleeting form of a wild hog as it disappeared into the brush. Before we could move again, another form, that of a brown piglet with a small curly tail, crossed the trail forty feet ahead and disappeared after the other.

We realized that the first animal was a sow and that her behavior was a display of maternal instinct as she sought to protect her piglet. Although we were in no particular danger, the hog's warning charge was certainly heeded, causing us to proceed cautiously for a hundred feet or so in the event that other offspring remained near. We did not see any other animals, however, and completed our walk without further hog encounters.

And Then There Were Six

Somewhere in the Smokies

October 4, 1982

Ed and I were high on a remote stream following a dim trail with the goal of retuning to our camp. Our thoughts were on supper and a relaxed evening after a day spent in off-trail exploration. The last thing on our minds was a wildlife sighting. Our minds were refocused, however, by rustling sounds in the nearby undergrowth that disturbed the silence of the forest through which we traveled. We immediately came to a full stop, listened as the sounds became louder and tried to pinpoint the source. Suddenly, a European wild boar burst from cover not more than twenty feet away and fled. The first hog was followed by another and another and another, until we counted a total of six fleeing animals. Thus, in a period of about thirty seconds, I counted more hogs in this single sighting than any other time during my years in the Smokies. This experience was somewhat disconcerting, but the pigs had no desire to share our company, and certainly we did not want to share theirs. We were glad to see them flee.

Panthers

The Profile Lingers in Memory

Big Cataloochee Valley

May 3, 1981

Jim C., Karen, Alice and I paused at an overlook beside the road entering the Big Cataloochee Valley and savored the beauty of the valley and the high blue mountains that loomed above it. While we were admiring this grandeur, Karen spoke excitedly, "Look in the road!" We all turned simultaneously and observed a large animal loping down the center of the road three hundred feet away. Then the animal paused and appeared to look toward us momentarily before climbing the bank and disappearing into the forest. During these moments of hesitation, we viewed the dark profile of the animal and were amazed at what we had seen. The animal appeared to be catlike in shape, and it had a long, drooping tail with an upward curve at the tip.

After the animal vanished, we excitedly exchanged our impressions of what we had seen. We were convinced that we had seen a panther. Like the Biblical Thomas, I had doubts. I wondered if the animal had been a large hound that strayed into the park from a nearby settlement, but the profile was catlike and the tail was too long for a hound. In addition, there had been other reports of panther sightings in Cataloochee and Big Creek, leading to the common belief that the animal was indeed present in these areas.

The dark profile of the animal lingers as a vivid image in my mind, and my doubts have vanished. I am certain that we saw a panther, a unique and rare sighting that few others have experienced in the Smokies. The quest to locate panthers in the Smokies has continued; however, questions still remain as to whether they truly exist in the absence of verifiable proof. As for me, I'm a believer—they're here!

As a footnote regarding panthers, friends Wayne and Carolyn Shepherd were on Roaring Fork Creek on April 24, 2009, along the side of the Roaring Fork Nature Trail near the "Place of a Thousand Drips" when they sighted a panther. Wayne describes the sighting as follows: "The panther appeared as a large dark-colored animal, and I observed its long tail as it leaped off the road. At the same moment, Carolyn observed a flash of white from the panther's underside." Such sightings support the presence of these animals in the Smokies.

Dogs

An Unexpected Companion

Lakeshore Trail

October 9–12, 1982

October 9—I walked through the tunnel at the end of the North Shore Road and traveled steadily until I reached Forney Creek, where I paused for a lunch that was consumed as a light rain fell, creating a whisper as it struck the leaves of the forest canopy. Following lunch, I moved in the continuing rain along the Lakeshore Trail, a route with comfortable ascents and descents. Travel was easy as I moved through a pleasant forest of green with shades of pastel color that marked the beginning of autumn.

My thoughts were immersed in the ever-changing trail scenes while I walked. The last thing I anticipated was encountering a hiking partner; however, I gained a companion as I approached Chambers Creek—one that remained with me for twenty-four hours. This companion was a young male hound, wearing a heavy red collar that bore no identification, which approached me from the opposite direction. Our greeting was casual. I spoke to the hound, and he reared up on his hind legs and whimpered—his version of "hello."

The hound was wet from the rain and very thin. Otherwise, he was a handsome animal. He stood approximately fifteen inches at the shoulder and had an orange coat and white markings on his chest and feet. He had a well-shaped head and long ears and displayed an alert, intelligent expression. How he reached this place on the north side of Fontana Lake miles from the nearest dwelling was a matter of speculation, but I had no doubt that he was a hunting dog.

As I continued, the hound followed me, remaining at my heels. In fact, he seemed content to follow me until he struck an interesting scent—then his hunting instincts took over, and he darted ahead, sometimes issuing a distant howl while on a track. After a while, however, he would return and take his place behind me again.

In time, I crossed Chambers Creek and continued to the Kirkland Creek Campsite, where I began preparations to spend the night, wondering how the hound would react to the downpour and also wondering whether he would join me in the shelter of my tent. I should have realized that the hound was quite self-sufficient. This became apparent when he curled up under a small hemlock tree that protected him from the worst of the rain. The hound did awaken in time for supper, and I shared my meal with him. Needless to say, he was most appreciative for this small kindness.

October 10—I awoke and prepared breakfast, which I also shared with my newfound friend; he had spent the night curled against a log fifteen feet from my tent. After breaking camp, we continued together again along the Lakeshore Trail. However, after lunch the dog strayed off on one of his many hunting excursions and did not return. I walked on to Hazel Creek, listening for the dog's howls, but I heard nothing.

October 11—Al W. joined me at the Proctor Campsite, and we embarked on an interesting hike that entailed a half-day of off-trail exploration. In the evening we enjoyed our pleasant campsite, but alas, we were not joined by the hound.

October 12—I met a backcountry ranger as we were leaving at the end of our outing and reported the lost dog in the hope that he could be rescued. Nevertheless, as Al and I walked to Fontana Lake to rendezvous with our shuttle across the lake, I was worried about the ultimate fate of this beautiful animal and regretted leaving him behind.

Our shuttle arrived on time, and we headed down the Hazel Creek channel. After we had proceeded only a short distance, we passed another boat with two occupants. They spoke to us as we passed, but their words were unintelligible above the sound of the boat's motor. Finally, realizing that we could not hear them, they pointed toward the bank to direct our attention to a movement there.

My heart rejoiced! There on the bank was the red hound with his tail wagging excitedly. I had grown quite attached to him and was relieved to be reunited again. We drifted to the shore where the hound willingly jumped into the boat, joining us for the return trip. I relayed to the boat operator the story of my meeting with the hound as well as my concern for the dog's welfare. I was gratified by his response. He told me that he would keep the dog at the dock in the event that the owner called for it. If no one claimed it, he said he would keep it with his own pack of dogs, as he was a hunter. Needless to say, I was relieved that the hound would be well cared for and pleased that I didn't have to end my outing without knowing the fate of this beautiful animal.

Black Bear Experiences

I have prepared a separate chapter on black bears rather than including them with other animals because of the number and nature of bear sightings and encounters I have experienced during my lifetime.

My earliest observation occurred when I was eight or nine years old. Our family was at the Newfound Gap Overlook, where I observed a young man with curly blond hair bend over and allow a yearling black bear to lick the hair tonic in his hair. Another time while camped at Smokemont Campground with my father and a friend, I was dispatched to get our water, and while engaged in this task I encountered a large bear standing upright in some rhododendron through which I had to pass. This was truly a Bill and Goliath moment that is still vivid in memory; however, in this instance the eight-year-old me turned heels and fled.

As an adult, I have enjoyed seeing bears, and some of my fondest memories are of off-trail sightings. Other encounters have been tense, and a few have been humorous. Regardless of the circumstances, I have always maintained a healthy respect for bears and kept my distance to the extent possible.

Signs and Sightings

An Apple a Day

Swallow Fork Trail

November 10, 1976

Jim W., Al C. and I left Walnut Bottom after a pleasant night at the campsite there and crossed Big Creek, intent on following the Swallow Fork Trail.

This was my first opportunity to walk this trail, and I looked forward to following it to Pretty Hollow Gap on Mount Sterling Ridge. We began on an old logging rail grade that passed through second-growth forest in an area once settled in earlier times. In addition to farming, Big Creek saw extensive logging, and the rail grade that we followed continued almost to Pretty Hollow Gap before continuing toward the Balsam range.

Before long, we came upon the remains of an abandoned apple orchard in what had been a mountain homestead. The limbs on the trees that remained in the small orchard had suffered considerable damage. They were bent, twisted and broken. It was evident that this place was a favorite of bears that apparently frequented it in numbers. They were responsible for climbing the trees to reach the apples that grew there, causing the damage we observed. Of course, it did not take a naturalist to identify the culprits that raided the orchard. Deep bear prints were everywhere in the soft soil beneath the trees, and piles of bear scat comprising the residue of eaten apples were scattered throughout the small orchard.

I had hoped to sight a panther reported to be on Big Creek in the vicinity of Walnut Bottom while we were there. However, I was pleased to settle for the interesting scene where the bears had congregated to enjoy apples, a scene I have recalled each time I have walked this trail in the years following my first visit.

"What Will We Do?"

Parsons Branch Road

June 15, 1980

After a night at Sheep Pen Gap near beautiful Gregory Bald and a descent by the Gregory Bald Trail, Alice and I reached Sams Gap and the Parsons Branch Road. We stopped here for a breather and then set off on a three- or four-mile road walk to our vehicle. The walk was pleasant, and we enjoyed being together in the Smokies on a delightful June day. Bears and bear sightings were the last thing on our minds.

Perhaps one should always expect the unexpected, however, because upon rounding a curve, I came upon a large black bear that I estimated to weigh 200 to 250 pounds standing in the middle of the dirt road ahead of us. I warned Alice, who was behind me, to approach slowly in order to observe the bear. Her first words upon seeing it, uttered in a shaky whisper, were, "What will we do?"

The answer was simple: we did nothing except stand still for what seemed like two full minutes. During this time, we looked intently at the bear and the bear reciprocated. So resolute was the bear in claiming the road that I began to wonder whether it would yield the right of way at all. Finally, however, the bear turned away from us and walked straight down the center of the road for three hundred feet until it disappeared around another curve.

I wanted to follow the bear at a safe distance, but Alice told me that she had heard yet another bear! I thought that a second bear sighting was unlikely and that her reaction was the result of being unnerved by the bear that had just ambled out of sight. Nevertheless, I hesitated at her request. In a few moments, I was glad that I had heeded her warning.

Suddenly, a second bear—almost as big as the first—climbed into the road from a marshy area below the bank. I hadn't heard the second bear at all and was impressed at Alice's keen sense of hearing. The second bear was noticeably skittish and immediately bolted into the forest when it saw us—a fluid blur of black fur and muscle—leaving big wet footprints in the dust. With the excitement of the bear sightings fresh in our minds, we continued our walk, discussing the unique experience we had shared.

A Shower of Bark

Brushy Mountain Trail

July 27, 1980

My goal for the day was walking to the crest of Brushy Mountain, and I climbed the Brushy Mountain Trail, enjoying the variety of scenery that seemed to change at every turn. Two hundred yards after crossing Trillium Branch, my progress was halted by a series of strange snorts and grunts. Surprised at these unexpected sounds, I scanned the forest below me in an effort to identify the cause. While I looked and listened, a new sound replaced the initial snorts and grunts. This time the noise I heard was the rasping sound of something scraping the bark of a tree.

I watched and waited and finally saw a small black bear cub no more than forty feet below me climbing the trunk of a large hemlock tree with awkward, ungainly clawing lunges. When this basketball-sized ball of brownish-black fur sighted me, it rapidly reversed direction and slid twenty feet down the trunk of the hemlock to the forest floor amid a shower of bark dislodged by its sharp claws.

I had to laugh at the antics of the small bear. However, I recognized that he who laughs first at a young bear may be leaving the last laugh to an irate mother.

This knowledge was sufficient to cause me to walk on without delay, concerned that the sow bear might be lurking near the trail. I proceeded cautiously for several hundred yards and was relieved that there no more surprise bear encounters during my outing.

Graceful Berry Picking

Silers Bald Shelter; Appalachian Trail

August 24, 1980

We had finished supper, and Robert and I relaxed following an enjoyable day on the trail. Before long, a half-grown bear visited the area in front of the shelter, curiously surveying the area with upraised head. A small red tag was affixed to each of the bear's ears. These identified it as a problem bear that had experienced previous human contact, resulting in it being relocated for its own protection. Certainly, it was not shy about patrolling the shelter area, no doubt hoping for a handout that was not forthcoming.

The bear ultimately tired of the futile search for human food and ambled toward the spring below the shelter. While I watched from a safe distance, the bear visited blackberry canes near the spring and began to consume juicy purple berries. The bear's agility and dexterity while engaged in this endeavor impressed me. Time after time, the bear would lift its paw and move a cluster of juicy berries to its mouth in a fluid motion before consuming them with a bite or two. The bear's skill surprised me, perhaps because I had never observed a bear feeding in a natural environment. I suppose, however, that all good meals have to come to an end. My enjoyment of witnessing the bear's meal ended when it sought the refuge of the twilight forest, leaving me with images of its gracefulness.

A Sound from on High

Low Gap; Appalachian Trail

October 10, 1984

After a night at Cosby Knob Shelter, I repacked my gear, ate a simple breakfast and began walking north on the Appalachian Trail. In time, the fog began to lift, and I witnessed the emergence of blue peaks that seemed to float in a sea of white clouds. As the sun brightened the mountains, I enjoyed the vivid colors of autumn.

About a mile north of Low Gap, my attention was diverted from the scenery by a movement in the highest branches of a large oak tree near the trail. I craned my neck and methodically scanned the branches to locate the squirrel that I supposed was creating all the commotion. Finally, I sighted the cause of the movement; however, it wasn't a squirrel as I had expected—it was a half-grown black bear.

To reach large acorns there, the bear maneuvered out onto small branches some forty feet above the forest floor that swayed and bent with its movements. I could hear loud crunching as the bear contentedly chewed acorns, caps and all. After the bear depleted the acorns on one branch, it moved to other limbs, limbs that appeared far too small to hold the bear's weight.

After a few minutes, the bear apparently detected my scent and began descending the tree's large trunk, creating audible scratching noises as its claws tore through rough bark. I had lifted my head to heed a sound from on high, but the bear's descent was my cue to depart, an action that required no second thoughts. Although the bear would have probably fled when it reached the ground, there was no reason to introduce stress into its life or, for that matter, into mine.

A Startled Bear

Snag Branch; Cosby Area

July 20, 1985

Before the Old Settlers Trail was cleared and marked, I made several walks to work out the route between Cosby and Greenbrier Cove. On this trip, I walked from the Cosby terminus of what became the Old Settlers Trail on an old path that evidenced some clearing in the last three or four years. The path passed through an old settlement and led to Dunn Creek, which I descended to Snag Branch—part of the puzzle of trails in the area.

I began an ascent along this small branch and passed through beautiful fern-covered glades that were most pleasing to see. In one of these, a movement caught my attention and brought me to a halt. There on the slopes above me was a large black bear that I had startled on my approach. The bear reacted to seeing me by breaking into a run, and its long strides quickly carried it around the ridge and out of sight but not out of hearing. The sounds of the bear's paws striking dry leaves and its massive body crashing through leafy branches attested to the fact that it was still on the run. The bear was a handsome animal, and I relished seeing its dark coat and massive form in its natural habitat. The bear's reaction indicated that it was not accustomed to human contact. I was glad this was the case and hoped the bear could live its life without sighting another human.

A Six-Bear Day

Hyatt Ridge Trail and Chasteen Creek Trail

August 29, 2005

After a rainy night at McGee Spring Campsite, Robert and I walked down Hyatt Ridge under drab gray skies, enjoying the scenery and appreciating the ease of downhill travel. One of the pleasures of the morning was the sighting of a sow bear with her young cub on Hyatt Ridge. Both quickly moved out of sight, permitting us only a brief glimpse.

We eventually crossed Raven Fork, where we paused for lunch before beginning the long but pleasant climb to the crest of Hughes Ridge, despite the rain that had begun to fall again. Viewing beautiful Enloe Creek and gazing at the ever-changing forest panorama made the time pass quickly. Once the crest was reached, we walked down Hughes Ridge to the Chasteen Creek Trail and made for the Upper Chasteen Creek Campsite, our stopping point for the evening.

A mile from the campsite, Robert, who was in the lead, motioned for me to halt, whispering that he had seen a bear on the high slopes of the cove through which we were descending. He was correct. He had indeed seen a bear, another sow, and like the first bear, she was not alone. This bear had three small cubs. Not unexpectedly, this bear fled instantly as the others had, allowing us only a quick glance.

Robert and I discussed our good fortune. We had seen six bears within a matter of a few miles. This was the good news. The bad news was that the rain had become a downpour, one that continued through the night and into the next day. The rain did not dampen our enthusiasm, however. We had enjoyed a six-bear day—a record for both of us.

Personal Encounters

A Bear in the Shadows

Ice Water Springs Shelter; Appalachian Trail

September 12, 1969

Larry, Kim and I had arrived at the old log Ice Water Springs Shelter, now removed, in the dusk because we had gotten a late start to our afternoon's walk. After arrival, we gathered a supply of damp wood for a fire that took the better part of an hour before we could coax the fragile flame into a sufficient blaze for cooking. In time, we were able to begin cooking over soft orange flames.

As we prepared our meal, a young black bear ambled into the shelter clearing and stood illuminated by the glow of our fire, which was reflected in its dark eyes. The bear sniffed the air with an uplifted brown muzzle and seemed to want to come closer but was reluctant to do so. The bear's reluctance was equally matched by our determination that it not invade our campsite.

Eventually, the bear faded into the shadows and left us alone. This departure was temporary, however. In a few minutes, the hungry animal again appeared in the orange glow of our small fire and studied us as it decided what to do. We resolutely stood our ground and eventually succeeded in banishing the bear. Our method was a simple one. We banged metal pans and pots with our spoons, creating a din of metallic music. This did it; the bear vanished for good.

I felt sorry for the bear, but discouraging it was far better than any other alternative available to us. Bear control measures have improved in recent years to help ensure fewer interactions between bears and those who visit the Smokies. This is as it should be.

"Is It a Bear?"

Big Walnuts Campsite; Eagle Creek Trail

September 13, 1973

Bears had never been a problem for Bob F. and me when we camped at Big Walnuts during our trout fishing outings; nevertheless, we always hung our food out of harm's way to avoid bear encounters. This trip was no exception—packs were suspended. Mine, which contained our shortening for frying fish, was suspended ten feet above the ground in a dogwood tree located a dozen feet from our tent. Perhaps "tent" is a loose use of the term. Actually, because I didn't have money at the time to invest in a proper tent, I had constructed a homemade affair out of clear plastic and duct tape.

On this particular morning, I was awakened about daybreak by a crashing sound outside our tent. I slipped quickly from my sleeping bag and crawled outside to investigate, although I had a suspicion about the cause. When I emerged, I was face to face with a large black bear that was standing upright ten feet from me in the doghobble that surrounded the tree in which my pack had formerly hung.

It was apparent that the bear had climbed the small dogwood and broken the limb from which I had suspended my pack. Despite my closeness to the bear, I felt no fear. "*Get out of here!*" I bravely shouted. In response, the bear swung a massive paw and snapped its teeth, creating a moist popping sound as its jaws rapidly closed. It was now quite apparent that the bear was not afraid of me either and that it was absolutely unimpressed at my effort to encourage its departure.

The bear's determination was disconcerting. It was obvious that it intended to hold its ground or, as a matter of fact, hold its shortening. This caused me to reflect on my own position. I was unclothed except for shorts, and it rapidly dawned on me that the bear had the distinct advantage in this mini-drama. Given this set of circumstances, I concluded that a hasty retreat was in order. What is the old maxim? "Discretion is the better part of valor"? Or perhaps Monty Python said it better:"Run away! Run away!"

I spun around in a perfect pirouette, reached into the tent to retrieve my boots and overalls and prepared to move away from the now angry bear. My movements aroused Bob, who mumbled sleepily, "Is it a bear?" Needless to say, I was unnerved by my encounter seconds before and hastily answered, perhaps with a bit of stress in my voice, "Yes, and he's a mad SOB." Now, I don't know how he did it, but Bob exploded from his sleeping bag and right through the end of my tightly sealed new tent, tearing plastic and duct tape asunder and creating an opening where none had been before.

I followed Bob, hopping and skipping as I donned overalls and boots. Then I moved to salvage my pack, which I could hear being torn in the midst of the doghobble by the now unseen bear. By the time I reached the dogwood tree, the bear was gone, leaving a shredded pack. The bear had taken our shortening as a reward for its boldness, leaving Bob and me shaking our heads over the encounter.

There were many long straight poplar trees around Big Walnuts, and good places to suspend packs were in short supply. The tree in which I had hung my pack was not a good choice but was the best available. In recent years, the park service has installed cables and pulleys at backcountry campsites for suspending packs. This arrangement is an excellent system and no doubt prevents many problems. If this had been present at Big Walnuts, I would not be relaying this story today. Although this experience was a bit disconcerting at the time, it had its lessons. As far as the bear is concerned, I can visualize the bear gathered with its family at the end of the day, saying, "A funny thing happened at work today."

Bear! Bear!

Upper Chasteen Creek Campsite; Chasteen Creek Trail

June 13, 1975

I was awakened at 7:00 a.m. by excited Boy Scouts shouting "Bear! Bear!" When I emerged from my tent, I encountered a scene of wild confusion. Several packs hung limply from a tree with their sides ripped and contents spilled. Other packs were on the ground. A trail of empty food packages indicated the path that the bear had taken. Scouts ran hither and thither, shouting and crisscrossing one anothers' paths, generally following the trail of papers left by the bear. Several boys aimed cameras toward the shaded forest intent on getting a photograph of the fleeing bear. Bruce breathlessly informed me that he was going after the bear.

The culprit and source of disruption was a half-grown bear. Now it may have only been my imagination, but I thought I saw the bear smile and then heard it issue a silly giggle as it contemplated the wild scene caused by its surprise raid. With this final gesture, the bear disappeared.

The first challenge that Bob W. and I faced was collecting the excited Scouts before they pursued the bear. Once we calmed the boys, we all gathered the scattered remnants of our food and gear and assessed the damage to determine how it would affect meals on the final two days of our fifty-mile hike. We concluded after our inventory that we had sufficient food by making menu modifications. As for our gear, my pack was most severely damaged, with tears matching those left by the bear on Eagle Creek.

How had this happened? This was a question that we addressed after everything settled down. We had hung several of our packs well off the ground in a large tree that leaned at a forty-five-degree angle as a result of being partially blown over. The bear had simply walked up the tree, and its weight had caused the tree to descend perhaps ten feet, allowing the bear easy access to our packs and their contents. It could have been worse. At least the boys had a good bear story to tell when they returned home.

It's Bad Luck to Break a Shoestring

McGee Spring Campsite; Hyatt Ridge Trail

May 29–30, 1976

Our gear was packed, and Sara, Bill and I prepared for an early departure for our trip to the Smokies. I dressed and put on one boot and then the other. As I tightened the shoestring of the second boot, the string snapped. There is nothing unusual about a broken shoestring; however, it brought to mind a superstition I had once heard from a forgotten source that it is bad luck to break a shoestring.

We drove to Cherokee, North Carolina, and stopped at our favorite restaurant, anticipating a hearty breakfast to start our day. We ordered, and in a few minutes our server returned, calmly balancing a tray with our order on an uplifted hand. Just as she reached the table the tray tilted; however, her quick reflexes prevented spilling the contents except for one bowl of grits that bounced across the table and onto the floor. Part of the bowl's contents spattered my overalls and one boot; however, the damage was minor, and I thought nothing of it.

We continued to Round Bottom, climbed to McGee Spring Campsite under intermittent showers and pitched our shelter, a tarp pitched in pup tent fashion between two trees. Our day ended with a simple supper of macaroni and cheese and a small fire to provide a bit of warmth against the dampness. We drifted off to sleep to the *tap-tap-tapping* of residual raindrops falling on our makeshift shelter.

I was awakened at daybreak by the sound of heavy breathing. The sound was familiar. I had heard it on other occasions and had no doubt that a bear lurked quite near. I sat up and shined my flashlight through the open end of our shelter, illuminating the form of a young bear that gazed at me from a distance of eight feet. The sudden flash of the light startled the bear, causing it to wheel about and scamper away.

My first thought was to check our packs, which were suspended from trees below camp, to determine whether they had been harmed. I put on my clothing, pulled on one boot and searched for the other in the jumble of gear at the bottom of the shelter. I couldn't find the second boot, but rather than waste time looking, I slipped a plastic bag over my shoeless foot and walked to our packs, which were unharmed.

I returned to the shelter and began a methodical search in our gear for my other boot. As I did so, a vague, nagging thought crossed my mind: *that bear stole my boot!* This seemed impossible. After further searching, I knew that the bear had poked its head into the shelter and indeed taken my boot—the one spattered by the grits—undoubtedly lured by the inviting scent. Sara and Bill were kind enough to search the woods about our shelter to see if the bear had discarded the boot, but they had no success in locating it.

Our original plan on our second day had been to walk to Tricorner Knob on a now abandoned portion of the Hyatt Ridge Trail; however, this was out of the question. The challenge that faced me now was not going ahead; it was returning to our vehicle almost four miles away without both boots. Admittedly, I was perturbed by the fact that an impudent young bear had dared to steal my boot; however, being frustrated served no constructive purpose in remedying the matter at hand.

After a few minutes of thought, I decided to manufacture replacement footwear. I accomplished this by cutting a sapling one half-inch in diameter—the only time I have ever cut a living tree in the Smokies—and dividing it into four sections the approximate length of my foot. Next, I lashed these pieces together with small cord to form a sandal that looked like a miniature raft. I put on several socks, covered these with a plastic bag and tied the sandal on my foot.

This makeshift substitute for my vanished boot worked perfectly, and I walked back to Round Bottom without difficulty. Fortunately, we did not encounter any other hikers, sparing me the necessity of explaining my unorthodox footwear.

Before my next outing, I went shopping for new boots accompanied by Bill. As I examined boots and commented about prices, Bill told me that the cost shouldn't be too high. "After all," he said, "you only need one boot."

In retrospect, although I have never been a suspicious person, I have been persuaded that a broken shoestring indeed causes bad luck.

Bird Sightings

Bird sightings are among some of my favorite Smoky Mountain memories. There are a number of reasons for this. There is the element of surprise—surprise at discovering a bird I've never seen before, surprise at some particular avian behavior and surprise at the intimacy of encounters when birds have come within a few feet of me. Then there is the grace of movement, whether in the form of dramatic aerobatics or a flurry of movement that catches one unaware and quickens the pulse. Of course, there is a matter of beauty. Every bird has characteristics that make it unique, including its song, whether rasping or melodic. All of these characteristics give pleasure and enhance the joy of being outdoors.

Hawks

On the Currents

Briar Knob; Appalachian Trail

October 6, 1982

Ed and I were favored by a clear, bright day marked by sun and blue skies. Our trail along the crest of the Smokies afforded endless views. At one of these we observed a large red-tailed hawk circling gracefully high above on air currents rising over the divide. We paused long moments and observed the hawk's lazy spirals and admired its picture-perfect grace and beauty.

This is just one of the many hawk sightings I have enjoyed over the years. Frequently, I have observed hawks gliding silently through the forest. I have observed at a distance what I believed were hawks taking wing from the forest floor after diving on some unsuspecting animal. The hawk that seemingly floated on the currents this day was special, made so by a perfect view of the bird's coloration and graceful flight framed against a blue October sky.

Owls

A First Time for Everything

Kanati Fork Trail

October 3, 1976

Sara, Bill, Susie (a friend of Sara's) and I reached the crest of Thomas Divide and, after a brief rest, began our descent along the beautiful Kanati Fork Trail in a forest where trees here and there displayed a palette of colors, a foretaste of the autumn season. Not far from the crest, we heard the distant hooting of a large owl that echoed from somewhere below us. The eerie hooting broke the silence of the late morning. We all paused and listened for a repetition of the call and were not disappointed. The owl periodically repeated its call, much to our enjoyment. Although I wasn't sure of the owl's identity at the time, a bit of research led me to conclude that it was probably a barred owl, an owl that is known to hoot during the day. Certainly, the owl contributed to our enjoyment of the day because it gave a hoot.

Magnificent in Flight

Little Dudley Creek

January 25, 1981

I began my day at Dudley Creek Stables and walked an abandoned trail, horse trails and segments of maintained trails in a circuit that took me as far as the Roaring Fork Motor Nature Trail, where I warmed in the sun on the steps of a reconstructed cabin and enjoyed smoking Old Danger before continuing back toward my starting point.

My return entailed a visit to an abandoned cemetery, where I studied the graves of hardy mountaineers who farmed the hills and coves through which I walked. A mile from my starting point, I saw in the distance the even strokes of a pair of strong wings. On first impression, I thought for an instant that the bird was a grouse; however, I knew in the next moment that the bird was too large to be a grouse. When it perched on a high limb seventy-five feet from me, I determined that it was a great horned owl, and I felt fortunate to be able to observe this magnificent bird. After perching on the limb, it turned its head for a few moments, reciprocating with its own observations. Then, to my regret, the owl flew silently out of sight.

An Excellent Sighting

Appalachian Trail West of Spence Field

October 5, 2004

We were a mile west of Spence Field when Sara, who led the way, experienced an excellent sighting. She observed a large owl glide across the trail in front of her and perch on a tree limb forty feet distant. She halted immediately and pointed out the owl to me. The owl, a barred owl, turned its round head toward us and gazed at us intently with dark black eyes while we studied its intricate coloration and feather patterns. The owl began to preen its wing feathers by repeatedly pulling them through its beak while we stood spellbound. These leisurely movements reminded me of the way a cat grooms itself with purposeful but slow and unhurried strokes. We had been serenaded by one of the owl's relatives earlier in our trip, enjoying the haunting calls that echoed across the mountains. In time, the owl flew into the forest, releasing us from its spell.

Ruffed Grouse

A Multitude of Grouse

Couches Creek

December 27, 1975

An old road trace along Couches Creek provided the route that Bob F., Bill and I followed into this once settled cove. We enjoyed the winter woods and anticipated the joy of doing nothing more than looking for signs of former habitation such as the outlines of old fields, trails branching away from what had once been the only route into the valley, tumbled-down chimneys and other similar evidence that marked a vanished settlement.

Well up the wooded valley we reached the site of a narrow field now overgrown in second-growth tulip poplar trees; the field was perhaps

Sara Hart Stewart on Mount Buckley at the beginning of an Appalachian Trail walk from Clingmans Dome to Fontana Dam, October 2, 2004.

one hundred feet wide and situated immediately beside Couches Creek. Rhododendron grew thickly on the steep mountainside beyond the creek, with leaves curled tightly serving as a natural thermometer to record the twenty-degree cold. While we paused here, I recited for Bob and Bill an account of once flushing a large number of grouse at this same field.

It was autumn several years earlier when I first explored Couches Creek. When I arrived at the old field, I flushed two grouse and then three more exploded from the leaves below me. Then groups of two or three grouse continued to fly toward the rhododendron across the creek, filling the nearly open clearing with fluttering brown wings. I counted twenty-five birds before I lost count; however, there must have been forty birds in all that filled the quiet forest with thundering wings.

I cannot account for this concentration of grouse. I have never flushed more than two together since. Certainly this was a remarkable experience, and one that I treasure yet. Notwithstanding, I have always wondered what attracted a multitude of grouse to Couches Creek.

A Disturbed Mother

Somewhere in the Smokies

June 7, 1985

I climbed the old logging rail grade that paralleled a small creek, enjoying a variety of sights and sounds along the stream. A sudden movement refocused my attention to the grade in front of me. It took me only a moment to realize that I had disturbed a grouse hen camouflaged with subtle patterns of tan, white and black, ideal protection in a forest with many colors and shades.

While I watched, the hen moved ahead on the old overgrown grade, feigning injury by dropping one wing and moving erratically. I had observed this behavior at other times and knew that the hen was attempting to distract my attention from her brood that hid nearby. In fact, it took only an instant for the mother's alarm to spread to her chicks, and in short order eight or ten tennis ball–sized young scattered in all directions depending on stubby wings to fly them to safety.

Although they did not know it, I meant them no harm. To avoid disturbing the birds further, I moved up the grade and away from the place where I had enjoyed discovering the mother and her chicks.

The Music of Autumn

Hughes Ridge Trail

October 15, 1988

The urge to enjoy an autumn weekend in the Smokies prompted me to select Pecks Corner Shelter for an overnight destination. I climbed the Chasteen Creek Trail and eventually reached Hughes Ridge and the Hughes Ridge Trail. As I walked along the crest of the ridge, I paused to admire the bright colors and to listen to the sounds. I heard the wind rustling the leaves, causing them to whisper with a dry rattle. I heard the sounds of katydids and an occasional acorn falling to the forest floor, striking with a faint thud. These were the sounds of autumn.

As I ascended toward Mine Ridge, I heard another sound. It began with a series of slow, muffled beats—almost pulses of air—that quickened until the sound was like the continuous beating of a distant drum. Then all was silent until the process was repeated again in a few minutes. This mysterious drumming, sometimes called "beating" by natives, was produced by a male grouse possibly to mark his territory and to serve as a warning for other grouse to keep away. The beating of the grouse combined with the other sounds I had been enjoying to produce the music of autumn.

Mutual Attraction

Sweat Heifer Trail

November 28, 2006

Ron and I were engaged in discussion as we descended the uppermost reaches of the Sweat Heifer Trail when Ron called my attention to a male grouse twenty feet below the trail in a stand of red spruce. The grouse was strutting in a zigzag pattern on lush green moss that comprised the forest floor. The grouse's brown tail feathers were fanned out like a deck of cards, and his neck feathers were fluffed about his head, feather duster fashion, creating a feathered circle the size of a softball. What a sight!

We paused for several minutes to enjoy this colorful display. The grouse in the meantime paid absolutely no attention to us, despite our nearness, and showed no inclination to fly. We watched him until he pranced out of sight before continuing on our way.

We hadn't gone more than fifty paces when we saw a female grouse also below the trail. Like the male, the female showed no fear and strutted along, issuing low clucks at regular intervals much like the ticking of a slow clock.

With our sighting of the female, all became clear. The male and female were obviously courting, and Ron and I had been privileged to observe part of their ritual. The opportunity for the two birds to meet seemed promising, but we were unable to wait until the marriage ceremony. I wonder if the two birds in their irritated state groused about this!

Red Crossbills

A Visit by Strangers

Pecks Corner Shelter; Appalachian Trail

November 6, 1976

A long day on the Appalachian Trail ended at the vacant Pecks Corner Shelter as dark approached. There was no time to loiter. Al C., Jim W. and I immediately began supper preparations and consumed a hot meal in short order. During supper, four or five strangers visited the shelter in search of food. They didn't stand on ceremony; they just moved right in as if we weren't present.

The strangers were the feathered kind, so we didn't mind their foray into our abode. These were extremely interesting birds of a type that I had not seen previously. They were reddish-gray in color and appeared to be slightly smaller than a cardinal. Also, their mandibles were crossed, giving their beaks an unusual, misaligned appearance. Most unusual was the fact that these birds appeared to be quite tame, feeding within two or three feet of us without any apparent fear. Needless to say, we enjoyed their company.

It is always exciting to have an experience such as this—the first observation of a beautiful bird. No time was lost in identifying these birds when I returned home. They were red crossbills. I learned that in earlier times these birds sometimes were called "saltbirds" because their fondness for salt caused them to visit areas in the high Smokies where cattle were salted.

I Believe We've Met

Pecks Corner Shelter; Appalachian Trail

October 16, 1981

Robert and I arrived at Pecks Corner Shelter late in the afternoon and set about selecting sleeping spaces, spreading our gear and starting supper.

After we had completed these chores, we relaxed and anticipated a pleasant evening after a day on the trail.

As soon as we had completed these preliminaries, we had visitors. Two birds with reddish markings and crossed mandibles flew into the shelter and busily began the search for food. I had met their relatives almost five years earlier at this same location and about the same time of day and immediately recognized them as being red crossbills. I relished this second meeting, and Robert and I watched as the birds went about their business of securing a meal. I haven't made other sightings of this bird since my night at Pecks Corner; however, I know where to find them in the future and will no doubt visit them again.

Pileated Woodpeckers

A Cunning Distraction

Baskins Creek Trail

June 19, 1983

A bit of searching allowed Alice and me to locate the unsigned Baskins Creek Trail and to begin our walk to the beautiful Baskins Creek Falls and beyond. We passed through green forest, enjoying the flame azaleas growing beneath the forest canopy, and admired the vivid coloration of the beautiful blooms that ranged from the palest yellow to the darkest orange.

This peaceful enjoyment of the magnificent blooms was interrupted by a raucous cry in the treetops that refocused our attention to a pair of pileated woodpeckers. These beautiful, large and colorful woodpeckers were impressive with their brilliant red topknots and distinctive black-and-white feathers. While we watched, one of the birds flew to its nest that had been hollowed out high in the trunk of an oak tree. The second flew to another tree sixty feet distant from the nest and lit on the side of the trunk with its back to us. From this position it began flexing its wings in a manner that repeatedly displayed the striking white feathered patches on the back of its wings. We were transfixed by this cunning distraction. The woodpecker was intentionally seeking to divert our attention from the pair's nest with its precious clutch of young by the semaphore movement of its wings. To avoid further agitating these beautiful birds, we continued our walk, discussing the marvelous experience we had just shared. We had both been impressed by feats of sleight of hand in the past; however, sleight of feather proved much more impressive.

Bird Sightings

Wild Turkeys

A Remarkable Comeback

Balsam Mountain Road

June 20, 2005

Ron and I had spent a day rambling in the mountains. Although neither of us had expected rain, a severe thunderstorm swept the crest of the mountain, forcing us to shelter for an hour under the edge of a boulder with barely space for two of us while thunder and lightning played across Balsam Mountain. After the worst of the storm passed, we continued our walk, spending the better part of the day walking in the rain.

At the end of our trek, we returned to our vehicle and found that a note had been left on our windshield by a ranger. The ranger's note advised us that the auto ford of Straight Fork at Round Bottom, now replaced by a bridge, was closed due to flooding. Subsequently, because our planned exit was impassable, we were advised to exit at the Balsam Mountain gate. As Ron and I returned, driving the wrong way on the normally one-way road, we were forced to halt to allow a hen turkey with four eight-inch-tall polts to cross the road in front of us. The hen held her gray head high, alert for any threat to her young, while the gray-brown polts moved with determination into the weeds and forest beyond, well camouflaged by their subtle markings.

When we continued, I reflected on the remarkable comeback of the wild turkey in western North Carolina. As a youth, I never saw turkeys, and I never saw them during my early trips to the Smokies. Now, however, turkeys are present throughout the Smokies. Even so, sightings of wild turkeys, the largest bird in the park, are always enjoyable.

Ravens

A Spectacular Aerobatic Display

Boulevard Trail

May 24, 1970

I enjoyed my walk along the Boulevard Trail; however, the most impressive feature was the final ascent of Mount Le Conte. Here the trail skirted sheer cliffs cloaked in sand myrtle with delicate pink-white blooms. The rolling expanse of Greenbrier Cove spread out below me, contrasting with the dramatic rugged heights above. The valuable moments along this section of trail were mine to enjoy, and I sat alone for a long time savoring the grandeur about me.

While I reflected on this beauty, I was treated to a spectacular aerobatic display by three ravens. They played on the updrafts from the valley below, gliding, diving and circling above me in playful flight accompanied by eerie croaks. Their movements were careless and free and seemed motivated by the sheer freedom and joy of flying. I will always remember these dark, soaring forms against a backdrop of crisp blue sky.

Slate-Colored Juncos

Angry Chatter

Albright Grove

April 11, 1977

My day entailed a walk of approximately twenty miles in the Cosby section of the park, along a series of trails that included the Snake Den, Maddron Bald, Albright Grove Loop and Gabes Mountain Trails. When I strolled through the Albright Grove, I admired the majestic virgin forest with its giant hemlock, tulip poplars, maples and other large trees and regretted the loss of much of the forest treasure of the Smokies during the logging era. However, I was grateful that the formation of the Great Smoky Mountains National Park ensured protection of a vast mountain preserve.

These thoughts were interrupted when a gray junco flitted from a green, mossy bank beneath a large hemlock tree. Closer examination of the bank revealed a carefully constructed, cleverly concealed nest recessed in it. The nest contained four delicate eggs. Mother and father were obviously upset at my violation of their privacy, and they voiced their displeasure by chattering angrily at me from a nearby bush.

Although I am not an expert at translating bird talk, the birds were obviously warning me to leave the vicinity of their nest. Needless to say, I wasted no time in heeding their angry warning.

Bird Sightings

Evening Grosbeaks

A Chirping of Birds

Near Buckeye Gap; Appalachian Trail

May 2, 1982

The Smokies are filled with surprises. Robert and I experienced one of these as we neared Buckeye Gap, our departure point for an off-trail segment on our Clingmans Dome–Elkmont walk. As we walked along, we were halted by a mysterious chirping sound that filled the forest about us with the reverberations of happy bird calls. It was a sound reminiscent of spring peepers—the small frogs whose calls are noted in early spring.

We craned our necks and scanned the forest overstory but could see nothing. Proceeding cautiously, we continued to gaze into the treetops. Finally, we were able to observe birds in twos and threes fluttering in the highest branches. While we watched, a flock of an estimated sixty to eighty birds moved about, chirping continuously. With some effort, we were able to determine that the birds had combinations of yellow, gold, white and gray feathers and that they had white wing patches that varied in configuration between males and females.

Neither Robert nor I was able to identify these birds, but we made mental pictures to aid in later identification. Upon returning home, I determined that these mystery birds were beautiful evening grosbeaks. According to *Birds of the Smokies*, these birds were first observed in the park in 1951. I was grateful that a mighty chirping of birds created a pleasant surprise and led to an acquaintance with a new feathered friend.

Belted Kingfisher

Sounds Along the Stream

Proctor; Lakeshore Trail

August 8, 1982

Hazel Creek was our destination for a few days of trout fishing, and Bill and I walked toward the former sawmill town of Proctor excited by the prospect of hungry trout that lay awaiting our lures. Along the way to Proctor Campsite, we startled two buzzards, which flew away with slow, graceful sweeps of their wings as they gained altitude. Later, we saw a hawk that flew at treetop level above the stream, uttering a shrill call as it flew.

In short order, we pitched our camp at Proctor and made our way to Hazel Creek and cast dry flies on the stream's clear waters, watching them as they drifted in the current toward the likely hiding places of trout. Nothing focuses one's attention as much as fly-fishing. It is all-absorbing. We angled intently, expecting a strike with every cast.

We could not escape, however, the staccato call of the belted kingfisher as this blue and white bird flew rapidly downstream a few feet above the stream's waters. Hearing and seeing this bird reminded me of the numerous times I had observed kingfishers while trout fishing and listened to their distinctive call. I paused and watched as this bird flew out of sight with bold, strong strokes of its wings. I was thankful for the kingfisher's appearance, for the memories it caused to resurface and for its contributions to our enjoyment of the day.

Winter Wren

A Complex Melody

Deep Creek Trail

July 5, 1985

Alice and I were high on Thomas Divide, descending the Deep Creek Trail through a magnificent forest. The misty fog that muted our views was slowly being replaced by the sun's rays, bringing the promise that our day would be bright and enjoyable. It was in this setting that we heard the joyous, melodic trilling of a small unseen winter wren—the virtuoso of the feathered musicians of the Smokies. The distinctive and delicate notes of the wren's musical call rose and fell. Perhaps it was expressing its own joy at the brightening of a somber morning.

Cedar Waxwings

Who Was That Masked Bird?

Laurel Gap Shelter; Balsam Mountain Trail

July 1, 1995

I seated myself on a log beside the fire circle outside Laurel Gap Shelter and enjoyed quiet conversation with a few others who were spending the night there. Then the unexpected happened! Those of us around the fire circle were joined by five others. They wore black masks and invaded my personal space without fear, moving within three feet of where I sat. Despite the masks, I noted that the invaders were immaculately groomed and very well mannered. In fact, I readily welcomed these strangers into our midst.

This was my first observation of cedar waxwings in the Smokies and an excellent one it was. It was delightful to observe at a distance of only three feet the color pattern and prominent crest of these beautiful birds. I was somewhat surprised, however, that they demonstrated no fear of humans and searched for food as if no one was about the shelter area. Unfortunately, the birds did not remain long enough for me to satisfy my desire to enjoy their beauty. They departed in their continuing quest for food.

Unidentified Birds

The Joy of Flying

Dry Sluice Gap; Appalachian Trail

November 25, 1978

Robert and I had chosen a cold November day for some exploratory hiking. When we neared Dry Sluice Gap, we paused to observe a flock of thirty to forty small, unidentified birds in flight. This in itself is not unusual. In this instance, the wind was blowing in continuous blustery gusts from Tennessee into North Carolina as it passed across the craggy crest of the Sawteeth. This small flock of birds flew just above the crest of the ridge, where they received the full brunt of the wind. Notwithstanding, the random formation of birds rose, circled and swooped in the wind, displaying intricate, elastic patterns as their swooping flights were repeated a number of times in ever-changing configurations. When viewed against a silver-gray sky, the birds were like intricately choreographed moving black dots. The effect was almost hypnotic as this small flock demonstrated its dramatic prowess in flight.

Snake Encounters

I never look for snakes when I walk in the Smokies; I only look for things that look like snakes! Thus, I continually scan the terrain ahead and examine roots and stray tree limbs that resemble snakes. Of course, to the extent possible I look before I step over logs and use care where I place my hands. I have cultivated these practices mainly as a matter of woods safety; however, in following them I also discover a snake from time to time. These discoveries add pleasure to any outing despite the fact that snakes have an undeserved negative reputation among many. By pausing to admire snakes, one can enjoy the complexity of their markings, the beauty of their coloration and the grace of their movements, not to mention their methods of defense.

Timber Rattlesnakes

Superior Powers of Observation

Smokemont Loop Trail

October 13, 1974

Alice, Sara, Bill and I embarked on the Smokemont Loop Trail, an ideal trail for an autumn outing. After a couple of miles, we crossed Bradley Fork on a long foot log and began ascending Richland Mountain, following the trail's meanders around the slope. As the grade steepened, we walked single file, with Sara bringing up the rear of our small procession. One by one we passed a gray, weathered snag beside the trail, scarcely paying attention to this element of the landscape.

Suddenly, Sara gave a startled shout: "A snake!" We all wheeled about, and Sara pointed at the snag that all of us had just passed, but no snake was visible. Or was it? Sara directed our attention to the well-camouflaged form of a heavy-bodied three-foot timber rattlesnake draped gracefully over the contours of the snag. Its muted colors blended perfectly with the gray wood and dull, dry leaves on the forest floor. This beautiful creature had escaped notice by all but Sara, whose powers of observation proved superior.

We all admired the snake from a safe distance. It was sluggish in the morning chill and showed no inclination to coil or strike. Because it seemed quite vulnerable due to its proximity to the trail, I lifted the snake from its resting place with a strong limb and placed it out of the sight of others who might harm it. I was glad that I had done this when, within twenty minutes, we met a group of hikers who told us they had killed a copperhead on the trail. Sadly, we found their victim later—a harmless garter snake.

"I Didn't Know You Could Dance!"

Twentymile Trail

August 28, 1977

We had descended from Gregory Bald into the Twentymile Creek basin first on the Long Hungry Ridge Trail and finally on the Twentymile Trail for the final segment of our multi-day walk. Robert and I were walking abreast along the old road that served as our trail when Robert suddenly broke into a strange chant and a foot-stamping shuffle. "Oh-Oh-Ah-Ah" echoed from Robert's mouth, and little puffs of dust boiled around his rapidly churning feet.

This strange behavior—the chanting and dancing—startled and puzzled me. Both were uncharacteristic for Robert. While I was trying to digest this situation, Robert stuttered, "Sn-Sn-Sn-Snake!" There it was—a fully extended rattlesnake approximately three and one-half feet in length. It lay stretched full length beside the road where Robert began his animated dance.

We set our packs quickly aside and obtained a camera to make photographs. The snake reacted to our photography session by coiling into striking position and beginning a vibrating rattle with its black tail. This was our warning not to interfere, and of course, we were happy to oblige. We left the snake unharmed and continuing its warning rattle. What an exciting way to end an outing!

Snake Encounters

Primitive Chanting

Springhouse Branch Trail

August 23, 1980

We had descended Forney Ridge and had traveled perhaps two hundred yards on Springhouse Branch Trail when it happened. Robert began an eerie, primitive chanting that resounded through the forest. Accompanying this chant was a reverse foot shuffling dance that sent Robert backing up the trail at a brisk pace. A stranger observing this strange behavior might have assumed that Robert was possessed; however, I was not puzzled by Robert's strange actions. I had observed them before. I knew immediately that Robert had encountered a rattlesnake!

Indeed, Robert had stepped directly beside a four-foot timber rattlesnake, which displayed its impressive length draped on a rotted chestnut log. The snake had a pale yellowish coloration with dark patterned markings that merged into a solid black tail tipped with yet lighter-colored rattles. It was an exquisite snake! Seeing it displayed on the chestnut log portrayed the snake in a most rustic and attractive manner.

We disposed of our packs and approached the snake carefully to obtain photographs to document our discovery. The snake quickly tired of all this and began to coil, accompanied by the menacing vibrations of its upraised rattles. This constant buzzing filled the air and could be heard when we were two hundred feet beyond the snake and headed for Forney Creek. This was a wonderful experience, and we were pleased by the opportunity to admire the beautiful rattlesnake.

Oblivious to Attention

Jakes Creek Trail

September 5, 1981

In order to get an early start for a circuit of approximately 17 miles, I arose at 3:30 a.m., drove 103 miles to my trailhead above Elkmont Campground and walked with the aid of a flashlight until dawn. My itinerary included all or parts of the Jakes Creek, Miry Ridge, Lynn Camp Prong, Middle Prong and Panther Creek Trails, plus an ascent of Blanket Mountain.

In early afternoon, I reached Jakes Gap for the second time on this circuit and began descending the final segment to my starting point. After walking the Jakes Creek Trail for ten minutes, I rounded a curve and observed at a distance a young man and woman—the first persons I had encountered all day. As I approached them, I noticed that they were peering intently at something on the trail. The something turned out to be a three-foot rattlesnake, which seemed oblivious to the attention it received.

I joined the couple in admiring the rattlesnake and photographed it. When the photo session ended, I selected a strong stick, slipped it under the snake and removed it from the trail. The snake never coiled throughout this process and slithered away rather contentedly, I thought, with the occasional rattle of its six rattles, a sign of mild agitation.

Northern Copperheads

No Escape

Noland Creek Trail

May 9, 1981

Bill and I were walking the Noland Creek Trail to Fontana Lake. As we passed though an area cluttered with a jumble of brush and debris left when the lake receded, I detected two forms directly in my path—copperheads! I took evasive action instinctively and immediately by jumping to my left and away from the snakes. In doing this, I bumped into Bill, who was unaware of the snakes and thought I had stumbled. He reacted by pushing me in the belief that he was keeping me from falling. His push again directed me toward the snakes. This resulted in a brief but furious period of pushing and shoving until I finally escaped both Bill and the snakes.

Watch Your Step

Proctor; Lakeshore Trail

August 9, 1982

When Bill and I completed our supper chores, I walked through the grassy area up the road a bit above the Calhoun House, envisioning how the area must have looked during the heyday of the Ritter Lumber Company, whose large band mill was located nearby. As I moved through the shin-high grass that covered the site, I proceeded carefully, recognizing the potential for snakes. This anticipation was well founded because I discovered a copperhead poised and alert nestled in the grass. I gave it wide berth and continued my ramble, pleased with my sighting.

This was the second copperhead I had seen in the past two days. The previous day while Bill and I were fishing, I had stepped over a copperhead while it lay unnoticed in my path as we skirted a portion of the stream. Bill, who followed me, narrowly missed stepping on the same copperhead but averted it by quick footwork. This first encounter probably helped me detect the second snake because I watched every step I took in the grassy meadow.

Eastern Garter Snakes

The Greeter Snake

Forney Ridge Trail

August 28, 1980

Robert and I were walking along the sun-warmed reaches of the Forney Creek Trail near Clingmans Dome, celebrating the first day of our multi-day trip, when we observed a large eastern garter snake sunning itself in the center of the trail. As we passed, the snake slowly slithered into a patch of trailside blackberry canes; however, it lingered long enough for us to observe the distinctive alternating bands of yellow and black that extended the length of its graceful body.

After a six-day ramble on- and off-trail on the North Carolina slopes, we trudged upward toward Clingmans Dome on the final day of our outing. When we reached the place where we had sighted the garter snake on our first day, we were surprised to find a garter snake there again. As a result, we concluded that it was the same snake. We discussed the fact that this snake had met us going and coming and decided that the snake was not a garter snake after all—it was a greeter snake.

Eastern Rat Snakes

You Look Comfortable There

Hannah Mountain Trail near Flint Gap

August 25, 1977

A pleasant morning's walk brought Robert and me to Flint Gap on the Hannah Mountain Trail, where we ate a dry lunch washed down with a few cups of water from a poor source south of the gap. As we walked on, we rounded a curve in the trail and came upon a large eastern rat snake that had draped and curled its long body in the top of a five-foot hemlock tree. I believe that if the snake had had the ability to speak I would have asked it why it chose that particular perch. Maybe the snake would have replied, "It's really comfortable here. Why else?"

A Skilled Climber

Boogerman Trail

June 24, 1979

One of the joys and rewards of Boy Scouting is the opportunity to share the outing experience with young men. On this particular outing, ten Scouts and I hiked the Boogerman Trail, identifying former signs of settlement and enjoying the large, beautiful trees along this pleasant trail. One of the entertaining occurrences during the day was the sighting of an eastern rat snake that was climbing a small tulip poplar tree. The snake moved slowly but effortlessly upward, spiraling around the tree and allowing us a close view of the rippling movements of the snake's body as it climbed upward. Most of the Scouts had never seen a snake climb a tree and were surprised to learn that they could climb. Hopefully, this was an experience that was shared with family and friends when the trip ended.

Northern Water Snake

An Unusual Catch

Noland Creek

April 24, 1982

Bill and I fished favorite stretches of Noland Creek with dry flies, and both of us caught six or seven fish. Bill numbered two keepers among his catch, but the balance of his and all of mine were undersized and duly released. Bill's most unusual catch was a snake that he spied washing downstream in the cold current. The snake, one that we presumed was a northern water snake, was cold and stiff and unable to escape the chilly water on its own. Bill noted the snake's predicament and deftly wrapped a loop of his fly line around the immobile reptile and lifted it to the safety of the bank. Once on dry land, the sluggish snake crawled slowly and almost painfully away.

The Queen and the Pretender

Proctor; Lakeshore Trail

April 24, 2004

A portion of the Lakeshore Trail between Eagle Creek and Hazel Creek had been rerouted, and Bill and I chose this occasion to walk this relatively new segment—a portion that we had not walked before. This new segment ended in a gap on the ridge and continued to Hazel Creek by way of Shehan Branch and Possum Hollow, following an old road we had visited many years before.

When we reached Proctor, we crossed the bridge at the Calhoun House and stopped at the end of the bridge to study an interpretive marker that described the Ritter Lumber Company complex that once occupied the area. While there, I idly glanced down at the grassy area beside the bridge abutment and saw a snake. At first I thought it was an eastern garter snake because of its yellowish markings; however, additional examination of the snake proved that my first assumption was incorrect. I couldn't identify the snake; it was a type I had never seen.

We left the snake undisturbed, walked on to the Proctor Campsite and pitched our camp. While Bill fished, I relaxed about camp. Later, on his return from fishing, Bill discovered another snake at the lower end of the campsite and summoned me to take a look. This second snake was black-brown in color and had a nose that was somewhat flattened. Additionally, the snake flattened and expanded its head menacingly when approached, causing its head to somewhat resemble that of a timber rattlesnake. We thought its mimicry was very effective.

Bill thought that the second snake was an eastern hog-nosed snake, but the identity of the first snake remained a mystery. Upon returning home, we confirmed the correctness of Bill's presumption and identified the first snake that we found as being a queen snake. Our outing was special in part because of our two-for-one experience—one trip and two interesting snakes. Yes, we indeed met the queen and the pretender.

Things That Buzz, Flit, Creep or Crawl

The Great Smoky Mountains National Park contains a vast number of life-forms. In recent times, the appreciation of this fact has resulted in an effort to identify every one of these, with the result that new species have been identified yearly.

Things that buzz, flit, creep or crawl often tend to escape notice unless a focused effort is made to appreciate and enjoy their beauty and uniqueness. I have admired dragonflies, water spiders, snails, salamanders, lizards, crawfish, butterflies, centipedes and many other insects during my rambles in the Smokies. Generally, my experiences with these life-forms have not been dramatic. However, like spices in food, they add savor and variety to the outing experience.

Bees

Whoa, Harry, Whoa!

Enloe Creek Trail

September 8, 1973

Bob F. had arranged for Jerome Parker to take us by horseback from the Tow String settlement on the edge of the park to Enloe Creek by way of Hughes Ridge. Not being a horseman, I experienced some anxiety about this arrangement. However, Jerome gave me some pointers on riding and assigned me Silver, a surefooted horse familiar with Smoky Mountain trails, and I soon lost my discomfort. Bob rode a horse named Harry, an equal to Silver in reliability and ability to traverse the narrow trails we traveled.

When we reached the Enloe Creek Trail, we began our descent toward Raven Fork. At the steepest places, we dismounted and led the horses as a matter of safety for both man and beast. Jerome was in the lead with his horse and a packhorse. I followed Jerome, and Bob brought up the rear of our small procession. Suddenly, the unexpected happened. Jerome's horse bucked and the packhorse bolted. My horse, Silver, pushed against me and attempted to break free. I realized in an instant that the horses had disturbed an underground yellow jacket nest and that the horses were being stung by swarming, angry bees. When Bob passed the nest, Harry caught the full fury of the bees.

Poor Harry broke free and galloped down the trail, leaving Bob behind shouting, "Whoa, Harry, whoa!" to no avail. Harry was eventually forced to halt behind Silver because the trail was too narrow for him to pass. Bob loped down the trail and reclaimed Harry, and we continued without further bee adventures.

The Droning of Bees

Andrews Bald; Forney Ridge Trail

August 23, 1980

Andrews Bald provided an ideal resting place for Robert and me, and we paused here to gaze into the distance at jumbled ranges of blue mountains and to sample the sweet, abundant blueberries on bushes scattered about the bald. In time, we dozed on a cushion of warm grass that carpeted the crest and enjoyed the constant droning of honeybees as they visited the filmy angelica near where we lay. What pleasure!

Puzzling Behavior

Thunderhead Prong

July 28, 1984

A day of exploration found Al W. and me on an old logging rail grade well up Thunderhead Prong. Following this grade, we began our descent back to our starting point and the end of our circuit. Eventually, we reached a fording of Thunderhead Prong and then a second fording of this same stream after another half mile.

Al announced that he was going to wade the stream when we reached the second ford and began the crossing while I evaluated alternatives for a dry passage by jumping from rock to rock. I paused, however, to watch Al before crossing myself. As he approached the deeper current near the far bank, he climbed a large flat rock and straddled a bent, overhanging tree that served as a bridge over the final few feet of stream.

The next few seconds were puzzling. Al hurriedly unstraddled the small tree and slid off the large rock into hip-deep water in one fluid motion. At first, I thought he had lost his balance. This thought passed quickly because Al appeared to have good footing on the stream bottom; nevertheless, he continued to behave strangely. He bent toward the water and began scooping up hatfuls of water into his nondescript red felt hat. Then he repeatedly splashed water on his face and head. Strange behavior indeed!

This flurry of activity occurred so suddenly that at first I could not comprehend any reason for Al's frantic splashing and thrashing. Then I spotted a gray cantaloupe-sized yellow jacket nest concealed in a leafy branch above the large rock Al first climbed. His head had struck the nest when he climbed the rock, causing the bees to angrily swarm out and sting him about his head and shoulders. When I realized what had happened, I moved to Al's assistance and began brushing bees from his hair and clothing.

The outcome of this misadventure was that Al was stung ten times and was fortunate not to have received more stings. He did not experience any adverse reactions other than the pain of the stings; however, this attack could have proved fatal to someone allergic to bee stings. In reflecting on this incident, I concluded that the Smoky Mountain hiker is much more susceptible to problems with bees than with poisonous snakes.

Butterflies

At Least a Dozen

Deep Creek Trail

April 17, 2004

There they were—a cluster of yellow swallowtail butterflies (probably eastern tiger swallowtails) beside the trail. There were at least a dozen within an eight-inch circle. All had their wings gracefully displayed—some fully extended, some held vertically and others held at angles in between, displaying the beauty and intricacy of their wing patterns. I admired this fluttering, trembling mass, marveling at the enjoyable kaleidoscope of yellow.

A visit from a butterfly while camped on Forney Creek, August 26, 1980.

KATYDIDS

The Forest Filled with Sound

Doe Knob; Appalachian Trail

October 5, 1984

I moved north on the Appalachian Trail and, after a period of serious walking, reached Doe Knob, where I paused about 4:00 p.m. for a rest. While I reclined against my pack, a solitary katydid began its call. Then another and another took up the call. Eventually, the air was filled with their continuous rhythmic, rasping cadence. The sound evoked the sensations of early autumn.

Gnats

Part of the Food Chain

Bote Mountain Trail

July 17, 1981

Spence Field was our goal, and we had reached the turnaround on the Bote Mountain Trail when we decided to stop for lunch at a pleasant setting. Then they found us—large gnats. At first, we encountered only the advanced scouting party. While a few of these stayed with us, the others went back to alert their brothers and sisters that food was to be had. Eventually, the whole cadre arrived, and the gnats circled our heads and periodically sampled exposed skin, leaving bothersome, itching bites. As it turned out, Alice and I had become part of the Smoky Mountain food chain. The gnats' persistence caused us to quickly dispense with lunch and move on to escape the pests' infernal biting. It was a matter of survival.

Spiders

Decorations

Straight Fork

September 18, 1993

I followed a faint and often obscure path up Straight Fork on an exploratory outing. When I was not enjoying the beauty of the stream, I admired the green of the forest with its ever-changing vistas. Breaking single strands of spider web was a common occurrence as I passed though undergrowth where spiders had anchored strands of web to the growth on either side of my overgrown path.

Not all webs were single strands, however. Some of these were elaborate gossamer webs of complex design that reflected the sun's rays, making them appear to be woven with the finest silver threads. A number were decorated with bold zigzag designs that were skillfully laced into the center of the web. Large spiders decorated with black and yellow markings, spiders that I later tentatively identified as being black and yellow agriopes, occupied the center of many of these webs. My father called these writing spiders because of their scriptlike web designs.

I frequently stopped to admire these creations, moving within inches to better study a spider's beautiful coloration and markings, as well as its weaving prowess. I bypassed each of these complex webs when I encountered them to avoid destroying wonderful works of art.

SNAILS

A Small Discovery

Bradley Fork Trail

April 24, 1988

My spring day hike began at Smokemont Campground and included segments of the Chasteen Creek, Hughes Ridge and Bradley Fork Trails for a walk of approximately fifteen miles. After completing the Hughes Ridge segment, I began descending the upper end of the Bradley Fork Trail, enjoying the beauty of Taywa Creek and the pleasant valley through which it flowed.

Well down the trail, I discovered my first snail of the year and stopped to admire it. It was truly a beautiful creature. Its delicate light tan shell had several concentric swirls, each smaller than the last. The snail that supported this graceful ornament was almost pink, with two swaying antennae. The snail moved imperceptibly as it crossed a damp stone decorated with an irregular pattern of green moss. There was an element of perfection in this small scene set in the vastness of the Smokies.

CRAWFISH

A Strange Dance

Raven Fork to Tow String Trace

July 3, 1982

For a short period, the Great Smoky Mountains Trail Map displayed a trail three and one-half miles in length that extended from near the park boundary along Big Cove Road to the Tow String Bridge across the Oconaluftee River. Apparently, it was not maintained, and locating it was difficult; nevertheless, I finally found the Big Cove terminus and followed its sometimes puzzling meanders.

It traversed woods and fields and eventually paralleled the Oconaluftee River, leading across a wooded knoll, where I paused to visit a small cemetery situated in a shaded clearing. While I surveyed this peaceful setting, I was surprised to see an orange-colored crawfish at the edge of the cemetery, seemingly far from its logical habitat.

When I stooped to examine the small crawfish more closely, it instinctively raised its pincers in a defensive gesture. When I stood, the pincers were lowered. When I stooped again, I was greeted with upraised pincers. I repeated the exercise of stooping and standing several times to test the reaction of the crawfish, and each time it assumed a defensive posture to do battle with the intruding giant.

When I thought back on this encounter in the cemetery, I was glad no one had observed my strange dance with the crawfish. If questioned about my movements, my explanation would have certainly been greeted with considerable skepticism, and my dancing support group would have no doubt expelled me for dancing the Crawfish Wiggle.

Beneath the Water

Silers Bald Shelter; Appalachian Trail

October 2, 2004

Our gear had been laid out, and Sara and I enjoyed an early autumn evening in the Smokies. Only a few chores remained, and while Sara worked in the shelter, I descended to the spring to obtain water. While engaged in this endeavor, I enjoyed watching a bright orange crawfish on the bottom of the spring pool—actually more of a wash pan–sized puddle. The crawfish deftly navigated the sandy bottom of the pool in search of food, moving slowly here and there in its search. I secured water for our meal and left my small companion to its quest, appreciative for the entertainment it provided.

Salamanders

Is That a Blush That I See?

Balsam Mountain Trail

August 11, 1974

Ten Boy Scouts walked ahead of me with red, blue and olive packs swinging as they walked. We had spent the night on the crest of Spruce Mountain and were headed to Laurel Gap. At noon, we reached Pin Oak Gap, where we ate a simple lunch before embarking on the final miles to our destination.

In time, we crossed Ledge Bald and passed Beech Gap, and somewhere beyond these landmarks, we made the big discovery of the day, or maybe the big small discovery of the day. There beside the trail was a red-cheeked salamander (Jordan's Salamander). I was thrilled at our discovery because I had never seen one before; however, I knew of their existence from my reading. The dramatic red cheeks of this small salamander contrasted dramatically with its black body. This rare salamander is known to exist only in the Great Smoky Mountains National Park, making this a special sighting. In a small way, the mountains became teachers of boys on this day long ago.

SKINKS AND LIZARDS

Enjoying the Heat

Bunker Hill

July 15, 1979

We drove through Cades Cove and then followed the Parsons Branch Road to the gated entrance of the road leading to Bunker Hill. As we began our walk, we were assailed by oppressive heat and humidity, which was particularly intense in the absence of the slightest breeze. Nevertheless, the opportunity to visit a previously unvisited part of the park—with its promise of new discoveries and the opportunity for Alice, Sara, Bill and me to spend time together—far outweighed any discomfort we might experience.

We sampled blueberries and huckleberries as we walked to Bunker Hill and took time to enjoy an abundance of mushrooms with endless varieties of sizes, shapes and colors, all blessings of the summer season. When we reached Bunker Hill, we climbed the fire tower for hazy views of distant mountains.

As we began our walk back to our vehicle after a simple lunch, we stopped to admire what we believed to be a five-lined skink. The skink, with its long iridescent blue tail, was sunning itself on the side of the cabin near the fire tower. As a boy, I called skinks scorpions, probably something I picked up from my father, and I believed that they were poisonous. Fortunately, I could tell Sara and Bill that the skink was harmless and dispel any youthful misunderstandings they might have had. The skink favored us by allowing us an opportunity to examine it briefly; however, it apparently feared the attention we paid it and hurriedly scampered away, depriving us of further opportunity to admire its beauty.

The Quick and the Dead

Goldmine Loop Trail

June 17, 2006

Sara had a free weekend, and we chose the Goldmine Loop Trail for our outing, an outing that began by passing through the tunnel at the end of the North Shore Road to reach one terminus of this pleasant loop.

We descended off the ridge to a small stream that passed a charming old house site that was situated in a gently sloping flat area beside the meandering small watercourse. Beyond this point, we reached an old road, probably a county road, that passed a marshy, rhododendron-covered area, which appeared to have several water seeps and small streams. This led us to Fontana Lake, which was nearly full, where we gazed on green waters that covered a valley that was once home to many citizens of Swain County.

Beyond the lake, the trail ascended steeply on a dry ridge. It was along this stretch that Sara discovered two eastern fence lizards. The first had dug a shallow burrow half the length of its brown body in the crusted earth beside the trail, and the lizard was partially hidden in this cavity. We discussed our find and speculated that the lizard was probably in search of food. Not far from the first lizard, we found a second cavity just like the first. This lizard appeared dead; however, this could have been survival behavior. Both sightings were unusual because in the past we had always observed fence lizards in a different setting, one in which they always fled at the least provocation. For whatever reason, these lizards did not move.

We enjoyed our walk and especially enjoyed discovering the eastern fence lizards, both the quick and the dead.

TURTLES

Turtle on the Divide

Indian Creek Motor Trail

May 20, 2000

An exercise hike seemed in order, so I drove to Deep Creek for a walk that included a portion of the Indian Creek and Indian Creek Motor Trails. It was pleasant to revisit a route that I had walked numerous times and to anticipate the landmarks and scenes that I knew I would enjoy once again. It had rained the previous night, the forest dripped with excess water and the trail had puddles here and there. The forecast called for the day to brighten, so rain was not a deterrent to my plans.

When I reached the crest of Thomas Divide, I stopped to admire a single pink lady-slipper growing beside my route. Droplets of water clung to the flower and radiated the sun in a sparkling spectrum of color, adding a gemlike quality to the beauty of this already marvelous flower. Later, I discovered an eastern box turtle. Like the lady-slipper, the turtle's black shell with delicate yellow markings reflected the sheen of the water, giving it a polished appearance. The turtle pulled its legs and head into its shell and then cautiously emerged from its shell with head and legs half extended as if trying to decide whether to continue its slow journey or retreat once more. I walked on, leaving the turtle to make this decision on its own.

Trout Fishing Outings

Trout fishing has always provided special pleasures for me. Catching trout was the appeal when I was a youth. As an adult, my motivations are more complex. I still experience the excitement of reading a stream to determine where trout are likely to be lurking and relish plying a dry fly or drifting a nymph in the ever-changing combination of pools, runs and eddies that varies with each stream. I enjoy testing my skills and reflexes when a trout is finally enticed to strike. I never tire in briefly viewing the beauty of a freshly caught trout; however, I haven't kept a trout in over twenty years, preferring instead to catch and release them.

Equally appealing is the beauty and mystique of trout streams in all seasons and in all their moods. It is pleasant to observe the changes in forest scenes, enjoy delicate wildflowers on the banks and gaze at the effects of light and shadow on a stream. There is the matter of solitude; it is always pleasant to enjoy quiet time on a trout stream. Such a day with the ever-present sounds of flowing water erases life's concerns—at least for a while—and makes it virtually impossible to concentrate on worldly matters.

Smoky Mountain streams become like old friends. I look forward to visiting them time after time. Like friends, I see changes in their lives over a period of years in the form of channel diversions, debris piles after floods and fallen trees that alter the fishing pattern in a favorite pool.

I have included in this chapter some of my favorite streams, although I have fished many others that are not mentioned. It should be noted that while there are many fine trout streams on the Tennessee side of the park, I have primarily restricted my fishing to the North Carolina side as a matter of travel convenience. Thus, I have not included any Tennessee trout streams in my narratives.

Big Creek

Unexpected Success

Big Creek

July 16, 2004

I first fished Big Creek—one of the clearest streams in the Smokies—with a friend when I was eighteen or nineteen years old. As I recall, our success on this first trip was limited, and I came away from that experience with the opinion that Big Creek was a hard stream to fish. Thus, I had my misgivings when Bill and I decided to give Big Creek a try. On the other hand, I knew from hiking along Big Creek numerous times and gazing into its pools that it had an abundance of trout.

We entered the lower waters and alternately fished stretches of the stream. I was immediately taken by the beauty of the foliage along the banks and the variety of stream-washed stones that served as the stream's bed. To my surprise, we began to catch fish!

Bill made an accurate cast, placing a dry fly in a rushing run. There was an immediate splash and he instinctively raised his rod tip and tightened his line, hooking a ten-inch rainbow trout. The fish darted in the clear water and glinted silver in the sun when it escaped the water in a mighty jump before Bill skillfully guided it into still water and quickly released it after admiring the splash of red on the trout's side. It was truly a rainbow of color. When released, it darted into the depths with the same energy it had demonstrated when first hooked.

Several other rainbows succumbed to Bill's skill after the first. I also caught several trout. One of these—a nice nine-and-a-half-inch rainbow—proved to be what Bill and I call a "mystery fish." Mystery fish are fish that are caught unintentionally. Although I wish I could claim that my superior skill was the reason for the catch, I did not realize that a trout had struck my dry fly as it floated through a promising run. It only became apparent that I had hooked a fish when I reeled in my line and found the trout on the other end.

So much for my highly touted angling skill, at least highly touted to Bill. Anyway, a fish is a fish in Bill's and my informal competition to see who catches the most trout. In actuality, Bill usually catches the most fish, as he did on this day. In these cases, his success can be easily explained by the fact that as a true sportsman, I always let him fish the best pools and runs.

Trout Fishing Outings

Bradley Fork

Heeding the Biological Clock

Bradley Fork

April 1, 1978

Just as some biological clock triggers the migration of birds and animals each year, an internal clock signals that the time has come to begin trout fishing. Possibly, swelling tree buds, early spring wildflowers and warming temperatures provide an external stimulus that sets the clock in motion. Nevertheless, whatever the cause, those who fish know the sensations and also feel this mysterious urge.

It was such a signal that motivated Bill and me to walk several miles up Bradley Fork in pursuit of trout. Although regulations at the time only permitted retaining trout in excess of twelve inches—and we didn't expect to catch any of these—the absence of other people and the beautiful scenery was sufficient to lure us to "fish for fun."

We each floated nymphs, including Secret Weapon, Tellico and Muskrat patterns, drifting them through beautiful swift-flowing water as we slowly

Bill on Bradley Fork holding a freshly caught rainbow trout, April 1, 1978.

waded downstream. Occasionally, our drifting lures attracted rainbow trout, and we caught several in the seven- to ten-inch range.

Bill proved more successful with his angling efforts than I. Although I did not know it at the time, this was destined to become a common occurrence in the years ahead. He chided me about my inability to catch as many or as large fish as he caught. In defense, I used my usual excuse of allowing him to fish the best waters, which was not the case at all. I was secretly pleased with his demonstrated skills and didn't mind the competition.

Cataloochee Creek

Angling Trip Stirs Memories

Cataloochee Creek

April 11, 1985

I crossed the grassy field below the picturesque Palmer Chapel Methodist Church, skirted a stand of woods and passed through low growth to reach the stream. The water was high and flowed rapidly, swelled by the runoff of melting snow; nevertheless, the water was clear and inviting.

I tied on a dry fly, although a nymph might have been more suitable given the cold April waters and the high level of the stream. The fluff of hair and feather drifted on the crest of turbulent waters and floated over the likely hiding places of waiting trout. While I fished, I noticed jagged chips of rotten wood in a shallow eddy, the work of a pileated woodpecker. I looked overhead and identified the dead tulip poplar tree that had yielded to this powerful woodpecker's search for grubs and insects. Rugged sycamore trees with their ragged bark and graceful hemlocks stood across the wooded stream border. Mossy stone walls left by those who had farmed the fields adjacent to the stream stood as a silent memorial to their labors.

When my attention focused on the stream, the water itself became a study. It was bright and clear one moment while receiving the full illumination of the sun. When passing clouds blocked the sun's rays, the stream bottom was concealed in darkness. Sometimes the combination of light and passing clouds changed the stream's reflection from gray to blue-green and then silver.

During the day, I thought about other trips to Cataloochee—some more than a quarter century earlier. These recollections included observing a pool come alive at dusk as trout went into a feeding frenzy as an aquatic hatch emerged from the stream's surface. I recalled fishing up toward the old steel bridge at the lower end of the valley, now replaced, and observing a man who was fishing from the bridge catch two pan-sized trout in succession. I hadn't even managed to get a trout to strike, so I envied his success. What was his secret? When I could not contain my curiosity anymore, I approached the man and asked what lure he was using. He responded casually, "white bread." This practice was illegal, of course, as only single-hook artificial lures were allowed. Alas, I had to settle for a fishless outing, preferring to use artificial lures rather than violate the fishing regulations.

One of my most treasured memories was meeting Mark Hannah, a legendary and respected park service ranger and native of Cataloochee. I recall Mr. Hannah as being a gentle, friendly man who was not too busy to sit by the campfire of two young men not yet out of their teens and pass the time of day.

By the way, I caught one small rainbow trout on this outing. However, it was a far better day for memories.

Deep Creek

Failure and Success

Deep Creek

May 31, 1981

Shortly after 7:00 a.m., Bill and I reached Bumgarner Branch and waded into Deep Creek intent on fishing around Bumgarner Bend. Cascades of pink-white laurel blooms flanked the stream, creating a delightful floral display. A faint gray mist floated above the stream, further enhancing the beauty of the blooms. We fished upstream, wading in high, fast water that made progress slow and difficult. Strikes were few and the effort seemed futile. These circumstances persuaded us to abandon our agenda and turn back, counting the day a trout fishing failure.

Our return to the Deep Creek turnaround at the end of the old Deep Creek road was via the old abandoned Deep Creek Trail, one with several fords. As I stood in one of these old fords along the trail, I cast my dry fly upstream onto water that was silver with the sun's reflection. A mere dimple on the silver surface signaled the strike of a trout. I set the hook with an instinctive motion of the wrist and recognized immediately that I had hooked a trout of larger than normal size. A fight of several minutes followed, punctuated by the fish making several runs and dramatic leaps. At length I lifted a brightly colored twelve-inch rainbow from the run. Success!

Before reaching the turnaround, we passed a former homesite. Pink roses the size of silver dollars grew about the site. These old rose bushes commemorated a mountain woman who first planted these colorful flowers to add a touch of color and decoration to a simple mountain home. Seeing the old rose bushes marked the pleasant end to our trip.

Trout Wisdom

Deep Creek

September 6, 1982

Bill and I walked up the Deep Creek Trail as day dawned over the mist-shrouded mountains and enjoyed a breathtaking sunrise accompanied by the symphonic sounds that echoed from Deep Creek's waters. In time, we stepped into the creek at Bumgarner Branch and were greeted by the shock of cold water on warm, dry feet. We soon adjusted to the cold and began a day of fishing using flies selected to match the natural insect hatch along the stream. Dark forms followed our flies occasionally and tell-tale splashes signaled striking trout. We caught both brown and rainbow trout and retained a few of these for the table. Many more fish escaped when our reflexes failed to respond with adequate speed.

In one deep pool, a trout that I estimated to be sixteen inches in length appeared from the depths and moved languidly toward my fly. It halted a foot away and eyed the blend of thread and feather while I waited poised and breathless for the trout's next move. The wisdom of the trout's years prevailed, however, and it slowly drifted into the blue-green depths when it determined that the fly had no nutritional value.

In the end, trout wisdom saved the day for the wily fish. I was left with a wonderful memory that I now cherish more than a hooked trout.

EAGLE CREEK

The Perfect Presentation

Eagle Creek

September 14, 1971

Midday came and Bob F. and I selected a sunny luncheon site beside a clear pool high on Gunna Creek, a tributary of Eagle Creek. The sun's rays penetrated the pool by which we sat and allowed us to scan its depths while we ate. After a few minutes, Bob issued a long, low whistle of exclamation and pointed to a large trout partially concealed by a smooth stone one and a half feet beneath the surface. We observed this fine specimen for several minutes; however, the temptation of the lurking trout was too great for Bob, and he declared that he was going to catch it.

With this pronouncement, Bob baited his hook with a piece of the fruit bar he had been eating, taking great care to break it into the correct trout-sized morsel. Next, he backed away and stealthily circled the pool to a suitable place for a cast, using great care to avoid alarming the trout by his movement or shadow. After ten minutes of carefully crawling into position, Bob had positioned himself in the most advantageous location for the ideal presentation of his bait before the large trout.

The trout had not moved and all was ready for the moment of truth. Bob swung the bait in a gentle arc above the pool, poised to drop it so it would drift just in front of the fish. Finally, the bait descended toward the pool, and in a second or two Bob's plan would come to fruition. Unfortunately, the bait struck a moss-covered rock immediately upstream from the fish and lodged firmly in the thick coating.

Bob's efforts to dislodge the hook were futile. Finally, he had to emerge from his hiding place and wade into the pool to dislodge his hook. Of course, this spooked the trout. It was gone for good. Aside from the fact that Bob's bait never touched the water, I must admit that his presentation was perfect.

Catching Any Fish?

Eagle Creek

September 11–12, 1972

Bob F. and I fished Eagle Creek and, as was our practice, we fished together, alternately fishing desirable stream segments. We changed positions when one of us caught a fish, stopped to change a leader or fly or reached a particularly inviting pool or run. This allowed us to experience the pleasures of both fishing and enjoying each other's angling efforts.

I recall the pleasure of seating myself on a fallen log and lighting Old Danger while watching Bob cast his fly skillfully into pools, runs and riffles. His fly would skim the surface and then disappear in a splash of water that signified the strike of a trout. The ensuing fight, punctuated by runs and jumps, frequently ended with the landing of a trout of sufficient size to retain for supper.

It is customary for fishermen who meet along the stream to ask, "Catching any fish?" or "Doing any good?" Although we did not see anyone to ask these questions, Bob and I could have replied, "We've caught one or two," the proper response to these questions. In actuality, our catches for two days are as follows:

	Bob	*Bill*
September 11	*11½″ Rainbow Trout*	*10½″ Rainbow Trout*
	10¾″ Rainbow Trout	*9″ Rainbow Trout*
	9½″ Rainbow Trout	*8½″ Speckled Trout*
	8½″ Speckled Trout	*7½″ Speckled Trout*
	7½″ Speckled Trout	*7½″ Speckled Trout*
September 12	*8½″ Rainbow Trout*	*11″ Rainbow Trout*
	8½″ Rainbow Trout	*9″ Rainbow Trout*
	8″ Speckled Trout	*9″ Rainbow Trout*
	8″ Speckled Trout	*8½″ Speckled Trout*
		8½″ Speckled Trout

At day's end on both days, we performed camp chores and built a small fire. While the fire burned to coals suitable for cooking, we rolled our trout in cornmeal and fried them in a fire-blackened steel frying pan. We consumed them steaming hot with deep-fried hush puppies and the dehydrated vegetable of the day. These were memorable meals, as well as memorable times with a good friend.

FORNEY CREEK

A Spring Hatch

Forney Creek

May 9, 1987

I drove to the end of the North Shore Road and began my walk to Forney Creek filled with the usual anticipation of catching a few trout. I had made no provision to keep any fish, preferring instead to fish for fun. Yet despite the fact that I would not retain fish, I felt a sense of excitement that had not been dulled by years of fishing. It was this excitement that served as my motivation for the outing, nourished by a week contemplating the trip.

My angling efforts began where Forney Creek emptied into Fontana Lake, and this is where I landed my first fish after a few minutes, a small rainbow. In time, I exited the stream and walked upstream for more than a mile to select another segment to fish. My angling approach was one of leisure. Before fishing one emerald pool fed by swift current, I seated myself midstream on a boulder, lit my pipe and proceeded to enjoy a smoke while I surveyed the pool for striking trout.

While I relaxed, an insect hatch began right before my eyes, much to my surprise. Brown flies with translucent wings escaped the pool's surface in a ritual as old as time and arose into the bright sunlight fluttering on new wings. It was intriguing to watch this natural phenomenon. This activity did not go unnoticed by the trout either. They began to feed as rapidly as possible on the winged meal emerging from the water.

I visually divided the pool into four-foot squares and evaluated the feeding activity in my imaginary grid. Employing this method, I could determine that one or two trout were breaking the surface simultaneously in each section, creating a display ranging from mere dimples on the surface to outright splashes from vigorous strikes. Upon completing my study, I selected a dry fly from my box that most closely replicated the hatch in progress, crept to the lower end of the pool and slowly worked my way upstream, casting into the lower reaches. I caught two eight-inch rainbow trout in short order before their antics while being played frightened the other trout, putting an end to further strikes in this spot. Thus, I continued my upstream angling, with the reward of other trout caught and released. I returned to my starting point late in the afternoon with memories of my day being replayed in my mind. Foremost among these memories was the image of delicate insects emerging from the beautiful pool and circling into the light of the bright sun.

Hazel Creek

An Electrifying Strike

Hazel Creek

September 27, 1980

After a morning of hiking and off-trail exploration, Bill and I returned to our camp at Sugar Fork, rigged our fly rods and walked down Hazel Creek to the Brown Hole, where we began fishing. After experimenting with several dry fly patterns, we began to catch a few trout on lures that were predominantly brown or gray.

After fishing the Brown Hole, we moved upstream to another beautiful pool. With care, I cast my fly into the current flowing into the pool so that it would float naturally before any trout that happened to be feeding there. My fly had drifted no more than four feet when I had a vicious, electrifying strike that snapped my leader in an instant. This happened so suddenly that I never glimpsed the trout that attacked my lure. All I was left with was the sensation of the taut line between my fingers before the line went slack. This strike still stands out in memory as the most aggressive that I have ever experienced.

Despite the fact that "the big one got away," Bill and I caught six trout between us. These were fried to perfection and made an excellent meal, the perfect ending to our day in the Smokies.

Landed by a Fish

Hazel Creek

June 18, 1981

Bill fared better than I as we fished from Fontana Lake to the Proctor Campsite. Although I caught a few trout, they were undersized and had to be released. Bill, on the other hand, had two keepers, causing me to fish seriously to match his catch.

Bill hooked yet another keeper in a beautiful run above the point where Shehan Branch enters Hazel Creek. The fish was a fighter with room to run, and Bill moved to midstream to better play it. As he did so, he lost his footing and landed in a seated position armpit deep in the current with arms uplifted, all the while holding his fly rod overhead in an attempt to hold on to his fish. Bill finally regained his footing just as the trout made an upstream run. Again, Bill lost his footing and took a second plunge. After five minutes and two wettings, Bill ultimately landed a beautiful eleven-and-a-half-inch rainbow trout with brilliant red stripes down its sides.

I had enjoyed this battle from a comfortable spot on the stream bank, curious to see how it would end. When Bill emerged from the stream thoroughly soaked but with his trout in hand, I chided him by telling him that it appeared to me that the fish had landed him instead of him landing the fish. Nevertheless, one couldn't argue with his success even if it did come at the price of a good wetting.

Bill's three fish were fried over an open fire and served with vegetables and biscuits, making an excellent meal for both of us. The fact that I had not contributed to the meal did not go unnoticed by Bill, who not so subtly bragged about his superior ability. Although I didn't like admitting it, I grudgingly had to agree with his assessment.

School House Trout

Hazel Creek

September 12, 2003

After coordinating schedules, Bill and I arranged a trip to Hazel Creek for a bit of trout fishing. We made camp at the Proctor Campsite and immediately returned to the stream to wile away the afternoon in pursuit of trout.

Both of us fished without success; however, as we fished near the School House Spring, Bill had a dramatic strike from a silver form that darted from the depths of a deep pool to make a purposeful attack on his dry fly, leaving

Bill playing a thirteen-inch rainbow trout in Hazel Creek, September 12, 2003.

a splash of clear water where the fly once floated. I could not determine the size of the fish that stuck his lure, but I knew that it was of decent size based on the bend of Bill's fly rod. First, it ran upstream before reversing course and speeding downstream into the next pool some seventy-five feet away. Without unduly tiring the fish, Bill followed it downstream and finally deftly guided it to the bank, where he knelt and removed the hook from a fine thirteen-inch rainbow. Then the fish was gently returned to the water. The School House Trout was gone in a flash, living to fight again another day. Or perhaps there would be no future fights if it learned its lesson well.

OCONALUFTEE RIVER

A Successful Outing

Oconaluftee River

April 9, 1978

The urge to enjoy the onrush of spring prompted Bill and me to visit the Oconaluftee River for a day of trout fishing. We waded into the cold water without waders but soon acclimated to the cold and focused on our fishing.

In short order, I caught two rainbow trout on nymphs that were ten and ten and one-half inches in length, respectively. Farther downstream, I had a hard strike that was telegraphed up my line like a jolt of electricity. I instinctively set the hook, and although I could not see the fish, I knew from the vigor of its resistance that a strong fight was to follow. Five minutes of sweeping runs and acrobatic leaps followed before I lifted a colorful twelve-inch rainbow trout from the water. Although the fish was of legal size, I released it in still water and watched it swim off just as I had released the first two fish I caught.

Moments later, I heard Bill shout above the sound of the gliding stream. I hurried to the green pool where he fished in time to observe him lift a thirteen-inch rainbow from the water. Afterward, I watched while Bill unsuccessfully tried to interest three trout in the sixteen- to twenty-inch range to strike in his lure. They were uninterested, however, just as I knew they would be from my own unsuccessful efforts to catch them on previous trips to the beautiful Oconaluftee River. Despite their lack of interest, we considered our day a success.

Trout Fishing Outings

Reward and Punishment

Oconaluftee River

March 18, 1979

Several days of warm weather prompted Bill and me to make plans to fish the Oconaluftee River. When we left home on our outing, the temperature was thirty degrees, inciting the sudden realization that in our zeal we had ignored the fact that the waters of the Oconaluftee would be bone-chillingly cold. Despite this knowledge, our optimism overshadowed our judgment.

When we arrived at the stream, we walked to one of our favorite fishing holes and ultimately began wading. Unfortunately, hip waders were not part of our fishing gear. When we stepped into the water and first felt the shock of cold on our feet and legs, Bill reacted philosophically by saying, "Well, you have to take the punishment for the reward."

We caught several small trout for our efforts. After three hours, however, Bill told me that he couldn't take the cold anymore and suggested we quit fishing. In view of our limited success, we decided that the punishment outweighed the reward in this case and returned to the warmth of home.

A Demonstration of Superior Skills

Oconaluftee River

March 28, 1981

The waters of the Oconaluftee River ran clear and high. Bill and I plied rushing blue-green pools and swift runs with Tellico and Secret Weapon nymphs in the hope of enticing trout to strike our lures. While fishing in one deep pool, I hooked a large trout, a fact that was evident by the resistance on the end of my fly line. The fish immediately sought the security of the bottom and remained there momentarily before making a powerful run to the end of the pool, a run that culminated in a mighty leap.

Bill coached me excitedly from the bank as I played the trout. His instructions were generally aimed at making sure the trout did not escape. He need not have worried. I played the fish carefully to avoid having it break my leader and finally coaxed it within reach after a few minutes. The valiant fighter was a brilliantly colored thirteen-inch rainbow trout. We admired the fish a few brief moments before I gently returned it to the stream. It was gone in an instant, free to haunt its familiar pool once more.

Throughout the afternoon, I caught and released several smaller trout, but Bill failed to catch a single fish. I made the most of his lack of success by proclaiming my superior fishing skills. My comments were payback for recent similar treatment at Bill's hands when his fortunes had exceeded mine. All's fair in love and trout fishing.

STRAIGHT FORK

The Grand Slam of Trout Fishing

Straight Fork

May 22, 2004

The temperature was sixty-four degrees, and the skies were partly cloudy as Bill and I began working our way along a beautiful section of Straight Fork, casting dry fly patterns in an effort to lure trout to strike. As always, we observed our traditional fishing pattern of alternating stream segments to ensure that both of us had an equal opportunity to fish productive pools and runs.

Although we had come to fish, there were many distractions. The remains of an old rail grade paralleled the stream, a reminder of a time decades ago when the forest wealth on the upper reaches of Straight Fork and beyond was transported to the mill at Ravensford for processing. The stream banks were green with thick moss and the forest displayed the fresh new leaves of spring. The stream consisted of an ever-changing combination of runs and pools, some the size of a washtub, that challenged us to make just the right cast to make our flies float like natural insects.

The sun played hide-and-seek, creating periods when the stream was in complete shadows. At other times, the sun brightened the water, completely illuminating the stream bottom and revealing a display of rounded, well-washed stones. I preferred the brightness because it allowed me to better observe my fly and detect the occasional strikes that occurred.

After a few casts, I experienced success. A slight splash indicated my first strike. I reacted instinctively, rapidly raising my rod tip to hook the trout, a reflex action that is automatic and beyond my explanation. I could feel the weight of a small trout on my line. I led it quickly to the bank, held it gently in wet hands to remove my fly and released it all in a matter of seconds, gazing at its beauty during the process.

The first fish was a brown trout with dull orange spots on its golden brown sides. The next trout I caught was an eight-inch rainbow with red stripes on its sides. The third trout was a speckled trout in the vernacular of the

Winter trout fishing in the Oconaluftee River, February 10, 2009.

mountaineer. It was approximately seven inches and displayed a milky-white underside and fin tips with bright pink-red spots on its sides.

I was thrilled by my success. One might wonder at this reaction to catching and releasing three small trout; however, this was the first time I had ever caught all three types of trout that inhabit the waters of the Smokies on one outing in all my years of fishing in the park. This was my trout fishing "grand slam."

Usually, a catch of rainbow trout or a combination of rainbow and brown trout is common in the lower elevation water of the park. At upper elevations, a catch of rainbow and speckled trout is possible. A catch of exclusively speckled trout is possible only in the highest waters. Thus, my grand slam was a fairly unusual feat, one that I'll probably never duplicate.

Remembering the Past

The Great Smoky Mountains National Park has been the home to humans for thousands of years. First, the mountains were occupied by American Indians, who left a network of trails, campsites and towns as evidence of their presence. They were followed by explorers and traders. Later settlers cleared the land and built homes and farms, expanded the network of trails and roads, constructed small mills to grind their grain and established churches and schools to accommodate their religious and educational needs. In time, loggers and miners moved into the mountains in search of natural resources. The loggers purchased large boundaries of timber, built sawmills and mill towns and extended rail grades to the very crest of the Smokies to harvest the abundant timber of the mountains.

Other uses were made of the Smokies. The Civilian Conservation Corps established camps, and young men entered the forest to build trails and roads and to perform other useful work. Fire towers were constructed on prominent peaks to allow spotters to identify and report forest fires, contributing to early fire suppression efforts. Hikers and campers ventured into the Smokies to explore the valleys and peaks, and the writers among them described their adventures. Others such as George Masa and Jim Thompson captured the beauty and mystique of the Smokies with their cameras.

The creation of the Great Smoky Mountains National Park ended development in the Smokies. The forest is reclaiming the land, and today the park appears largely untouched by human hands. Although the scars are healing, the signs of humans are evident throughout the park, even in the most unlikely places.

I have enjoyed looking for these signs during my outings in the Smokies. Reading the land, so to speak, has helped to educate me and to develop an understanding of patterns of settlement and land use through the years. This study has allowed me to mentally weave the fabric of mountain life in all its many dimensions. Ultimately, reading the land has helped me to understand and remember the past.

Roads and Trails

Which Is the Real Asbury Trail?

Asbury Trail

February 23, 1975

Mark, one of the senior Scouts in my Boy Scout troop, chose as his Eagle Project the blazing of the historic Asbury Trail, a trail named for Bishop Francis Asbury, a renowned Methodist minister and circuit rider who followed the trail across the Smokies in the early 1800s in his historic travels to save souls and spread Methodism. In preparation, Mark contacted the district ranger for permission to blaze the trail, determined acceptable blazing practices and recruited and trained two teams of Scouts in project logistics. He was influenced in the selection of his project by the fact that our troop experienced a period of bewilderment during our first traverse of the Asbury Trail. He was determined that others would not duplicate our difficulty in following the old path.

One of Mark's teams began its work at Cove Creek Gap, and I worked with the other team, which began blazing at Mount Sterling Gap. Pairs of Scouts with stencils and cans of yellow paint placed evenly spaced blazes on trees beside the trail to mark its route and make it possible for others to enjoy it in the future. The work was well organized and went smoothly. I enjoyed our slow descent as we worked our way to the steel bridge located at the bottom of Big Cataloochee Valley, our rendezvous point.

As we descended, I noted that the old trail we blazed had followed several different courses in previous years, evident from leaf-covered depressions here and there that divided and rejoined the main route. These worn routes were always close together and showed how the trail had been shaped by past travelers who avoided blowdowns and other obstacles by going around them. I wondered which of these several paths Francis Asbury actually followed when he passed this way.

In pondering this question, I concluded that it really didn't matter which was Asbury's original route. I recognized that the Asbury Trail was a living thing with a life of its own, always changing to suit conditions and the convenience of the traveler. Each person who had passed this way had influenced this historic route in some small measure, just as a fine group of young men did on this bright February day.

Why a Path Here?

Somewhere in the Smokies

February 7, 1976

Our goal on this cold winter day was a partly off-trail trek that entailed walking the length of a small creek and then climbing beyond its highest springs to intersect with a maintained trail. Once on this trail, we planned to follow it to a high crest before returning to our starting point via the trail. With this in mind, Bill and I ascended the old road trace through a once settled valley that eventually ended at the last homesite in a high cove. The natural topography of the cove channeled the tumbling waters of the creek downward through a bleak forest. We continued our ascent into untracked forest beyond this last homesite.

Eventually, we reached a small watercourse at the base of a ridge spur, plunged through a patch of thick rhododendron and began climbing the spur to the crest of the ridge through fairly open hardwood forest mixed with a bit of laurel and patches of briers. To our surprise, we found a faint path on the spine of this ridge! This now became our route, and we followed it upward, detouring around blowdowns and other obstacles as we climbed.

Why had a path existed on this remote ridge? This question was the subject of discussion as Bill and I plodded along. After considerable deliberation of possible reasons, we finally concluded that the early residents of the valley below had employed this route to drive their cattle to a nearby summit that was once cleared to provide summer pasture. Thus, if our assumption was correct, we were retracing a portion of a herding route that retained a historic link with the past.

At length, our faint path crossed an oak-covered knoll and intersected with the maintained trail, which we followed to the snow-covered crest before turning back. Our outing had been a success in more ways than one. First, we had accomplished our off-trail goal. Additionally, we made a discovery that helped us better understand life in a time before the formation of the Great Smoky Mountains National Park when farmers had driven their cattle to graze on an open, grassy pasture.

In Search of an Old Trail

Somewhere in the Smokies

May 13, 1988

An early map of the Smokies documented a trail that once climbed to a high ridge along an unnamed tributary of a stream feeding into a picturesque valley. This trail intrigued me, and I had often contemplated locating and following it. On this pleasant spring day, my yearning to discover this old trail was about to become reality. Several hours of walking on a maintained trail brought me to a ridge and my departure point for a day of exploration with the goal of discovery.

I began the off-trail segment of my outing by walking down the ridge until I reached the point where the old map indicated that the trail had left the ridge to reach the unnamed tributary that I was seeking. Thus, I abandoned the ridge here and descended steeply, without finding any semblance of the trail I sought, into a forest that was green with new growth. This preoccupied me as I picked my way downward, admiring trees with small leaves and early wildflowers.

At an elevation of 4,300 feet I reached a spring in the center of a gently sloping high cove. Before long, I encountered moss-covered crossties and rusting rail spikes marking the location of a logging incline built to remove timber from the steep slopes flanking either side of the narrow valley that I was following downward. During my map study before my walk, I wondered why the trail had not maintained a higher route versus following the valley. Now the answer was clear. The old logging incline had served as the most logical route to the ridge for the early hiker. It served for the most part as a ready-made trail.

Using my altimeter for reference, I left the incline at approximately 3,700 feet just as the trail of the past had and set a parallel course around the slopes without finding evidence of the trail I sought. That is, no evidence was found until I reached a side spur of the main ridge, and there it was—a rudimentary trace that made a very steep descent to the valley through which I had made my approach earlier in the day.

At day's end, I had seen no contemporary human signs on my off-trail jaunt. The only prints I saw were those of a medium-sized black bear in the damp, dark loam beside the small stream that was flanked by the white blooms of trillium. I had enjoyed a day of solitude and experienced the excitement of unlocking the mystery of an old trail. I will always recall the experiences of this day whenever I study my map of this remote place.

Homes and Farms

A Historic Parade

Big Walnuts; Eagle Creek Trail

September 12, 1970

Bob F. and I camped at Big Walnuts, a campsite that derived its name from several old walnut trees northeast of the site. In our rambles about our camp, it became apparent that others had preceded us here, creating a virtual parade of history.

Indian hunting parties had no doubt spent brief periods here on their hunting sojourns. Much later, white settlers inhabited the flats along Eagle Creek, farming the fertile soil and allowing their livestock to roam the forests. When the logging era flourished, hardworking loggers extended a rail grade past our camp almost to Spence Field and cut and removed the timber, leaving a decimated forest in their wake. All of these times were now in the past, however, and Bob and I witnessed the healing hand of nature that was softening the scars created in other times. Now only a few relics remain to remind us of the past at Big Walnuts.

A Visit with Quill Rose

Eagle Creek Trail

September 12, 1973

Trout fishing was the motive that resulted in Bob F. and me being on Eagle Creek; however, while there, we suspended fishing for a while to visit the long-abandoned homesite of Quill Rose, a notorious mountaineer and distiller. Quill, mentioned by Horace Kephart in *Our Southern Highlanders* and by Rebecca Cushman in *Swing Your Mountain Gal*, as well as by other writers, is legendary in Smoky Mountain lore.

Visiting his abandoned farm now grown up in trees gave us the impression of stepping back in time. A portion of a neatly laid stone chimney remained where his cabin of hewn logs had stood, and a rock-bordered plot near the cabin site marked the bounds of a garden that supplied the family's needs. Beyond the cabin site, there were rows of rocks cleared from the land to create terraced fields for the planting of a corn crop. A stream nearby would have been the logical place for Quill's still where he turned his corn to liquor, but the exact location eluded us.

We had only our imaginations to breathe life into this pastoral setting, and this was enough. Our visit with Quill Rose was most enjoyable. After all, the opportunities to rub shoulders with a legend are most infrequent.

These Were Not Random Marks

Big Fork Ridge Trail

July 25, 1976

Alice, Sara, Bill and I enjoyed a circuit over several trails in Cataloochee, all of which provided reminders of the small farms that populated this beautiful valley. We enjoyed the beauty of the broad fields in Cataloochee Valley where our walk began, admired the Woody House and noted the formerly settled places along a portion of Caldwell Fork. Our last segment in the series was the Big Fork Ridge Trail, an unlikely place to find additional evidence of farming. We were surprised, however, to find an unusual sign, one that would have escaped the notice of most if not all who traveled this trail.

High on the ridge, we passed a dead chestnut tree perhaps twelve inches in diameter with an unusual feature. Many years before, someone who was well practiced in the use of an axe had left a series of cuts completely around the circumference of the tree. This practice, called girdling, was employed to "deaden" trees, a land-clearing practice employed by landowners to push back the forest and clear land for crops and pasture. Often extensive areas were girdled. Such places were called "deadenings."

We all studied these marks, the first and last such marks I have seen in the Smokies, and discussed what they were and why they were made. These few simple axe marks told a story and provided us with an important lesson about the past.

Stepping Back in Time

Meigs Mountain Trail

October 27, 1977

The steady drumming of rain on our tent awoke me at 4:00 a.m. As I lay awake for a few moments listening to the pleasant sound and appreciating the warmth of my sleeping bag and the comfort of a dry tent, I wondered what weather lay in store for Bill and me on the day ahead. Fortunately, by dawn the rain had ceased; however, the forest, now largely devoid of leaves, was gray with fog and sodden from the previous night's rain. Notwithstanding the damp and cold, the mood of the morning was perfect for an enjoyable walk.

After a simple breakfast, Bill and I left our camp at King Branch and walked toward Elkmont on a wet path, talking quietly about the trails that we would walk on the second day of our multi-day outing. Little did we know that a surprise lay in store for us before we reached our next trail junction.

Upon rounding a bend in the trail, we were treated to a completely unexpected sight. Far below us was an old farmstead. It consisted of an ancient house painted white, a weathered gray barn and rows of neatly aligned bee stands, all surrounded by green pasture. We had the feeling that we had been transported back eighty years in time. This picture-perfect scene might have qualified for one of the many excellent photographic studies on Smoky Mountain scenery. In actuality, however, this remnant of the past, I learned later, was a life estate—one of the last in the Great Smoky Mountains National Park—granted to the farm's owner to allow him to live his last years in the park. In time, this farm was destined to vanish, like hundreds of small farms before it, and return to the forest from which it was originally wrested.

Coming suddenly on this pastoral scene was one of the pleasant dimensions of our day. I can still visualize this beautiful, unique setting as if it were yesterday.

A Remote Cabin

Bone Valley Trail

September 1, 1978

Robert and I walked to Sugar Fork from Fontana Lake and prepared our camp. With ample time remaining in the day, we decided to visit the historic Hall Cabin some two and a half miles distant. To achieve this end, we followed the meanders of an old road along Bone Valley Creek that passed through an area of former settlement. Overgrown clearings and faint paths leading away from the road reminded us of a time when homes and farms spread along the stream. After wading the creek several times, the road circled away from it and ended at a gray, weathered log cabin, the last remaining cabin on Hazel Creek—although similar cabins once existed throughout the valley.

The Hall Cabin was situated on a gentle slope within the sound of Bone Valley Creek. In another era, cornfields would have spread away to the creek and an orchard would have probably occupied the pastures. Of course there would have been a garden and a barn, and other outbuildings would have rounded out this mountain farm. A stand of nonnative aspens now replaced a portion of the old cornfield, and weeds grew elsewhere.

Robert and I seated ourselves on a crude bench on the cabin porch and reflected on Forrester Ridge, a part of the mountain vista available to us from the porch, while we rested in the warmth of September sunshine. Here we enjoyed a quiet interlude only interrupted by the occasional low droning of insects and let our imaginations transport us back to the day when the farm was an active, thriving enterprise.

A Historic Homestead

Little Brier Gap Trail

December 29, 1979

We walked along the old road past abandoned fields and faint road traces leading to vanished homesites. Eventually, we reached a grassy clearing at the base of Cove Mountains. In the midst of this clearing stood a gray two-story log cabin with adjoining one-story kitchen backed by the mass of the mountain. This had been the home of the Walker sisters, four self-sufficient sisters who remained on the old homeplace after the death of their parents and after other siblings had left. These sisters became famous in their own right, and much has been written about them.

As the cabin was open, Alice, Sara and I entered and walked into a large room adjacent to the kitchen. This room had served as an all-purpose area where the sisters lived, worked and slept. Overhead was a loft accessible by a ladder nailed to the wall. A large mud-chinked fireplace dominated one wall, and it had no doubt served as the focal point of activity and fellowship at day's end. The smoke from the fire that was kept burning constantly had darkened the wood rafters and ceilings and left a pleasant lingering smell in the room, reminding us of the sisters' life there, although the cabin had been unoccupied for years.

The drafty cabin had once been papered with newspapers that served as both decoration and an element of protection from the probing fingers of the wind. Tattered fragments of these faded and stained papers remained here and there. One of these had a recipe for apple pie that boasted that the pie would "make a grouchy man smile." Certainly, this comment made us smile. We had no doubt that the sisters' mountain culinary skills would have made anyone smile.

A few yards east of the house was another log structure, a combination corncrib and toolshed. The only other structure remaining was a nearby springhouse, which had served as a place to store food and keep it cool. The source of water was a beautiful circular spring basin of carefully laid stones.

We vicariously savored the life of the sisters on this bleak winter day. We admired the strong, independent women who had maintained the many skills and technologies that allowed them to master the hardships of life on a remote, picturesque mountain farm.

An Old Homestead in a Clearing

Indian Camp Branch

January 25, 1981

Old trails contain surprises. This walk on an abandoned trail was no different. I began in darkness, experienced an exquisite sunrise and enjoyed the trail's meanders as I followed its gentle turns. My travels led me to Indian Camp Branch, where my surprise awaited. There in a clearing was a pile of logs, the remains of a cabin that had collapsed of its own weight after years of neglect. Remnants of old fields stretched above and below the ruins, providing an outline of the bounds of the farmstead.

I paused for a time and surveyed the jumble of logs. What secrets did they harbor? I imagined that they held the untold stories of a mountain family's life on the shoulder of the mountain, one filled with their joy and their sadness. The story was one of hard work and simple pleasures. It contained a range of emotions associated with birth, death, times of hardship and times of warmth and love. All of these elements were present. However, I could only wonder about them. There was a melancholy feel about this place, and I felt a touch of sadness as I continued my day's exploration.

A Vanished Settlement

Little Cataloochee Trail

May 31, 1981

Little Cataloochee was what has been termed an "island community" in that it was largely self-contained and only loosely connected to other settlements in the area. Walking there has always given me a sense of what life was like in the pre-park era because many remnants of the past are present throughout the valley, and one can visualize the ebb and flow of life patterns simply by walking through it. This was our goal. Karen, Jim C., Alice and I were there to immerse ourselves in the community's history.

Hannah Cemetery, sheltered by large oak trees, was our first stop. Here we gazed at the graves of those who, for the most part, lived their lives in Little Cataloochee. The Hannah Cabin, our next stop, with its gray logs, brick chimney and broad puncheon floors, was a reminder of the earliest homes in the settlement. Beyond, we passed through the vanished settlement of Ola, named for Will Messer's daughter. Mr. Messer was the most prominent citizen in Little Cataloochee, and Ola was the commercial center of the community with its store, blacksmith shop, mill and barns. Mr. Messer's home sat nearby, marked at the time of our visit by a lilac bush full of purple fragrant blooms.

As we continued past Ola, we reached a small spring on the right of the road that served to quench the thirst of those who traveled this way in another time. There we began the climb to the Little Cataloochee Baptist Church, a place where many of the valley's citizens worshiped. The church is situated on the crest of the ridge. Its cemetery, spread out on the slopes below, was flanked with rows of stones to memorialize past residents.

As we continued up the valley, we passed old fields and homesites such as the Cook place. The stone foundation of the apple house stood here, a reminder of a time when the valley was prominent in the production of apples. Beginning here, we made a steep climb to Davidson Gap, where we paused to eat crisp apples and reflect on what we had seen during our walk.

It didn't require much imagination to piece together the Little Cataloochee puzzle. In fitting each piece together, we were able to visualize a way of life as it had existed in other times.

The Remains of a Farm

Somewhere in the Smokies

March 14, 1987

I walked a remote path beneath hemlock trees that shaded my way and gave a somber look to the forest. Rhododendron provided a different shade of green in contrast to the hemlocks, and the bare branches of hardwood trees predominated beyond the hemlock growth. The arrival of spring was a feature of this late winter day. Spring that day was more like a sensation than any visible sign. Perhaps it was the touch of warmth in the air or the way the sun's rays illuminated the bare forest. Regardless of the reason, the feeling and promise of the new season was present.

Remembering the Past

My walk led me to the remains of an old farm in a high cove. The site had been selected with care by someone who appreciated the more gentle lay of the land here and its potential for becoming a fine homestead. The site caused me to wonder when the cove had first been visited and about the men and women who committed their labor to wrest the land from the forest. As I studied the site brightened by the sun radiating from a cloudless sky, I also felt the appeal of this place—a feeling that must have been experienced by the first settler here. I fancied that I could have selected the cabin site, recognized the value and convenience of the nearby spring and seen the potential for creating pastures in the midst of the forest.

A few remnants of the farm remained. I noted a depression in the bank that would have been a root cellar. This sheltered place would have protected canned goods and perhaps turnips, apples and potatoes. Beyond were the rotted remains of a log barn, which held livestock below and hay in the loft above. Perhaps even a small crop of burley tobacco hung there in the rafters to cure.

Near the barn was the site of the now vanished home. A tumbled pile of moss-covered bricks marked one of the home's two chimneys. The other had consisted of precisely laid stones chinked with mud. Only six or seven feet of this chimney survived. Two relatively sound sills yet remained. These sturdy beams, hewn by broad axe, rested on stone pillars. Everything else had disappeared; it had melted into the earth.

As I surveyed the broader setting, I could see a fence line marked by a few gray fence posts, and I could identify some of the vanished fields by the second-growth timber that grew in them. What a beautiful place! It was a special pleasure to visualize the independent people who had lived here along with their pattern of living with its many challenges and joys.

Churches and Cemeteries

The Little White Church on the Knoll

Little Cataloochee Baptist Church; Little Cataloochee Trail

April 9, 1977

Alice, Sara, Bill and I, along with two of the children's friends, Tim and Susie, had dinner on the grounds at Little Cataloochee Baptist Church, although our meal was quite modest compared to meals served here at the gatherings of past Little Cataloochee residents. While we ate, we gazed at the small cemetery that stretched below the church with its neat rows of graves. What a peaceful setting!

Following lunch, we visited the church's sanctuary. A simple lecturn decorated with a small bouquet of pink plastic flowers occupied the front. A center aisle divided two rows of wooden benches, and a cast-iron stove manufactured in Knoxville, Tennessee, that was also located in the front, was available to provide warmth on cold meeting days. Except for the stove and flowers, all was stark white.

The exterior of the church was also painted white, as was the modest belfry. At one time, the church's bell summoned the valley's citizens to worship here and possibly tolled the death of someone in the community. It was quiet on this beautiful day.

I felt a sense of reverence as I stood in the sanctuary. It was a place that served as a symbol of the strong faith that dominated the hills and coves of the Great Smokies. Years later, I visited York Cathedral in England and must say that I found Little Cataloochee Baptist Church its equal in the sense of reverence evoked.

Flowers in September

Sugar Fork Campsite; Hazel Creek Trail

September 27, 1980

We planned to spend the morning in exploratory walking and our afternoon trout fishing in Hazel Creek. With that agenda in mind, Bill and I left our campsite at Sugar Fork and set off for our first objective, Higdon Cemetery.

This small cemetery, typical of many scattered throughout the park, contained fieldstone grave markers without legible markings, based on our cursory survey. Its remoteness attested to the simple, hard life of the mountaineers who inhabited the hills and coves of the valley through which Hazel Creek flows. Despite the fact that this burial ground was located in a remote location, there was no doubt that those buried here were not forgotten. Bright plastic flowers that resembled their natural counterparts were placed on the graves. They seemed perfectly natural here, except that they were blooming in September, well past the growing season of their natural brothers and sisters. These symbolized the strong ties that remain in the hearts of families who yet maintain a spiritual bond with their ancestors. These families come each year to keep the graves clean and marked in order that the past will not be forgotten.

The First Child Born in Gatlinburg

Bales Cemetery; Baskins Creek Trail

June 19, 1983

An old trail led Alice and me to beautiful Baskins Creek Falls, where rays of summer sunshine heightened the white cascading water that tumbled over the gray stone face of the falls. This view was framed by green leaves, which rustled in the breeze. I might add that this was a welcomed breeze because it brought some relief from the humidity that seemed to hang in the air.

After this interlude, we climbed back to the trail and walked to the Bales Cemetery near the Roaring Fork Motor Nature Trail. The crude original fieldstone markers here had been replaced by formal markers. One of the most interesting of these bore the following legend:

Caleb Bales
B. 1829 D. 1914
Married Apr. 1861
Elizabeth Reagan
B. 1838 D. 1912
Daughter of
Daniel Wesley Reagan
He Was the First Child Born In Gatlinburg, Tenn.
B. 1802 D. 1892

This grave offered a small but worthwhile history lesson and gave a perspective about settlement in the Gatlinburg area. Conversely, it reminded us how much history has been lost and of the fact that each of the graves in this quiet cemetery concealed stories largely lost to history.

Meticulous Workmanship

Somewhere in the Great Smokies

January 27, 1985

On a bitterly cold day, Robert and I passed through a narrow, grassy valley that was formerly settled but now grown up in even-growth tulip poplar trees. Our path led us past a cemetery that contained many graves. A number were marked by crude, unmarked fieldstones. Others were professionally finished marble stones bearing dates as early as the 1820s, attesting to the long settlement in the valley.

In addition to the crude markers and marble stones, there was a third type. These were hand-crafted markers created by some unknown mountain artisan whose caring, meticulous workmanship was apparent in the handsome works present here. These works of art were fashioned out of slabs of smooth native stone. Some of these gray, lichen-encrusted markers were three and a half feet tall and perhaps eighteen inches wide. Their tops were rounded, as were their edges. Their shape and proportions gave them a graceful appearance. The names and dates of birth and death for the deceased were precisely chiseled into the stone. Additionally, some of these markers displayed decorations of hearts and flowers formed with a distinctive flourish.

I reflected on these handsome works that portrayed the pride, skill and craftsmanship of the maker. I also found something symbolic in them. They bespoke of a proud, strong people who lived and farmed the valley and mountain slopes above. These people gave substance and character to their community, state and nation. They passed positive traits and values to descendants, who possess them today.

A Message from the Grave

Somewhere in the Smokies

September 21, 1986

Alice and I walked through a grassy grove and into a moss-covered cemetery. Most of the markers here were fieldstones that added simple dignity to this quiet place. Many were too worn to reveal names. Others contained legible names, many that are common in surrounding communities today, and the dates of birth and death of the deceased. A number of markers were those of children whose early deaths left us with feelings of sadness and regret for families who had experienced the tragic loss of their deeply loved little ones whose lives were just beginning. We were also reminded just how fragile life really is.

One of the most interesting stones that we observed expressed a thought-provoking message that contained an eminent truth. It read:

Remember man as you
Pass by as you are now
So once was I as I am
Now so shall you be there
Fore prepare to follow me

While this dour advice was worthy of thought, we didn't dwell on it, in favor of savoring the warmth and beauty of the day, a blessing for the living. Notwithstanding, our day had included an unexpected message from the grave.

Sacred Ground: A Historic Cemetery

Proctor Cemetery Lakeshore Trail

June 27, 1993

I camped at the Proctor Campsite with friends and relished the opportunity to enjoy the beautiful site, fish the familiar waters of lower Hazel Creek and enjoy a time of fellowship with Tom D., Jim S. and Jim's son, Parker. The history of Proctor also had its special appeal. Spending time at Proctor provided the ideal opportunity to remember this rich history and to visit some of the sites that recalled the past.

Part of my ritual when camped at Proctor has been to visit the Proctor Cemetery, and this trip was no exception. Thus, we all walked to the Calhoun House, crossed the hill beyond and followed the old road to the cemetery entrance. A short path led to the cemetery itself, which spreads over the brow of a ridge spur, ending where the slope of the mountain steepened. Neat rows of stones, both marble and fieldstones, marked the final resting places of those who had a connection to Hazel Creek.

Not surprisingly, the Proctor Cemetery was carefully maintained as usual. There was one new addition to the cemetery, however, that I had not noticed on previous visits. A new marker had been added, so recently in fact that rain had not fallen on the red clay soil exposed in its placement. This new marker honored Moses Proctor (1794–1864) and Patience Rustin Proctor (1801–1870), the first settlers on Hazel Creek.

This new marker consisted of a base and two upright marble squares with the names of Moses and Patience, topped by a rectangular marble slab with legend describing the significance of the graves. The legend read:

PROCTOR

THE FIELD STONES IN FRONT OF THIS MONUMENT IDENTIFY THE GRAVES OF PATIENCE RUSTIN AND MOSES PROCTOR, THE FIRST SETTLERS ON HAZEL CREEK, THEIR FIRST CABIN BEING ERECTED ON THE LOCATION OF THE PRESENT CEMETERY. MOSES WAS THE FIRST PERSON BURIED HERE.

After visiting these graves, we walked among the others and reflected on the beauty and solitude of this mountainside cemetery. We reflected on the significance of this place. We were on sacred ground, ground steeped in the history of Hazel Creek.

The Cataloochee Reunion

Palmer Chapel Methodist Church; Cataloochee Valley

August 14, 1994

Each year, the Cataloochee Reunion is held at the Palmer Chapel Methodist Church located in the beautiful Cataloochee Valley. Former residents, descendants of those who once populated the valley and friends of Cataloochee cross the high mountain gaps to reach this isolated valley that became part of the Great Smoky Mountains National Park. I attended at the invitation of John Palmer, a friend and distant cousin, whose family once lived in the valley.

The morning was a time of excitement. Families gathered, exchanged hugs and handshakes and engaged in friendly and sometimes animated conversations, catching up on family news events since their last meeting together. Amidst these activities, baskets of food, covered dishes and dessert plates were spread on long tables in preparation for the dinner on the grounds that was to follow.

The formal activities began with a service in the church. Every pew was filled, and people stood around the walls, outside on the porch, on the steps and in the yard beyond. The service was called to order, and after the opening prayer and welcome, the names of Cataloochee family members who had died since the last reunion were read. After the reading of each name the church bell was tolled once in memory of that person, a symbolic act that moved me deeply. A hymn singing followed this, and many voices filled the sanctuary with rich song as all joined in the singing of familiar tunes.

Following the benediction, individual families gathered together to enjoy a bountiful meal. I joined the Palmer family and was treated to an excellent meal of home-cooked food and the family's warm fellowship. When the meal was completed, I accompanied the Palmers for a ritual drink of water from the spring that once served as the water source for the Beech Grove School.

I was grateful to John Palmer and honored by his invitation to be part of the historic Cataloochee Reunion. It was a wonderful day of fellowship and very meaningful for me. Ending my day with the symbolic drink of water from the Beech Grove Spring was the perfect way to toast the Cataloochee Reunion and the Palmer family, who had made my hours in Cataloochee so enjoyable.

Education

Early Smoky Mountain Education

Little Greenbrier School; Little Greenbrier

December 29, 1979

The alarm sounded at 5:00 a.m and jolted Alice and me awake. Alice mumbled, "Let's lie here a little longer." Initially, I had wanted to arise at 4:00 a.m., so getting up an hour later had been a compromise on my part. After an incoherent debate over whether to arise or remain in bed, Alice mumbled again, "You get up and I'll follow you." With this faltering start, we began our day.

Fortunately, Sara arose without similar resistance; her protestations would come later, however. When we reached Metcalf Bottoms, Sara didn't want to leave the warmth of our vehicle to brave the morning cold. "Why don't we just ride around all day," she questioned. Finally, after reassuring Sara that the day would warm up and that our walk would be an enjoyable outing, I was able to achieve a reluctant consensus among the members of my small party. Thus, we began our walk along the road into Little Greenbrier Cove in crisp thirty-degree air. The sun's warmth and the exertion of our walk removed the discomfort of the cold in a few minutes, and we were glad to be up and about.

Before long, we reached the Little Greenbrier School, situated in a level flat near a tumbling steam. The one-room structure constructed of gray, hand-hewn logs served both as a school and a church, and a small cemetery surrounded by a hand-split picket fence attested to this latter use. Inside the old school were rough benches with dates and initials carved into them dating to the 1920s, although the school was in use long before then. The blackboard was fabricated of wooden boards nailed to the back wall of the building. These had been painted black, creating a literal "black board."

A study of old maps documents the fact that small schools like this one existed throughout the area that was to become the Great Smoky Mountains National Park. Now the only schools that remain are the Little Greenbrier School and the Beech Grove School in Cataloochee. These schools, while not perfect in the education they provided, reflected the fact that the citizens of the Smokies valued education and encouraged their children to participate in the opportunities these schools provided. This is a reflection of the importance that education played in mountain life, contrary to the stereotyping that has plagued mountain people throughout the years.

We lingered at the old school for a while, imagining the shouts and laughter of students who gathered here and sat on hard benches engaged in study. The Little Greenbrier School was empty and quiet on this cold December day. The noise of youthful voices was missing, now only a memory of a distant past.

Milling

Once They Were Common

Slab Camp Branch; Forney Creek Trail

January 23, 1972

At one time, tub mills were common throughout the Smokies. These small mills were crude and slow, and their output was small; however, they allowed families to produce sufficient cornmeal to meet their needs and perhaps those of their neighbors. This was an important convenience when larger mills may have been miles away. Seeing one of these original mills had never crossed my mind; however, Bob F. and I were to discover one before our day ended.

We walked down the Forney Creek Trail, maintaining a steady pace in order to rendezvous with the man who was to shuttle us across Fontana Lake. Although our schedule allowed little time for exploration, we made a brief side trip a short distance up Slab Camp Branch and discovered a deteriorating tub mill there beside the branch. Although we didn't recognize it at the time, we were quite possibly looking at the last original tub mill in the Smokies.

Our mill was a crude structure approximately eight feet square and constructed of quartered logs. There was a low doorway that permitted entry, and inside were two small millstones, approximately two feet in diameter, mounted on a platform three or four feet above the branch. A wooden shaft connected the stones to a handmade wooden turbine constructed from a log three feet in diameter and one and a half feet deep, situated at water level. The turbine was mounted parallel to the water. The whole affair was operated by diverting the flow of the stream onto the turbine, causing it to rotate the shaft, which turned one of the millstones in order to grind the corn being fed into the mill.

This deteriorating structure reflected the capacity of an unknown craftsman to take native materials and create a small but functional mill. We left this interesting place reluctantly but carried with us the mental images of our unique discovery.

Mill Evokes Memories

Mingus Mill; Mingus Creek Trail

April 22, 2001

A spring walk along Mingus Creek promised wildflowers, the beauty of a fast-flowing stream and signs of past settlement. There was the special appeal of Mingus Mill, one of the historic mills in the Smokies. For these very reasons, Miegan, Alice and I had chosen this pleasant stream for our walk and a simple picnic shared together while seated on a mossy boulder well up the creek.

When we reached the millrace to Mingus Mill on our return—a millrace dug into the earth above the mill that merged into a framed trough that delivered water to the mill's turbine through the penstock—we crossed the creek and followed the shady path to the mill. The mill, with its gray board sides and split shake roof, was as I had always known it and seeing it again evoked memories of past visits.

My first recollection, the first time I ever saw the mill, was with my father in the late 1940s when I was nine or ten years old. We stood in the grassy clearing in front of the old mill, which I seem to remember was not operating at the time, and experienced a sense of its history and importance as a community institution. It was a social center in the valley, where the valley's citizens talked and shared stories as they awaited their turn to have their corn ground. How interesting it would have been to have witnessed a day at the mill.

I remembered a cold January visit to the mill when Alice and I were twenty and not yet married. The mill stood in winter shadows, and long, diamondlike icicles hung from the suspended portion of the millrace that connected to the penstock. We admired the old structure and enjoyed the winter solitude that was apparent there.

At other times Alice and I have visited the mill with Sara and Bill, sometimes to admire the workings of the mill and at others to buy a bag of cornmeal, coarse meal always reserved for cornbread. I always enjoyed the cadence of the gears and watching the stones turn as they dispensed a thread of ground meal that descended to the hopper below.

Although I did not interject these memories into our conversation while we studied the old structure, they came readily and vividly to mind. As I mentally recalled these past visits, I realized that in a small way Mingus Mill is threaded into the fabric of my life.

DISTILLING

Two Nails and a Bucket

Somewhere in the Smokies

Ed and I spent the morning climbing a steep ridge to a high gap, tracing one of the old trails from a turn-of-the-century hand-drawn map. As we made our ascent, I felt a connection with the mapmaker, knowing that early in the last century he had climbed and meticulously mapped the old trace we followed.

Rather than return to our camp the same way, we selected an off-trail route that entailed descending along a stream that passed through what was at the turn of the century a well-populated valley. Thus, we walked along a maintained trail for a while and in time left it to descend into the head of a cove. There we found a seepage of cold water—one of the high springs giving birth to the stream that we followed. We drank freely of this delicious, cold water while we rested on a log near the source and enjoyed our forest setting.

We made a strange discovery during this pause. A rusting tin bucket lay near the water source, and two nails were discovered nailed into the log on which we sat. They were rusty and had been nailed there many years ago. Because we were in such a remote place, a place not visited by humans for years, we were puzzled by these artifacts. Why were they there?

Of course, we could only speculate about the answer. Our guess was that we had discovered the site of a long-forgotten liquor still. The site was certainly ideal. There was a supply of fresh, clean water, a good supply of wood to stoke the fire beneath the still and a remote site. Perhaps the tree had been felled to conceal the still, and the bucket was a remnant of the still's operation!

Distilling was quite an art, and considerable value was placed on good, properly made white liquor, liquor that was as clear as the water of the nearby spring and produced a good bead—tiny bubbles—when shaken. It was a favored drink in the mountains and also used in homemade medicines. Were we correct in our speculation? Possibly. This may have been the place where a mountain farmer who took pride in his craft produced a supply of liquor. At any event, we had two nails and a bucket to support our claim.

Herding

Once a Pasture

Becks Bald

February 11, 1989

My walk began at Smokemont Campground before 8:00 a.m. The temperature was twenty degrees, and I wore a toboggan, gloves and several layers of clothing as defense against the cold. I passed through the campground, walked along Bradley Fork and finally climbed the familiar trail along Chasteen Creek toward Hughes Ridge. Ice froze on my mustache and beard as I walked, much like the icicles that had frozen on the edges of the streams I passed.

I reached the crest of Hughes Ridge mid-morning and walked to Becks Bald, a rounded summit to the south of the point where I first crested the ridge. From Becks Bald, I viewed the main crest of the Smokies from Clingmans Dome to Mount Guyot. The main divide appeared dark blue and was framed by the grays and browns created by the bare limbs of hardwood trees in the foreground.

After admiring the distant panorama, my focus narrowed to my immediate locale—Becks Bald. The summit of this mountain mass is wooded, not bald as its name implies. However, at one time this top was indeed a grassy high-elevation pasture. It was a place where cattle were driven to graze in the summer, attended to by herders who salted the cattle and looked after their welfare. Jerome Parker told me in 1973 when we passed this way on a horseback trip to Enloe Creek that the herders had sheltered under Enloe Rock, a large rock overhang with a spring underneath. Becks Bald, like Nettle Bald across the valley on Thomas Divide and Hyatt Bald on Hyatt Ridge, was all grassy expanses once; however, the forest has encroached on these formerly bald areas, leaving them bald in name only.

It was a bleak, cold day, and it was hard to envision cattle here. They once freely roamed these slopes when Becks Bald was an inherent part of an agricultural system in another era.

Vanished Highland Pastures

Lead Cove, Bote Mountain, Jenkins Ridge and Appalachian Trails

March 25, 1989

My mind was already on Spence Field, De Armond Bald and Blockhouse Mountain as I walked on the Lead Cove Trail through a forest awakening to spring. Trout lily, with its speckled leaves, covered the ground in a cove lush with new spring growth. I paused to enjoy a wood anemone growing in moist leaves beside the trail. In another place, I paused to admire a small cascade of crystal water flowing over green, moss-covered cobbles in a forest yet devoid of leaves. Perhaps the most rewarding experience was the song of a winter wren, heard but unseen, whose trilling filled the forest with its complex melody, a melody that reminded me of phrases played on a piccolo.

I reached Spence Field at 10:00 a.m. It was covered with golden brown grass and clusters of serviceberry trees and other growth. The border of this open meadow consisted of rhododendron, green against the drab grass. The skies were blue overhead and seemed boundless. I enjoyed crossing this open expanse, one of my favorite places in the Smokies, and imagined how the field had looked when it was summer pasture to hundreds of head of livestock. Cattle, sheep, goats, mules and horses kept the field manicured, giving it the appearance of a well-kept lawn.

Passing beyond Spence Field, I walked the Jenkins Ridge Trail to Haw Gap. This high gap at an elevation of 4,925 feet was my departure point for both De Armond Bald and Blockhouse Mountain, which lay to the right and left of the gap, respectively. I chose De Armond Bald for my first ascent and made a short climb to the crest, which was covered in rhododendron. I pressed through this growth and descended one-tenth of a mile beyond the crest. To my surprise, I reached the remnants of a grassy area, perhaps one-half acre more or less, largely overgrown by blackberry canes and briers.

After an examination of this remnant of a once more expansive bald, I ascended Blockhouse Mountain to another opening slightly larger than that on De Armond Bald. This opening was covered in golden grass that extended to the crest on slopes that were otherwise wooded—another surprise.

The creation of grassy balds in the Smokies has been the source of much discussion and debate. As I retraced my steps, I recognized that the open areas on Spence Field, De Armond Bald and Blockhouse Mountain are closing in as the forest and other growth slowly encroaches on them. Certainly, livestock played an essential role in preserving the balds. However, with the end of herding in the mid-1930s, the balds that were once highland pastures are slowly vanishing.

Logging

A Feat of Engineering

Grassy Branch Trail

April 16, 1979

As Robert and I sped toward Tennessee for a planned walk to Mount Le Conte, my car's engine began to sputter and knock, and there was an appreciable loss of power. Although the engine continued to run, its irregular rhythm caused us to abandon our original plan. Rather than forego the opportunity to walk altogether, we drove to the nearest trailhead, which happened to be the Kephart Prong Trail, and made the decision to walk to Charlies Bunion after considering the options available to us.

As the hours passed, we walked the Kephart Prong and Sweat Heifer Trails to the Appalachian Trail, which we followed to Charlies Bunion. After a period spent admiring the panorama there, we continued to the Dry Sluice Gap Trail and finally to Grassy Gap and the Grassy Branch Trail, progressing toward the completion of a circuit of approximately fourteen miles.

Beginning at Grassy Gap, we descended through a second-growth forest that had not yet leafed out. The forest floor, however, was carpeted with a cover of spring beauty whose flowers gave a snowy appearance to the slopes. Farther down, we paused to view what had once been a high logging railway trestle. It had been approximately 150 feet long and spanned a hollow that was some 60 feet deep. It had been constructed of long, straight chestnut logs supported by log cribbing. Theses logs, now collapsed and rotting below, served as a reminder of the engineering feats that enabled steam locomotives, skidders and log loaders to move slowly to and from the high ridges to remove timber from the very crest of the Great Smokies.

These remains were not obvious and were slowly melting into the earth after weathering here for many years. With their ultimate disappearance, the memory of a substantial trestle that once stood here will also vanish just as the logging era that spawned a period of destruction in the Smokies ended.

A Visit to a Vanished Town

Proctor; Hazel Creek Trail

June 7, 1988

We were transported by boat from the Fontana Marina to the boundary of the Great Smoky Mountains National Park, where we followed an old road along Hazel Creek toward the Proctor Campsite admiring the delicate clusters of pink-white rhododendron that adorned the slopes on one side of the road and the clear waters of Hazel Creek on the other. The forest overhead was fully green with maturing leaves that added the final touch of perfection to this scene.

Alice and I had a few hours before we were due to return to the marina, and I had planned to use these hours effectively with a whirlwind tour of Proctor to acquaint Alice with both its beauty and its history. With these goals in mind, we continued up the stream and entered another time.

We ambled past the hill where the Proctor School once stood and enjoyed the coolness that we experienced in the shadows of white pines that now occupied the school's ball field. Beyond, we entered the bounds of the sawmill town of Proctor, built by the Ritter Lumber Company early in the century to meet the needs of those who worked in the nearby sawmill. Employee housing, a clubhouse, a commissary and other buildings once occupied the overgrown fields along creek. Next we visited the site of the sawmill, with its overgrown millpond and other vestiges of industrial use. The most prominent remainder was a portion of the brick kiln building, whose high walls were partially vine covered much like those of an untended formal garden allowed to go wild. The sun's rays were diffused by tall trees, creating a soft lighting that enhanced the beauty of these ruins.

We retraced our steps to the Calhoun House with its long porch. This white frame house, shaded by massive oak trees, faced Hazel Creek and offered both a delightful view of the stream as well as a place to listen to the perpetual whisper of the steam as it glided by. Beyond the old house, we climbed upward to Possum Hollow and to the Proctor Cemetery, where we reverently examined markers with chiseled inscriptions, as well as unmarked fieldstones that commemorated the lives of those who formerly lived here.

We lunched at the Proctor Campsite under tall white pines that we had admired earlier and observed the aimless swirling of the stream as it flowed past the campsite. While we relaxed, we discussed Proctor's history, first as a site frequented by American Indians, then as a farming community, later as a logging boomtown and now as a jewel in the Great Smoky Mountains National Park. We found it hard to comprehend on this quiet day that the fields and forest through which we'd walked had once been the home to one thousand people when Proctor thrived as a bustling mill town.

The Creation of Place Names

Somewhere in the Great Smokies

January 30, 1993

My hikes with Woody were always rewarding. His effervescent personality, delightful wit, knowledge of the Smokies and keen powers of observation made any outing with him enjoyable, as well as a learning experience. This off-trail walk was no exception.

Woody, who was intimately acquainted with this remote section of the park, led me across a low ridge and into a gentle hollow where a home had once stood. A partially collapsed log structure made of rough saddle-notched logs was all that remained of past occupancy. The woods were bare, and the site had a lonely, forlorn appearance as the old structure was gradually rotting away.

Old homesites are commonplace in the Smokies, so this discovery, although interesting, was not unusual. The unusual awaited, however. Beyond the homesite, as we followed a trace along an unnamed branch, Woody called my attention to a rusting circular saw blade some four feet in diameter that was propped against a tree. Now, this was a real find! Although I had seen a piece of blade from a band mill and one or two crosscut saw blades, this was the first time I had ever seen a circular saw in the Smokies.

The circumstances leading to the abandonment of the blade were to remain a mystery. What was certain, however, was that the blade had been part of a portable logging operation that involved moving the mill to the logs versus the logs to the mill. This technique allowed the logs to be harvested and converted to sawn lumber in an effective and expeditious manner.

Many years had passed since this rusty blade had sawed its last board. However, it did serve one final purpose. Woody told me that he had christened the unnamed branch we followed "Saw Blade Branch" when he first found the blade sometime in the past. Yes, the branch was given its unofficial name after Woody's discovery. That's how place names are created!

One in a Million

Somewhere in the Smokies

July 18, 2005

We had abandoned the maintained trail, Ron and I, in favor of following one of the many rail grades in this large watershed. Although ventures such as this have their challenges, such as climbing steep inclines and penetrating thick rhododendron growth that frequently claims old rail grades, among others, there are also rewards.

It is rewarding to determine how the rail grades were engineered to climb to the very crest of the mountains and to identify skidder sites and incline grades, making it possible to determine how a particular area was logged and how the logs were moved to rail grades in preparation for transportation to the mill. For me, perhaps the most rewarding aspects of rail grade exploration are the joy of being off-trail, finding beautiful open sections of rail grades, witnessing exquisite small streams that were once spanned by rails and discovering some forgotten logging relic that has a story to tell about the physical aspects of logging or about those who devoted their lives to this endeavor.

On this particular day, Ron and I discovered one of the relics of logging. We were crossing a small stream when we discovered two parallel hewn timbers that apparently carried a rail grade to a nearby logging incline. This in itself was not unusual because old timbers survive to this day when immersed in water or otherwise kept wet. Most amazing in this instance was the fact that an intact crosstie spanned the parallel logs, and this crosstie had a rusting rail on it held firmly in place by an iron rail spike.

Although I have seen many crossties, rails and spikes during my rambles in the Smokies, this was the first time I had seen them connected just as they had been on the day they were laid. Also, this was a first for Ron, who is a leading expert on Smoky Mountain logging.

In the future when I use the phrase "one in a million," I will define it in terms of crossties, rails and spikes. Our observation of an intact crosstie, rail and spike had to be a one-in-a-million chance in the Great Smokies.

Amazing!

Somewhere in the Smokies

March 15, 2006

Ron, Marilyn and I walked through a flat area beyond the small stream, seeking some sign of Champion Fibre Company's rail grade, one constructed early in the last century that had crossed the high cove we were exploring. Despite our collective efforts, the grade eluded us. Ultimately, I moved to the slopes across a narrow valley, hoping to find the grade there, but no sign was visible. Then I looked up the slope twenty-five feet above the flats in which I stood and saw the grade there.

It all became apparent then. Those who engineered the grade had elevated it by means of a long log trestle that made a sweeping, gently ascending arc across the entirety of the valley to reach the elevated slope on the mountainside. This trestle, simply named "number 16" on Ron's 1920 track map, must have been an amazing structure that had spanned approximately 750 feet between each side of the flats.

I gazed at the valley and visualized the rustic trestle with its log supports and timbers bearing crossties and rails and imagined the labors required to complete this marvelous feat of logging engineering. The only thing missing in my mental picture was a logging locomotive spouting plumes of smoke as it slowly descended across the trestle with its load of logs destined for Champion's mill at Smokemont.

Civilian Conservation Corps

Remembering the CCC

Kephart Prong Trail

July 18, 2005

Ron and I climbed the Kephart Prong Trail, looking forward to a day in the mountains. Near the beginning of our trip, we paused to examine the remains of a former Civilian Conservation Corps (CCC) camp. A stone and masonry signboard with its blank face, a stone water fountain, old boxwoods and a massive chimney are the primary remains of this once active camp. The orderly bunk rooms, mess hall and associated buildings have long since vanished here and in many other places in the Smokies where similar camps were erected.

I reflected on the importance of the CCC in the Smokies. Young men who staffed this camp and others like it made a significant contribution in building roads, bridges and trails and performing other useful work throughout the park. The CCC also helped shape the lives of many men, as well as providing support for their families at a time when the nation struggled to emerge from the effects of a crippling depression.

As we passed through these silent remains, I realized that I owed the CCC a debt of gratitude for the lasting imprint that this institution left on the Smokies. Thanks to the CCC, I and many others have been able to enjoy the Great Smokies on trails that are a lasting memorial to its many contributions.

Fire Towers

High Rocks Fire Tower

Welch Ridge Trail

August 26, 1980

After a morning walk along the Cold Springs Branch Trail, mostly along an old Ritter Lumber Company Rail grade, Robert and I reached the crest of Welch Ridge. Our next goal was to visit High Rocks. The trail between Cold Springs Gap and the short connector to High Rocks provided ample opportunity to enjoy blackberries that grew in abundance beside the trail. We consumed these delicious purple berries by the handfuls until we could eat no more. This feast was one of the simple pleasures of our day's walk.

Shortly after midday, we suspended our packs in beech trees and walked toward High Rocks along a trail approximately a half mile in length. At its end, we climbed a carefully laid set of shaded stone steps and continued to High Rocks, a stone mass at the end of Welch Ridge. A metal fire tower and abandoned warden's cabin covered in gray weathered shingles occupied the crest.

At one time, towers such as this one occupied a number of prominent peaks in the Smokies and served as observation posts to allow the detection of forest fires throughout the park. Times had changed, however, and the cabins and towers were being phased out in favor of fire monitoring through the use of airplanes. This shift brought with it the demise of the towers and the rustic cabins that once sheltered the fire wardens, and now only a few towers remain in the Smokies.

Robert and I ultimately left the summit with a memory of High Rocks fire tower in our minds on this hot August day. The tower served as a reminder of a time when dedicated wardens scanned the surrounding mountains for fires and reported their locations to contribute to early suppression. It would have been unimaginable to these persons and others charged with the protection of the park at that time that the day would ultimately arrive when certain fires would be allowed to burn under supervision to duplicate a time when fires were a natural part of the cycle of the forest, one that had its positive effects in creating a diverse and healthy forest.

Special Places

First Visit to Mount Le Conte Lodge

Boulevard Trail

June 1971

Robert, Elizabeth, Alice and I planned an overnight stay at Mount Le Conte Lodge, the only lodge within the bounds of the Great Smoky Mountains National Park. This was our first trip to Mount Le Conte, and everyone looked forward to visiting this beautiful portion of the Smokies. Our trip along the Boulevard Trail to reach the lodge was filled with exquisite views, wildflower sightings and the cool sensation of hot faces pressed gently into luxuriant damp green moss.

After crossing the High Top of Mount Le Conte, we descended to Le Conte Lodge, an assemblage of gray, weatherworn buildings. On arrival, we were welcomed with cups of delicious, steaming hot chocolate and given our cabin assignment. Our small cabin was furnished with a double-width bunk bed that was constructed of fir trees harvested on the site. A small wood heater stood in the corner along with a supply of balsam billets for fuel. A few chairs and a small table constituted the balance of our furnishings. A pail of water and a dipper had been placed on the table and crude shelves supported a kerosene lantern. What more could one ask?

After we settled in and explored a bit, we returned to the lodge and awaited the supper call. When dinner was announced, the dining hall quickly filled with guests from all walks of life and from many parts of the United States. Simple introductions were sufficient to begin an evening of fellowship.

This was the first of a number trips to Mount Le Conte; however, this one stands out most vividly in my memory. It marked the beginning of a close friendship with Robert and Elizabeth that has lasted until the present. This trip has special meaning for another reason. It satisfied a childhood yearning to visit the crest of this mountain, a yearning that first developed when my father and I walked to Alum Cave when I was eleven. A trail sign at Alum Cave pointed toward Mount Le Conte. It seemed then to be a mystical place. It still seems so today.

A Memorable Breakfast

The Mountain View Hotel; Gatlinburg, Tennessee

May 13, 1978

Alice, Sara, Bill and I met Anne Broome for breakfast at the Mountain View Hotel prior to a walk with Anne in her beloved Greenbrier Cove. Our meeting place was suggested by Anne, and I welcomed her recommendation and the opportunity it created to visit this historic hotel, established in 1916 by Andrew Jackson Huff.

While we waited for the dining room to open, we strolled about the spacious lobby. It was furnished with comfortable chairs, and it contained interesting displays of traditional mountain crafts. The walls were hung with paintings of mountain scenes that enhanced the yesteryear charm and character of the hotel—character that only comes with age and use.

Our breakfast was served by a pleasant server, and it lived up to the hotel's reputation for serving excellent meals. Country-cured ham, grits, scrambled eggs, hot biscuits, fresh butter, honey and rich coffee comprised our repast. This was a truly memorable meal and one that fortified us for a delightful outing in the Smokies. Our time with Anne during this glorious meal was filled with warm conversation and an opportunity to visit with one of the truly great women of the Smokies.

Off-Trail Excursions

Some of my most enjoyable Smoky Mountain outings have involved trips into the wild, away from maintained trails, a few of which I share in this chapter. Such outings usually have had as their object exploring forgotten manways, abandoned trails and old rail grades left from the logging era. Occasionally, however, I have pursued routes that were previously untracked, at least in recent times, motivated by a desire to see the sights and experience a wilderness visited by few.

Other motives also influenced my off-trail rambles. I explored to get a sense of Smoky Mountain history. I crossed the Smokies on what was once part of a network of American Indian trails in the Southeast; followed rail grades to obtain a sense of how logging was conducted in the Smokies; sought out paths to retrace the footsteps of my Smoky Mountain heroes Horace Kephart, Paul Fink, Harvey and Anne Broome and George Masa; followed creeks into coves that were settled well before the coming of the park to get a feel for where and how life was lived in remote places; and sometimes I have explored simply because I was intrigued by a faint line of dots on a map.

Often these trips into the wild have been physically demanding and have caused me, especially when entangled in an impenetrable thicket of rhododendron, to question my sanity. Fortunately, I have had friends and hiking companions who shared my zeal for visiting out-of-the-way places and who joined me on many of these trips. These companions have helped to make even the most rigorous of these treks rewarding. Certainly, after a day immersed in the wild, I have experienced a feeling of accomplishment and exhilaration that is difficult to convey to others. I hope, however, that the reader will at least vicariously share what it is like to venture into the wild.

Finally, it is imperative to recognize that off-trail adventures are often extremely difficult and that they pose dangers and risks, including loss of life. Subsequently, such outings should be undertaken only by those who are prepared for the challenges involved. Consistent with the risks involved and to protect sensitive areas, I have provided limited information about these outings.

North Carolina Outings

A Strenuous Day

Somewhere in the Smokies

The forest was cold, and gray shadows shaded the snow-covered slopes about us. Rhododendron leaves were curled tightly against the twenty-five-degree cold. Six inches of frozen snow crunched underfoot, supporting our weight briefly before collapsing with each step. The day embodied all the elements of winter to test Robert and me as we embarked on a faint manway, intent on following its meanders to the crest of one of the ribs that branch off the crest of the Smokies.

Initially an old overgrown rail grade enabled us to follow the manway; however, snow obscured our path beyond the end of our grade well up the slopes, and except for a faint but discernable undulation in the snow, we would have lost the trail completely beyond this point. We did, in fact, stray away temporarily in patches of snow-laden rhododendron only to locate the trail beyond these barriers. Eventually the manway crossed the headwaters of a small stream high on the mountainside in a narrow "V" and began ascending a series of switchbacks along a well-defined narrow dug pathway that angled steeply upward.

The years had not been kind to the old, unused manway. Many blowdowns, some of significant size, blocked a portion of the path. These barriers, combined with snow, now ten inches deep, slowed our progress appreciably. Occasionally, we straddled fallen logs or crawled under those that we could not straddle. When neither of these approaches was practicable, we laboriously climbed around the obstacle, struggling to gain footholds on steep, icy slopes.

Above us loomed our goal—the crest of the ridge. The snow-covered crest was barely distinguishable when viewed against a background of silver-gray clouds. With eyes skyward, we struggled onward and upward, taking turns breaking the trail through heavy snow now a foot deep. This was a slow, laborious process, and our final ascent of eight-tenths of a mile required one hour and fifteen minutes of struggling through the snow and against the force of gravity.

At last we reached the crest. The view there made the day's exertions worthwhile. A high, thin cloud cover veiled the sun, but there was no haze and views seemed unlimited. Clingmans Dome, Mount Buckley, Silers Bald and Thunderhead were visible to the west as were Mount Kephart, the Balsams and Mount Guyot to the east. These views in themselves were sufficient rewards for a day exploring an almost forgotten manway.

The Unseen Hand of Nature

Somewhere in the Smokies

Robert and I left our campsite and walked to our jumping-off point for our off-trail jaunt. Many years before, an old path had ascended from a historic valley to reach the high divide on which we stood. Using map and compass, we attempted to pinpoint where the old trace lay because it was our intention to locate and follow it as others had in times past.

Initially, we found what we thought was a semblance of a trail and explored it until it became obscure and branched into a series of game trails that gave no clue as to the proper route. As a result, we abandoned our search and picked our way down the steep slopes into the hollow, which widened out below the crest. Once in the hollow, we separated and sought the best way through the tangle of growth and blowdowns—"best way" being a process of trial-and-error forays into the undergrowth to find the most feasible path through the maze of rhododendron and fallen trees. Unfortunately, sometimes there is no best way.

Before long, we reached the headwaters of a branch, and a short way down the branch we discovered decaying logs approximately ten inches in diameter and eight feet long laid horizontally across the small watercourse. These logs formed a crude skidway that had been employed many years before to move logs from the upper slopes to the rail grade that was somewhere below us. In another ten minutes we reached this grade, and it served more or less as our route for the next several hours.

In terms of the physical aspects of travel down the stream, now a creek, our route crisscrossed the stream a number of times. Sometimes, we walked in the stream, and at other times we were compelled to force our way through thick rhododendron when no other feasible route was available. At other times, fallen trees, combined with the rhododendron, caused us to scout alternative ways to go around or through the obstructions, resulting in frequent false leads into impenetrable growth that we were hoping to bypass. These struggles were compounded by the fact that we carried backpacks that had to be wrestled through the various barriers that barred our way.

Despite our struggles, we passed our morning in a world of spectacular beauty. To appreciate this grand scene, one must visualize majestic trees, the remains of rotting chestnut stumps left from the logging era, wild and tumbling streams rushing down steep verdant slopes to join the stream we followed and subtle shadings of light and shadow over the whole. There was the effect of elevation. We could look down the widening valley before us and view pale blue skies through the trees. Throughout our passage, we were impressed by the unseen hand of nature that was reclaiming a forest that had been scarred by the invasion of the logging industry, an industry that had once removed all the marketable timber in the watershed through which we passed.

After several hours, we emerged from the forest and into a beautiful grassy clearing. We paused here for a well-deserved rest and allowed ourselves to be transported back to a time when this clearing was the site of a mountain farm. As we gazed at the mountains that surrounded this grassy glade, we discussed our satisfaction with the outcome of our morning's adventure. Fortunately, the balance of our day was along trails free of obstacles. We counted this as a blessing.

Oh, the Glory

Somewhere in the Smokies

The Great Smoky Mountains National Park has numerous areas that beg a visit. Sometimes an interesting place name inspires an outing, or sometimes just the lay of the land compels a visit. In this instance, I had often studied the maps of this remote area and yearned to make a firsthand visit. Thus, I included it on my "Most Wanted" list of places to visit in the Smokies. Now after weeks of planning, Robert and I stood on a high ridge ready to embark on a trek into a basin far below. We were armed with map, compass and altimeter and with a bit of knowledge about where we were going; however, off-trail travel entails elements of uncertainty and surprise. Thus, we were unable to completely anticipate what awaited us or where nightfall would find us if there were complications in our plan.

At the start, we followed a side ridge for a time. Although no one had visited this ridge in recent times, bears had not ignored these high slopes. Here the bears, free from human interference, lived as kings and queens of a wild domain. Their signs were evident. We found a circular bed filled with thick leaves in a natural bowl-like depression. There was considerable scat on the slopes, indicating the bears' use of the area.

In time, we left the ridge and descended steep slopes, seeking a route that offered the least resistance through the tangle of rhododendron below. This tactic ultimately resulted in a further descent into a dark, hemlock-shaded ravine. No feasible choice existed now except to continue over blowdowns and rocks that choked the way and to wade the shallow waters that flowed through this crease in the mountains. This was a physically demanding place. It was not made easier by the thirty-five-pound backpacks that we carried.

Robert and I wasted no time in separating to seek the best way out of our undesirable situation, wondering how we had managed to get ourselves into such a plight when the map contours seemed so rounded and gentle. This phase of our search eventually enabled us to bypass the worst of the maze and led us to an open mountain slope with pleasant gentle contours where there were many large chestnut stumps left from the logging era. What a glorious and beautiful place.

We enjoyed a sense of pleasure at being in this place that had once been populated by big trees. The loggers who worked here no doubt enjoyed a level of ease in removing the logs from this remote cove. The signs of logging activity that we noted here meant that the source for moving logs to the mill must be close at hand. So it was. We stumbled upon a faint path that led to a small opening in the forest and to the headwaters of a stream. The rail grade was located here with its attendant strands of rusty brown logging cable and pieces of shiny black coal. These artifacts remained from an era when steam locomotives crept into this place to remove the timber wealth from the slopes.

After enjoying this pleasant spot for a few minutes, we were faced with making our way to a maintained trail several miles distant. We decided that the obvious choice was to follow the rail grade, and although it seemed obvious enough to begin with, we somehow strayed off it—probably at some rhododendron-choked creek crossing where a now vanished trestle once stood. Regardless of the cause, this error led to a time of squirming along rhododendron-choked animal trails that slabbed around the steep slope above the creek. Animals are efficient travelers, however, and their paths followed the contour of the slope, which was some consolation despite the difficulties of travel.

After a time of negotiating the challenges of this overgrown place, we rediscovered the old rail grade again. "Rediscovered" may be too generous a term for stumbling across it again. In any event, we followed the grade through the long hours of afternoon, not knowing where or when we would emerge at a trail marking the end of our cross-country trek. Eventually, however, we reached a trail and arrived at our campsite about 7:00 p.m.

We had spent a glorious afternoon. Notwithstanding the passage of the years, the rigors and hardships of this day have not been forgotten, although they are part of my happy memories now. I especially appreciated Robert at day's end, as well as now, because of his willingness to explore this forgotten place and because in all our times together he never complained about the hardships we encountered.

Choosing a Difficult Route

Somewhere in the Smokies

We stood on a high top after an early morning climb of several miles. We were surrounded by tall fir and hardwood trees that reached skyward like pillars in a Gothic cathedral. My eyes followed the lines of straight trunks to a thin cover of spreading limbs, and I felt a sense of reverence as I surveyed this majestic scene. A nearby spring issued cold, clear and pure water, and I drank from the spring before leaving the known for the unknown more as a symbolic gesture than from thirst.

Our destination was a remote manway; however, Al W., Rob and I shunned the traditional route to this place. We opted instead to descend the unnamed watercourse spawned by the waters of the spring to one of several forks of a larger tributary some distance from us. When we reached the larger tributary, we planned to descend it along a faint manway. We did not know what to expect on this first segment of our trek but nevertheless plunged into the roughs and gingerly picked our way over ice-covered stones in the margins of the spring branch and pushed through matted rhododendron with tightly curled leaves that reacted to temperatures in the mid-twenties. The sun's rays had not yet reached this north side, and the slopes were painted in frosty blue shadows that emphasized both the cold and the wild terrain through which we traveled.

In time, we reached the small tributary that we were seeking. The forest here grew to the very edge of the rushing stream, and in surveying the lay of the land, we determined that a dry path was not available. Our most feasible option, although one we dreaded, was to wade the cold water of the creek rather than force our way though dense undergrowth on the banks. Thus, wading and edging our way along the banks when possible, we descended the stream.

The mountains surrounding us were wild and beautiful. The slopes seemed a jumble of growth, yet nature's landscaping displayed order and perfection befitting of such a wild place. Tall spruce and hemlock trees, thick green rhododendron and gray lichen-covered rock outcroppings all blended in a perfection that was exciting to behold. Nevertheless, the scene was somewhat foreboding in that easy passage was denied.

The stream flowed between steep slopes in an endless variety of pools, runs and small cascades. Wind-thrown hemlock trees lay across it and dammed the waters into waist-deep pools. Small speckled trout darted before us as we invaded their sanctuary. After a time of wet, difficult travel, we reached a larger stream, where we paused for lunch and reflected on the sights and sounds of the wilderness. Our stop was brief, however, as several miles of rugged travel awaited us.

We located with some difficulty the old manway that we were seeking and began following it along the larger stream. This proved a three-person task at times. The path variously veered to the streamside, plunged into rhododendron and climbed over low side ridges covered so thickly in doghobble that solid footing was not possible on this springy mass. Considerable physical effort was required as we continually crouched, bent, twisted, crawled and climbed as we negotiated the obstacles along our obscure route.

We were rewarded for our efforts by grand views of the stream as it tumbled over its varied course. Low waterfalls, gliding runs, small pools, boulders and tall trees provided ever-changing scenes. All of this was framed by steep mountain slopes that loomed above us and displayed under luminous tarnished skies.

Late in the afternoon, we stumbled upon an old trail that led upward and away from the stream. It had lain abandoned for years, and none of us had ever explored it; however, we knew where it led. Thus, we climbed away from the stream, its echoes fading as we climbed, and eventually reached a maintained trail after a rigorous uphill battle through the undergrowth.

It was dark when we reached our starting point after many hours and many miles along a difficult route in the depths of the Smokies. Although we were wet from our stream encounters, scratched and bruised by the undergrowth and physically tired from our exertions, our day in the wilderness had been worth the hardships we had experienced.

A Christmas Day's Ramble

Somewhere in the Smokies

The family spent Christmas in Sylva, North Carolina. Gifts had been opened, Christmas dinner served and family members were reading, playing with gifts and napping. Although remaining indoors was appealing, I drove to the

Smokies for a quiet walk in the park. My goal on this outing was exploring a rail grade some miles distant. It was a pleasant enough day to walk, although the forest seemed lonely and forgotten under gray skies. The weather was unusually warm, and a blustery wind thundered across the ridges, reminding me that winter still held dominance over the mountains.

Eventually, I descended on a path in which water flowed in shallow rivulets on its passage to the valley below. Lush green moss grew in thick beds beside my path, thriving on the dampness. The moss presented a pleasing contrast to the dormant forest. As I enjoyed the winter variety, my thoughts wandered to an abandoned rail grade that awaited me, one that I recalled from past walks.

Abandoned trails, old rail grades and traces of paths discovered while on jaunts in the Smokies tend to remain in my memory. These places often reveal their beginnings, but they do not easily give up the secrets of their endings. Thus, my memory of these places, and this one in particular, only served to lure me to explore its meanders in order to learn its well-kept secrets. I was soon to learn that unlocking these secrets was not easily achieved.

In time, I shunned my path and ventured along the overgrown rail grade into unknown territory. Rugged steam locomotives and other steam equipment once labored to reach these high mountain slopes where the sound of loggers' axes and crosscut saws signaled the harvest of the rich forest. No man-made sounds intruded on this quiet afternoon. Only the old grade and rusting strands of logging cable bespoke of the logging era. There was no evidence that the old grade had been used for foot travel; however, animal trails revealed frequent wildlife visitation. Blackberry canes and briers grew in profusion, alternating with thick rhododendron, although there were a few open sections. Notwithstanding the natural impediments that I faced, I maintained a steady pace, working my way around the folds of the mountains past one ridge and then another. In these folds, water flowed over gray stone in small, filmy white cascades. Each of these places added an element of charm to a bleak panorama, and I paused often to mentally record these images.

Although I had carefully studied my route, I had neglected to bring my map and was unable to identify landmarks with precision. My regret at not having a map was reinforced when I reached the end of the rail grade. It terminated in a rhododendron hell and the beginning of a trackless area that had to be traversed to make my way back to the trail originally employed at the beginning of my walk. The mountain slope ahead was uncomfortably steep, and the rhododendron was thicker than any I have ever encountered since. Faced with these barriers, I briefly entertained thoughts of returning the way I had come, but these thoughts quickly passed.

The undergrowth barred easy progress. Fallen trees were intertwined with the rhododendron in a maddening maze made worse by the steepness of the slope. At times, I wormed my way through this tangle on my stomach, setting a target of six or eight feet ahead at a time. At others, I crawled on hands and knees, and where possible I climbed upward, stooping and twisting through the thicket and listening to the rasping sound made by the undergrowth brushing against my clothing.

As I faced nature's obstacle course, the prospect of becoming bewildered and spending the night on the mountain entered my thoughts. I was warmly dressed, however, and prepared to weather the night out if necessary, so this prospect was not alarming. My only regret was the concern that my absence would cause my family. Also, I regretted not telling Alice, who knew where I was walking, to wait until the middle of the next day to report me missing to avoid creating a hardship for park personnel.

Although I was uncertain of my exact location, the worst consequence of an error in judgment would be to mistake a side ridge for the main ridge I was seeking. In this case, I would have descended into a watershed far below. I recognized this possibility, however, and as I approached the ridge above me, I climbed, keeping to my left another small ridge that I believed would lead me astray if I crossed it.

Once I attained the upper reaches of the ridge, I faced the moment of truth. I had to make a decision to climb farther or descend. Outcroppings of blue-gray stone lay ahead, creating additional barriers to travel. Below me was either the trail I sought or a difficult descent into the watershed that I hoped to avoid. Darkness approached rapidly, and there was no time to tarry.

I reasoned that my trail was below me, so I crossed the ridge and climbed downward over moss-covered slopes through a bleak forest. After descending 100 to 150 yards, I spotted the trail, a sighting that caused a sense of relief and affirmed the correctness of my assumption about my location.

It was almost dark when I reached my starting point. My time on the mountain had been challenging but enjoyable, heightened by the opportunity to explore unfamiliar territory. My brier-scratched limbs were a minor price to pay for knowledge of a forgotten rail grade.

A Line of Dots

Somewhere in the Smokies

A line of small dots on an old map of the Smokies intrigued me because it indicated the existence of an abandoned trail extending from the headwaters of a prominent stream to the crest of a major ridge. Additional research revealed further information about this abandoned trail, one originally christened many years earlier with a forgotten name.

Armed with a small amount of information and a large amount of curiosity, I left my starting point at 6:00 a.m. determined to penetrate the backcountry and tackle the trail of the past. I witnessed the coming of day on my walk, felt the pleasant cool of early morning and enjoyed the ever-present sound of the rushing water beside my route. In time, I located the old path that I sought and followed it through mature forest with large specimens of hemlock and tulip poplar trees and exquisite scenes of tumbling clear water flowing near my route.

As I ascended off-trail, I tracked my progress by counting streams that entered the watercourse that I followed from the left and right. Eventually I made a final stream crossing, sought out the continuation of the old trail and prepared for my ascent to a ridge crest, a climb that entailed an elevation gain of 1,800 feet in the next two miles.

It was 10:00 a.m., and based on my rate of travel thus far, I estimated that I would reach the crest of the ridge by midday. As I climbed above the stream that had paralleled my route, I encountered rhododendron, briers and blowdowns that slowed my progress considerably and caused me to conclude that my estimated arrival time on the crest was overly optimistic. It was impossible to travel more than a few feet at a time without facing some impediment. Thus, I moved over, under, around and through dense growth, sometimes in maddening tangles, reminding me that I owed a debt of gratitude to park maintenance personnel for preventing all trails from deteriorating as had this old trail.

Eventually, I reached a switchback and then a second on the crest of a side ridge. Travel here became somewhat easier, and I eventually slabbed around the side of the main ridge that I was seeking, still facing moderate difficulty. My water had been consumed by this time, and I began to search for a source of replenishment. One of the pleasant memories of this day was the discovery of a small trickle of water above my path. I forced my way to it, sat in the afternoon sunshine and drank cupfuls of cold, clear liquid while gazing on the majestic crest looming above me.

After a continuous battle with the undergrowth, I reached the top of the ridge and stepped into a maintained trail at 2:00 p.m.—a hard-won destination. As I looked back toward the old trail I had been following, it seemed to have vanished entirely. It was as if the trail never existed! Its obscurity and the undergrowth that concealed it contributed to this impression. I turned toward my starting point and began my eight-mile return walk, welcoming the comfort of the maintained trails I would follow. As day drew to an end, I had the satisfaction of gaining firsthand knowledge of a line of dots on a map.

Beauty Compensates for Hardships

Somewhere in the Smokies

Marv and I set a plodding pace over a carpet of dry yellow leaves that had succumbed to the winds of autumn as we climbed to the crest of a mountain perhaps one and a half or two miles off-trail from our starting point. Once on the crest, we followed the meanders of the mountain, climbing across small knobs on the faint semblance of an old manway in the hope of being able to follow it to the crest of a much higher mountain well above us that was our goal.

Old paths give up their secrets grudgingly, and Marv and I often separated to search for the best route around wind-thrown trees, dense hemlock growth and tangles of laurel and rhododendron. "Here it is," was the oft-heard shout as one of us rediscovered the manway after losing it as we snaked our way along the crest. Despite the remoteness, we noticed fragmentary remains of a chestnut fence, which attested to the labors of mountaineers on the ridge in the distant past.

Travel on the crest involved traversing hundreds of feet through tunnel-like growth that arched over game trails that comfortably admitted bears and other wildlife but severely barred convenient human passage. Bending, twisting and pushing through the tangle was the norm. In addition to the challenge of penetrating the tangles of undergrowth, periods of rain and sleet began as we reached higher elevations, introducing another dimension to our walk. Passing showers forced us under protecting hemlock boughs for shelter. This made little difference, however, because wet undergrowth dampened us just as effectively as the continuing rain.

The wild beauty along our route more than compensated for these hardships. Rhododendron limbs grew in ever-changing, latticelike patterns, their trunks damp and faintly red with the effect of the moisture. Leafless trees wore garments of lichen and moss that almost concealed their form and strength. Wet laurel and rhododendron leaves appeared silver in the muted gray of morning light. Occasional openings in the foliage allowed us to gaze at a distant divide whose expanse was cloaked in thick clouds. Wisps of fog rose like plumes of smoke from intermediate ridges, and the sun's infrequent rays created a pattern of light and shadow on the panorama of mountain and valley before us. Ahead, the summit we were seeking rose before us, crowned by spruce trees whose jagged tops, softened by smoky haze, topped the crest.

After one final climb, we pressed through a thick growth of blackberry canes and stepped into a small opening on top. The wind blew briskly here, chilling our skin damp with sweat and from prolonged exposure to wet undergrowth. Movement was essential for warmth, forcing us to move on after a brief rest. Upon leaving the crest, we followed an abandoned trail that eventually led to maintained trails that would lead us back to the point where we began our walk. At the end of the day, the sun turned the clouds above the horizon to an alabaster sky of gold and orange.

TENNESSEE OUTINGS

The Path Vanished

Somewhere in the Smokies

Robert and I reached the gap that was our jumping-off point after an early morning walk of several miles. While Robert waited, I walked several hundred yards to a spring to replenish our water supply. I cleared leaves away from the thumb-sized bubble of water and captured the cold liquid. As I did so, I wondered how many times others had paused to drink at this source when it was a common stopping place for Smoky Mountain herders, hunters and hikers.

The principal objective of our outing was to trace, if possible, an old trail that led into Tennessee. Indeed, we initially found and followed what we believed to be this old manway; however, to our disappointment, the path seemed to vanish below the gap! Rather than search aimlessly for it, we opted to descend straight down the mountainside through fresh spring growth that included pungent-smelling ramps, a much-favored mountain delicacy.

Prior to our walk, I had penciled on my topographic map the old trail we hoped to follow, noting the elevation of stream crossings and old logging rail grades. As we descended, we began to verify map references with periodic altimeter readings, confirming the general accuracy of our route.

The Tennessee slopes were exquisitely clad in fresh green colors. The rushing waters of a nearby stream splashed playfully downward, offering occasional views of white cascades and small waterfalls. At about 4,400 feet, we reached an abandoned logging rail grade, well overgrown in places, which served as our trail. At length, we reached an almost indistinguishable switchback in the grade that led to a larger stream and eventually to a maintained trail, ending the off-trail portion of our walk.

The day was growing late as we followed trails and, finally, an old road to our destination. Our day ended with Robert and me sharing the satisfaction of completing a walk of approximately seventeen miles through beautiful Smoky Mountain scenery, including a visit to a forgotten path.

Physically Tired but Mentally Refreshed

Somewhere in the Smokies

Al W. and I met at our predetermined meeting place and began a jaunt that would lead us through a wild and scenic portion of the Great Smokies seldom visited by others, one that would entail considerable physical exertion to complete our planned circuit. In short, we planned to ascend a remote stream and then a spur ridge and, finally, return via another stream.

We began by passing through a forest of majestic trees that appeared to have escaped the effects of logging. The dense forest canopy reluctantly admitted the sun's rays, creating a sensation of twilight in the forest glade through which we walked. There was something sacred about these stately trees, and we paused often to reflect on this grand panorama.

When we reached the stream that we planned to ascend, we substituted the soft forest floor for a stony route leading directly up the watercourse. The boulder-strewn stream was nestled between steep ridges. Sometimes our progress was relatively easy. At other times, it was tortuous. We picked our way upward, sometimes wading and sometimes climbing mazes of moss-covered boulders. At other times, we made difficult detours through tangles of rhododendron. Often the spray of water dampened our skin as we clambered around small cascades and waterfalls.

Travel was always slow, and our steps were chosen with care to avoid an inadvertent fall. We continually zigzagged as we moved ever upward; I was impressed with the fact that for every foot gained in a direct line it seemed to require two in a different direction. Nevertheless, the rewards far outweighed the difficulty.

We gazed at jumbles of stone decorated with moss and splotches of gray lichen, which was bordered by luxuriant forest growth. The sun probed this deep valley and created a silver luster to the faint mist that floated above the stream. The streamside vistas were a mixture of trees, thick rhododendron and other shrubs. Although the scenes were pleasant to view, they were at the same time rugged, foreboding and full of challenge for anyone venturing away from the watercourse.

After gaining approximately one thousand feet in elevation on our ascent, we reached our point of departure from the stream. Our next target was a low swag on the crest of a ridge looming above us. Although the distance was not great—approximately a half mile—reaching the swag involved a steep climb and an elevation gain of approximately nine hundred feet. At first, the forest was sufficiently open to allow unobstructed travel. This open terrain quickly gave way to heavy rhododendron, which slowed our climb significantly and forced us into the bed of a shoulder-high gully that had a rivulet of water flowing through it. We scrambled up this route, our best alternative at the time, until it became so choked with fallen trees and debris that we had to return to the slopes for our ever-steepening climb.

We reached the crest after two hours and fifteen minutes of extremely rigorous travel, somewhat to the left of the swag, our intended target. Al led the way down the ridge to the low point or swag and then moved down the slope on the opposite side of the ridge. After a few minutes, Al shouted, "Good news!" when he heard the echo from the rushing waters of the stream that was to be our return route.

The balance of our afternoon was devoted to descending the slopes above the stream, admiring its myriad cascades and wild beauty. It was dark when we finally completed our walk. We were physically tired after the rigors and challenges of our day but mentally refreshed by the beauty and wild grandeur that we had surveyed.

A Visit to a Beautiful Hideaway

Somewhere in the Smokies

I crossed a large stream twice to reach an old logging rail grade that would serve as my route for a portion of my journey. As I climbed the grade and along the stream that paralleled it, I passed small side streams with colorful names, all of which had their beginnings on a high ridge above me. Moving yet higher, I passed through nearly open wooded glades that offered splashes of red and yellow color contributed by bergamot and coneflower. The sun filtered into these glades, gave additional richness to the green growth and intensified the brilliance of the flowers.

Higher up, I passed through an area that was thickly overgrown with small saplings, weeds and briers and littered with wind-thrown trees. Negotiating this maze was laboriously slow and necessitated crawling under or climbing over fallen trees or, on occasion, walking along the straight trunks of fallen trees several feet above the ground to avoid the tangle.

When the stream I was following bore away from my route, I abandoned it and climbed upward through a rhododendron-choked corridor that was not more than a crease in the folds of the mountains. A faint trickle of water ran though it and nourished a growth of heavy green-black moss that felt like a lush carpet underfoot. This route eventually led toward a high gap that entailed a further elevation gain of eight hundred feet. Higher still, the slopes became more open, and I eventually stepped onto a maintained trail, ending the first of two off-trail segments on my walk.

I walked south now with my mind set on visiting a valley far below on my return. In fact, this valley was the principal goal of this outing. Along the way, I made another steep climb by trail and enjoyed visiting with familiar landmarks and gazing at prominent nearby peaks that I had climbed on numerous occasions in the past.

Eventually, I reached a gap and exited the maintained trail. I initially descended though nearly open forest, well rooted by European wild boar, into undergrowth that became progressively thicker. My route led me into the beginning of a small hollow that collected the waters from high springs that fed the watercourse I had climbed at the beginning of my outing. I continuously forced my way through the undergrowth as I moved sharply downward on a jumble of moss-covered stones. The volume of water grew as more springs contributed their flow into the drainage, and I was treated to a variety of small cascades and pools as the stream plunged down the steep slope.

The most significant difficulty I faced on my descent was passing across the face of a damp, moss-covered rock to reach the stream bed twenty feet below. The slopes on either side were steep and thick with impenetrable growth, making a detour nearly impossible. My first choice to descend this barrier was thwarted when I recognized the risk of a serious fall. Subsequently, I selected an alternate route that involved skirting the upper portion of the rock to reach a small fallen hemlock tree. Using the trunk to steady myself against a fall, I finally was able to lower myself to stream level and grateful to be past this precarious obstacle.

Once past this difficulty, I reached a relatively level portion of a high valley. This was a beautiful place, in effect a hideaway that beckoned me to tarry and revel in the beauty here. Although the prospects here were indeed pleasant, I could not linger beyond a few minutes because several miles of travel lay ahead.

Upon completion of my largely off-trail trek, I experienced a sense of well-being at the end of a long day. I felt blessed to have been able to enjoy a pleasant time in the Smokies and felt fully rewarded for my efforts.

Entering the World of the Unknown

Somewhere in the Smokies

I joined sightseers who paraded through the Smokies intent on enjoying the beauty and uniqueness of an interesting portion of the park. My primary interest lay beyond this locale, however. My destination was a cove that I had often mentally visited during map studies. Now I was about to visit it in person.

I parked and walked a while on a maintained trail until I reached a faint trace bearing right away from the trail—a trace filed away in memory from seeing it on other trips here. I exited the trail, passed through a screen of hemlock trees and entered the world of the unknown. This world had been intimately familiar to settlers, however, who in earlier times had homesteaded the slopes of the cove that lay above me.

The trace I followed led to a small branch that carried the name of the cove and through a forest of tall trees that admitted sunlight, creating a dappled pattern of light and shadow on the forest floor. There were many hardwoods here, including many large maple trees, and I admired them while I climbed.

For a time, I became one with the cove's past and moved slowly, savoring the sounds and sights about me. A few piles of stone attested to early field-clearing efforts and suggested that the site of a cabin stood nearby. The accuracy of this assumption was confirmed when I found the largely tumbled-down remains of a hand-laid stone chimney. Only these stones served to mark the place of a long-vanished cabin. Nearby was the rusty scythe blade that symbolized the daily labor required to wrest a living from the stony slopes nestled in this horseshoe-shaped basin formed by two ridges.

Animal signs were more common than signs of human occupancy. I noticed where an animal—probably a bear or skunk—had dug up three underground yellow jackets' nests to unearth the tasty grubs. A few yellow jackets still remained in these places, and I passed with care to avoid disturbing them. Deer tracks were noted frequently, evidencing their regular trafficking here. Most interesting were the claw marks of a black bear that were left in the gray trunk of a large broken chestnut tree when the bear ascended the tree. I wondered if this was a den tree in which a bear hibernated in the hollow top to escape winter's ravages.

The old trace became faint high in the cove, and I was forced to become more attentive to its meanders. Old trails such as this one are sly and easily slip away when one is distracted. I resolved not to let this happen. Nevertheless, it disappeared despite my attention to it, and I was forced to climb without the path along the steepening slopes through sun-splashed forest glades, selecting a route that would lead me to the crest of one of the ridges above the cove. Well below the ridge, a startled deer, a young buck with velvet antlers, darted before me with the sun glinting on its sleek body.

I bore right, angled higher and higher along the side of the ridge and eventually climbed straight upward to the crest at an elevation of 3,800 feet, according to my altimeter. Here a pronounced game trail became my route, and I began ascending toward the high point of the ridge, which was approximately one mile away. As I climbed, I appreciated the fact that the animals that traversed this ridge had chosen a route that avoided the thickest growth, making travel fairly easy for them and me.

My ascent of the highest point afforded passage through several fern-filled glades. In one of these I discovered highbush blueberries with an abundance of ripe blueberries growing on them. The berries grew so thickly that I could pick a dozen at a time by gently cupping my hands over the ends of the branches. This technique yielded several delicious handfuls, which I consumed on the spot. Later, I discovered another bush that was severely bent and broken by the weight of a black bear that had been just as interested in the juicy berries as I.

I reached the rounded crest of the highpoint of the ridge in time and followed a compass bearing to a gap intersected by a maintained trail. Four hours had passed since I first embarked on the off-trail segment of my walk. During this time, I had stopped often to admire the variety and beauty of the forest. I now had an appointment to keep with one of the historic landmarks of the Smokies before I returned to my starting point. Upon passing the old trace on my descent, it was silent. Earlier in the day, when I first passed, it had whispered, "Follow me," an invitation that I had heeded.

The Forks Less Taken

Somewhere in the Smokies

Al W. and I joined others for an off-trail ascent of a stream with two forks. Both of these forks proved the fork less taken as there was no evidence of humans ever having passed this way.

Our route consisted of following an irregular jumble of lichen- and moss-covered gray stones scattered randomly in the stream. Looking up the stream, however, there were only stones—no water was apparent. Yet, the water was there, splashing downward through this stony maze. Rhododendron flanked either side of the stream, and tulip poplar, hemlock and maple trees created an overarching cathedral-like ceiling of soft green over the splendor of the cove through which we climbed. Rays of sun filtered by a filmy morning mist brightened individual clusters of leaves while leaving others in shadows. Here and there wildflowers grew along the stream's borders. The delicate purple flowers of monkshood captured our attention, and we admired their beauty.

After passing the highest springs of the right fork, we pressed through a waist-high growth of young trees, blackberry canes, hobblebush and ferns interspersed with fallen fir trees. Once past this barrier, we chose a lunch destination that afforded excellent views of the very ribs of the Smokies.

After lunch, we returned to the headwaters of the left fork of the stream that we had ascended during the morning and descended to the small springs that spawned the increasingly larger stream that we followed downward. These high slopes were a veritable fairyland. With each bend of the small stream, we were treated to vistas that left us awed by the richness and variety of the scenery.

The stream itself was our trail. Its bed was made up of worn upthrusts of stone covered by dense dark green moss that cushioned our steps. The water flowed in multiple small channels as it sought passage through the myriad stones that attempted to bar its way. At times, the stream flowed along an almost level course for several yards. Here and there beautiful shallow pools collected crystal water and held it for fleeting seconds before it poured out on its meandering course. Some of the pools had no visible outlet, and the water percolated through sand and gravel, causing the stream to disappear entirely, only to mysteriously reappear several yards down the slopes.

The breathtaking quality of this pristine forest had its scenic opposites, however. We eventually entered an area of destruction where the forest of the steep mountainside to our right had lost its fragile hold on the smooth stone upthrust on which it tenuously rested and slid and tumbled, crashing into the narrow valley through which we traveled. This massive landslide had left a gray tangle of earth and tree trunks in wild disarray. The stone upthrust, now devoid of growth and moist with water, glowed with the patina of unpolished silver as the afternoon sun reflected off the bare rock. At the crest several hundred feet above us, the forest was whole and there trees stood as dark sentinels above their fallen members.

With piles of trees jumbled at all angles and in all directions, we were challenged to find a way through this puzzle. No obvious route was apparent. We ultimately chose a zigzagging course, walking from one fallen tree to the next, often ten feet above the stream that ran beneath us. On occasion we would descend to a lower level to select a straight tree trunk that we could follow thirty or forty feet before selecting another tree to follow for a few more feet. Upon reaching an occasional impasse, we floundered through thick rhododendron growth that bordered the slide debris. Travel was indeed slow. Yet this wild place was fascinating by comparison to the soft, gentle forest along the upper reaches of the valley.

At the end of the day, Al and I were truly rewarded for traveling the forks less taken. The sore muscles, scratches and bruises were a reasonable price to pay for an excellent day in the Smokies.

Bewildered and Defeated

I am proud to proclaim that I have never been lost during my off-trail outings in the Great Smoky Mountains National Park. I must admit, however, with a modicum of humility that I have been bewildered on more than one occasion. Yes, in these instances I was merely uncertain about where I was, where I was headed and how to reach my desired goal. Becoming bewildered has never been a source of embarrassment for me. After all, some of my Smoky Mountain heroes such as Paul Fink and Harvey Broome in their respective books *Backpacking Was the Only Way* and *Out Under the Sky of the Great Smokies* also describe adventures that involved uncertainty about where they were. Becoming defeated was the result of being unable to complete a planned trip because of difficulties encountered along the way. Fortunately, the number of times I have been bewildered and defeated has been few.

Becoming lost in the Smokies is indeed a serious matter, and those who hike the trails or venture off-trail should recognize the dangers and take precautions to prepare for them.

Bewildered

Missed by a Mile

Somewhere in the Smokies

From time to time, I had studied maps and envisioned a cross-country hike from one of the valleys of the park to the crest of a high divide. The most logical route for this trip entailed ascending a major stream for a time and then a second stream and finally a third to reach the heights. Also, in contemplating this trip, I concluded that it was feasible to make it a two-day outing, with one night spent at a campsite in the backcountry.

The day finally came to make this trip. I left my jumping-off point with a light pack on my back, followed the first stream and then reached the other in short order. An old rail grade lay alongside this second stream. This now served as my route. I made steady progress with the expectation of reaching the crest of the divide by mid-afternoon.

The creek that paralleled my route was beautiful. I enjoyed wildflowers along the stream, watched trout swimming in small pools, observed a mother grouse and her small clutch and was entertained by the music of the stream. These were simple pleasures, but they were grand entertainment for me. About 2:00 p.m., as I neared the point where I expected to exit the rail grade and strike out for the crest, I heard a roll of thunder on the high ridges above me and observed that the sky was growing dark and threatening. As I stood in the rail grade with the threat of rain imminent, I debated about which way to continue. After a few moments, I decided to leave the grade and climb over a low rhododendron-covered ridge spur in the belief that this was the correct route. In short order, I reached a small watercourse, which was joined by a second a few feet above me, neither of which looked like a suitable route to follow. As I stood in the twilight of the forest, made ever dimmer by heavy undergrowth and accumulating thunderclouds, I decided that it was time to consult my map. Unfortunately, I couldn't read it! I even shined the beam of my flashlight on it but still could not make map details. While I was engaged in the effort, heavy drops of rain began to splash on my map, followed by a general downpour. My rough field notes tell the rest: "Two p.m., 4000 feet, heavy rain, sky dark, rhododendron, route uncertain."

Given the lay of the land, I chose the route of least resistance and climbed toward the skyline along relatively open slopes. When I was within one hundred feet of the crest, I reasoned that I would find the trail there if I had made the correct decisions, or correct guesses, at each of my turns. Indeed I reached the trail after one and a half hours of tramping since leaving the rail grade.

I was pleased to have reached a maintained trail but puzzled because I was not in a gap, as I had expected to find myself. I reasoned that my route put me nearer my campsite and turned left in hopes of soon reaching it. After a bit of walking, however, I reached a switchback in the trail that I did not recall as being on the trail that I thought I had reached. Nevertheless, the switchback was familiar to me. I now knew where I was, and it wasn't the trail I was supposed to be on at all!

I unpacked my sodden map, which I could now read in better light, and discovered that I had exited the rail grade too early and chosen a route that led me to the wrong trail. Instead of reaching the crest of the divide that was my goal, I had reached another ridge approximately a mile northeast of my planned campsite. I had missed by a mile.

I was embarrassed by my error, but there was nothing to be done about it at this point. Thus, I turned back, retraced my steps and ultimately reached the campsite and an end to my day's rambles in a driving rain about 5:30 p.m. I suppose there are several lessons to be learned from this account, but they are obvious and I will not state them here. The main lesson I learned from this experience, however, was that *I needed glasses*! I have worn them ever since.

This Can't Be Right

Somewhere in the Smokies

I stepped from my warm vehicle and into the chill of a twenty-eight-degree morning. Frost covered the ground and rhododendron leaves were curled and limp in reaction to the cold. The sky was clear, however, and the day held the promise of good weather. I was embarking on a walk that I had contemplated from time to time when studying maps of the Great Smoky Mountains National Park. My chosen route entailed ascending two streams to reach an old high-elevation rail grade that I planned to follow into a gap to intersect a maintained trail that I would follow back to my starting point.

Initially, I followed an abandoned logging rail grade that lay near the first stream I was to follow. It led through a forest of bare, leafless trees where rhododendron and fir trees were the main source of color. It led me to several crossings of the stream, which I managed with relatively dry feet by using sturdy limbs picked up from the forest floor to steady myself as I carefully crossed a random pattern of steppingstones.

At length, I reached the second stream I was to follow. Climbing this watercourse provided pleasing vistas of small cascades and long stretches of rushing water, which flowed around fallen trees and the myriad wet stones that choked the small channel. The sun brightened my little valley, and its rays created a distant line between light and shadow on the mountains above me as the sun made its daily passage over the Smokies. I watched on more than one occasion as ruffed grouse, when startled from their hiding places, flew erratically through thick rhododendron. I observed the sun illuminating the golden feathers of a large hawk that glided silently overhead. These were the special rewards of the wilderness.

The stream I followed grew progressively smaller, and I was forced to climb directly in the stream channel because of the heavy growth on either side. Even then the rhododendron overhung the stream, requiring force to penetrate the stiff branches. Finally, I reached a side stream entering the creek. I paused here to verify my altimeter reading with this landmark and was puzzled because my altimeter read lower than my map elevation! The same was true at the next stream, creating an element of bewilderment. Before long, I reached a distinct rail grade; however, my altimeter reading was four hundred feet lower than this grade.

How could this be? I had observed care in properly setting my altimeter at the beginning of my trip and couldn't understand the elevation differences between landmarks and my altimeter readings. I thought perhaps there was another rail grade farther up the slopes and that, perhaps, the grade I had located didn't show on the maps. I was now faced with a choice to follow the rail grade or climb on in search of another grade higher on the mountain. I resolved to do the latter. This decision entailed a very steep climb through thick undergrowth that included a battle through blackberry canes more than an inch in diameter.

When I reached the point that I expected to find a second rail grade, there was none. In fact, I was on top of a ridge. After another two or three minutes fighting briers and rhododendron, I was surprised to step into a well-used trail in a gap 150 feet from a campsite! I walked to this campsite to rest for a few minutes and to smoke Old Danger before beginning my walk back to my starting point. While I relaxed, I evaluated the cause of my bewilderment about my altimeter readings. I could only conclude that sometime during the day my altimeter, which I carried in an exterior coat pocket, had been struck a glancing blow as I pushed through the undergrowth. This, I believe, caused a change in the dial setting, leading to erroneous readings. I suppose, however, all is well that ends well. On a positive note, I concluded that my failure to walk the old rail grade as planned provided a reason to return to the Smokies for further exploration.

A Startling Discovery

Somewhere in the Smokies

I planned to climb from the headwaters of a remote stream to the crest of a ridge, where I expected to locate an abandoned trail that would become part of my circuit back to my starting point. As I walked, I welcomed the blue sky that replaced the silver-gray clouds of early morning and thought this a good omen for my off-trail outing.

When I reached the appointed place, I struck out for the old trail. While the distance in this segment was only eight-tenths of a mile, my ascent entailed a climb of 1,400 feet through what was certain to be dense growth. The section began pleasantly enough, however. I walked through a sun-dappled forest that entertained me as I traveled. Then the climbing started. I made several probes into impossible tangles of rhododendron before I finally settled on a none-too-suitable but passable route. I was never out of rhododendron, but this was only part of the problem. A continuous maze of fallen trees intermixed with the iron-strong rhododendron limbs battled me at almost every step. I was seldom in the open and spent my time twisting, stooping, fighting and floundering upward.

Eventually, I could see sky over the crest of the ridge and moved toward it, thinking the crest was where I would find the abandoned trail I was seeking. Finally, quite near the top, my way was blocked by a large fallen red spruce tree. I moved right and then left trying to find a way around this fallen forest giant. Then I made a startling discovery. I was standing on the trail!

Yes, I had reached the trail and would have no doubt overlooked it in its disguised condition had it not been for the fallen tree that barred my way. The hand of fate prevented complete bewilderment in this instance. I had invested three and a half hours to climb less than a mile, but the effort was worth it. Now I had only to follow the abandoned trail and ensure that it did not slip away from me. Thus I tracked the trace for approximately one and a half hours before reaching a maintained trail. After an eleven-hour walk, I reached my starting point. My outing might have been longer, however, had I not made the startling discovery at a fallen tree.

Defeated

A Sample of Hell

Somewhere in the Smokies

Ed and I were intent on locating and following an early trail between the point it departed from a maintained trail to its connection with another several miles distant. Although the trail wasn't shown on maps, we knew of its existence and planned to devote two days of our outing to exploring it.

On our first day of largely off-trail travel, we located the old trace after a serious search and spent the remainder of the day tracing its course. At times, we had to guess where the trail lay, and in one of these places we spent two hours negotiating the faint manway, often blundering into a maze of false leads that defied us to locate its inconspicuous meanders.

On the second day of our quest, the old trail appeared to vanish completely, and we found our right of passage immediately challenged by thick rhododendron and wind-thrown trees that choked the base of the ridge we were attempting to ascend. We forced our way through this trackless undergrowth and found every motion blocked by some barrier. Often the trunks of massive fallen red spruce trees provided the best route for a few feet. Once back in the rhododendron, each step was a hard-fought achievement complicated by the bulk and awkwardness of our backpacks.

Hour after hour passed as we fought the battle up steep rhododendron-clad slopes. This maddening experience gave vivid meaning to the term "hells," used by mountaineers to describe such rhododendron jungles. Finally, after four and a half hours of this tortuous travel, Ed and I rested in a small opening and assessed our chances of reaching our planned destination by nightfall. By our best reckoning, we had only traveled less than a mile for all our efforts. We reasoned that we would be overtaken by darkness on a dry ridge and well short of our goal if we continued. Not to continue would mean not achieving our goal of walking the old trail to its conclusion. We weighed the options available to us and reluctantly agreed that not proceeding with our climb was the reasonable choice.

Making this decision was the easy part! The difficult part was making our way to a maintained trail and a backcountry campsite. As it turned out, we had five more hours of off-trail walking that included some serious climbing to work our way out.

We ultimately reached a campsite and hurriedly prepared camp as the last rays of the autumn sun bathed the nearby ridges in a golden glow. After a long, hard day, we could finally relax to the comfortable sound of our stove while supper was being prepared. As darkness settled about us, our conversation dealt with our failure to achieve our day's objective. The past two days had been an adventure, however. We had experienced the wild, beautiful terrain and the rewards of precious time spent in the very heart of the Smokies.

Defeated by a Leafy Foe

Somewhere in the Smokies

It was raining when Al W. and I began our walk. Skies were gray and a faint mist was in the air. The rain foretold a bleak day with no hope for sunny relief. Before long, we turned along a stream and climbed past old homesites. Our spirits were not dampened by the weather, however. While we walked, my mind moved ahead more rapidly than the physical pace Al and I set. It lingered on the faint beginnings of an old abandoned trail—the one that we would attempt to follow to a point on a high divide.

When we reached the trace that marked the beginning of the abandoned trail, a place I had often observed on past walks here, we exited the trail and struck out on a journey into a drab, dripping forest where each twig, rhododendron leaf and hemlock bough shed its accumulated water on us. The old trail trace was visible, however, and I was optimistic about our ability to follow it despite the steady drizzle. My early optimism quickly waned. The rhododendron grew denser, and we were reduced to a slow pace due to wrestling with this leafy foe. This battle resulted in our having covered a half mile in our first hour.

Al had formerly walked this route as a teenager in the 1940s, but he had few recollections of the route. We did have information from old maps that indicated that our route generally followed the left side of the stream that lay along our path. We plodded along on this assumption but soon found that the trail crossed to the right of the stream. The fact that there had been a trail here was confirmed by an occasional sawed log, a sure sight of former trail maintenance. After a while, this maintenance effort was no longer evident—nor was the trail. We had lost it!

We reached the confluence of the right and left forks of the stream that we were following and realized that our ascent would be more difficult than we first anticipated. Nevertheless, we continued our plodding search for the best way through the tangle. Sometimes we were on the right of the right fork of the stream and sometimes on the left. Sometimes our route ascended higher on the slopes to avoid obstacles. At other times, we moved closer to the stream, and infrequently we moved with relative ease through fairly open forest.

The sight of the drab forest did not escape our notice. There was a subtle beauty here. Wet rhododendron leaves reflected the gray of the sky with a glistening sheen, tree trunks were flecked with silver lichens, fallen logs were coated with a cushion of damp, musty-smelling moss that seemed to come alive in the moisture and the forest floor was soft to the step as we walked in the fallen leaves of autumn. These visual treasures were set against the solitude of the mountains, a quiet broken only by the sounds of the stream and the patter of falling rain.

Al and I spent six hours in our off-trail segment and had only progressed two miles. Reluctantly, we concluded that we would not accomplish our goal in the remaining daylight. Given this circumstance, we abandoned our route and began the steep climb to the crest of a ridge to our right, where we knew we would intersect a maintained trail.

After a brief rest on the ridge, we continued on across a high peak, skirting patches of snow in the trail and walking for another six miles or so to reach the end of a long day. Although we had been defeated by a leafy foe, we had spent a few hours in a part of the Smokies where few ever venture.

Weather

Rain, wind, cold and snow can create challenges for the outdoorsman. For those improperly prepared, these conditions can create extreme discomfort and even death. Conversely, weather extremes can add an element of challenge and pleasure to an outing provided one exercises judgment and caution and is outfitted with proper clothing and equipment.

In my own case, the weather has been my instructor. It has persuaded me to periodically upgrade my outdoor clothing and backpacking equipment to better withstand the forces of nature. It has tested my mettle on occasions when temperatures dropped uncomfortably low or excessive rain dampened my spirit and body. The elements have reminded me that the forces of nature are always in control, far surpassing my own power and capability. Finally, weather in all of its dimensions has provided me with a score of pleasant memories.

Rain

The Joy of Rain

Ramsey Cascades; Ramsey Cascade Trail

August 7, 1976

A small vacation provided Alice and me with an opportunity for a day hike in the Smokies. We chose Ramsey Cascades as the destination for our walk, a preferable alternative to participating in the popular amusements in Gatlinburg, Tennessee. With our destination selected, we drove along the shady road by the Little Pigeon River past bathers splashing in the stream's cool waters and continued to Middle Prong and road's end. Beyond this point, we followed a gravel path and eventually reached the well-worn trail to the Cascades.

Our route followed the creek, crossing it periodically on footlogs. Beautiful forest surrounded us, and we periodically stopped to admire groves of arrow-straight tulip poplar trees that contained specimens five and six feet in diameter. Throughout the climb, we enjoyed the vivid sensations of the forest, never tiring of the variety of patterns of light and shadow created by the sun filtering through the trees.

Anticipation grew as we approached the Ramsey Cascades and the sounds of falling water. Finally, we came in sight of the massive stone face with its sheer film of water plummeting to the rocks at the base. Rich forest framed the Cascades like a jewel in a finely crafted setting. The beauty and grandeur of the scene was beyond adequate description. We remained below the Cascades for a long time in an effort to fully absorb the timeless sounds and sensations of this Smokies landmark.

Skies darkened as we began our return trip, and large raindrops began to fall. These were not ordinary raindrops—they were giants among their kin. At first they appeared to fall randomly. Then the intensity grew. At first, the force of the rain on the leaves created a whisper that matched the music of the nearby stream. Then the rain became a downpour that overwhelmed the stream sounds as it penetrated the leafy canopy above us. This sudden rain drenched us thoroughly, but we reveled in the deluge and the opportunity to walk in a Smoky Mountain storm. Fortunately, the air was warm on this August afternoon, and the rain on our exposed skin was rather pleasant. Although many of my rain encounters left me chilled and uncomfortable, this was a wonderful exception and one of my fondest memories of rain and of a time of joy shared with Alice.

Hurricane Katrina

McGee Spring and Upper Chasteen Creek Campsites

August 28–29, 2005

Upon reaching the McGee Spring Campsite, Robert and I immediately dropped our backpacks and began surveying the site to select the most suitable location for our small tent. This would seem like a simple task; however, Hurricane Katrina was moving toward the Gulf Coast, and we anticipated that we would spend a wet night as rains associated with this storm moved into western North Carolina. This meant that each tent site had to be evaluated for the likelihood of flowing or puddling water. Unfortunately, there was no perfect place to pitch a tent, and even the most desirable spots had a slant to them with the inherent threat of some impact from the storm.

We selected the best site we could find and pitched our tent. Once this was done, we selected another site one hundred feet uphill from the tent for our cooking location. Here we tied a head-high rope between two trees and stretched a light plastic tarp over the rope to a create a simple cooking shelter. Portions of broken logs served as adequate seats. Next we visited the spring and collected water. These chores were completed just as the rain began to fall in earnest. We spent the afternoon under our fragile shelter talking and enjoying the sights and sounds associated with the storm.

After a simple meal, Robert and I entered our small shelter, climbed into warm sleeping bags and drifted off to sleep to the sound of the rain on the tent. The rain continued all night with variances in cadence—sometimes heavy drumming and at other times in a light patter.

The rain had stopped by morning; however, by early afternoon, after we had crossed Raven Fork, the rain began again and continued during our

Robert Hill, longtime hiking partner, at McGee Spring, August 28, 2005.

crossing of Hughes Ridge and until we reached the Upper Chasteen Creek Campsite. Upon arrival, we repeated the activities of the previous evening—selecting a tent site and pitching our cooking shelter. Supper was prepared as the rain pelted down and puddled about the campsite.

It rained hard all night; however, we were fortunate and experienced only a small amount of water in our tent. Little did we know that while we slept Hurricane Katrina was wreaking its unbelievable damage on New Orleans and the Gulf Coast. It was only after we returned home that we learned that one of the worst natural disasters in United States history had occurred during our outing. Our thoughts and prayers went out to those who suffered tragically from the storm. Our own wet outing was inconsequential.

Wind

Any Port in a High Wind

Mount Cammerer

November 9, 1976

Jim W., Al C. and I spent the night at the Cosby Knob Shelter with eight others. We awoke to a cold morning. The temperature was twelve degrees, and the wind roared with fury over the ridges sweeping the sky clear of clouds. We dressed warmly against the onslaught of the wind and headed north on the Appalachian Trail. Despite the cold, we enjoyed an easy downhill trek that entailed descending to Low Gap. From there we climbed again, plodding along in the cold and wind.

When we reached the trail to Mount Cammerer, we made a brief departure from the AT to visit the Mount Cammerer Fire Tower. This fire tower was unique. While other towers in the Smokies were perched atop tall steel structures, the Mount Cammerer Tower was constructed on a rock outcropping formerly known as White Rock. It had a commanding view of Cosby, Tennessee, and the surrounding mountains. The tower's foundation was constructed of neatly laid stones. A wooden room sat on this foundation. From a distance, the tower had a squat appearance on its stony perch.

The wind blew at a sustained forty miles per hour as we approached the tower, freezing our skin and causing our eyes to water. Toboggans protected our heads and bandanas protected our faces. Nevertheless, these precautions were less than adequate on Mount Cammerer's exposed crest. Fortunately, we found that the door to the fire tower was unlocked, and we stepped inside. The place was like an icebox; however, we had escaped the driving wind. We were most appreciative for this cold but protective shelter. This respite gave special meaning to the saying "any port in a storm." Eventually, we returned to the Appalachian Trail and, as the day wore on, descended onto calmer slopes; however, as I thought back on our earlier experience at the fire tower I realized that we had been glad to settle for "any port in a high wind."

Unsafe to Linger

Unnamed Ridge Between Noland and Peachtree Creeks

April 4, 1992

Al W. and I had decided on an exploratory walk from Noland Creek to Peachtree Creek along a route that would entail crossing a side ridge of Noland Divide. The first part of our walk involved easy travel up the old road paralleling Noland Creek. Wildflowers and shrubs were beginning to bloom, and we identified hepatica, bloodroot, yellow and purple violets, cutleaf toothwort and the pink blooms of redbud, blooms that brightened the drab forest. Yellow forsythia also bloomed in old homesites, reminding us of former residents who planted these decorative shrubs to enjoy their beauty in early spring.

After one and a half hours, we turned right off the old road and began the off-trail segment of our walk, following an old trail that climbed out of the valley. In time, we left this trail and struck out toward the ridge crest. From this vantage, we were able to view Andrews Bald in the distance, identifiable by a distinct band of golden grass that contrasted with the fir and hardwoods that fringed the bald. When we looked southward, we viewed Fontana Lake, whose waters reflected the color of the clouds.

This setting sounds peaceful enough; however, our ridge proved to be an unsafe place for us to linger. High winds, absent on the lower slopes, swept the crest in repeated waves that sounded like a freight train rushing toward us at full speed. Gusts of an estimated forty to fifty miles per hour were the rule. The wind bent the hemlock boughs, revealing the pale underside of the needles. And trees swayed dramatically, causing rotten limbs to fall about us with heavy thudding sounds. Some of these limbs were large enough to easily cause serious injury or death. Prompted by this danger, we moved rapidly into the Peachtree Creek drainage and the safety of the protected lower slopes.

Our trip down Peachtree Creek was uneventful. The sound and feel of the howling winds remains a vivid memory. Certainly, the threat was real, and our flight was the only proper response to the danger posed by the winds on the crest.

COLD

Unexpected Cold

Double Spring Gap Shelter

May 10–11, 1969

I took a leisurely walk from Clingmans Dome to Double Spring Gap, enjoying the openness of the terrain about Mount Buckley and the dark green of the fir trees beyond. The day was mild, and partly cloudy skies seemed to pose no threat of foul weather.

When I arrived at Double Spring Gap, I spread out my sleeping bag, arranged my gear and wandered outside to explore the area about the shelter. I admired the delicate yellow flowers and mottled green leaves of trout lily that grew in profusion near the shelter, and I gazed at Fontana Lake in the distance and the rich views of blue mountain ranges beyond. Eventually, my thoughts turned to supper, and I gathered sufficient downed wood for a supper fire. I nursed flaming splinters into a small fire and enjoyed the warmth and glow of the flames that banished a portion of the darkness in the shelter that I had completely to myself.

At dusk, the skies grew gray and a brief shower swept through the gap. Later, rain fell in torrents, whipped by wild winds blasting over the crest from Tennessee. The air became noticeably colder, and the rain turned to sleet, creating a new rhythm on the shelter roof. I was protected, however, and enjoyed the serenade of the elements that lulled me to sleep.

I awoke cold and uncomfortable sometime during the night. At the time of this trip, I could not afford proper camping gear and used a family hand-me-down sleeping bag that was largely unsuitable for any but summer use. And even though I wore all of my clothing for extra warmth, I was unprepared for the unanticipated change in the weather.

I lay cold and uncomfortable through part of the night and welcomed the faint silver in the sky as a new day dawned. I weighed staying in my sleeping bag for a while longer but concluded that my best option was to arise and rekindle my fire, which I had banked the night before. Thus, I arose, started my fire and prepared breakfast. This meal fortified me for my climb back to my vehicle.

I stepped from the shelter onto frozen ground and braved sustained winds that whipped peppery ice crystals against my exposed skin. There was bittersweet enjoyment in these two days, days that displayed the temperament of Smoky Mountain weather. There was also a lesson in this experience. Weather in the Smokies often changes suddenly and dramatically. Staying alive during such occasions is often a matter of anticipation and preparation. My preparation for the cold had been marginal but adequate; others have perished in similar conditions.

If I Live

Beard Cane Campsite; Beard Cane Trail

November 28–29, 2003

Sara and I planned a four-day backpacking trip in the Cades Cove area beginning the day after Thanksgiving that would duplicate a trip that Sara, Bill and I had taken when they were quite young. We drove to Cades Cove and proceeded slowly around the Cades Cove Loop Road, enjoying the beauty of the cove framed by leaden skies.

We began walking along the Cooper Road in intermittent rain and sleet, requiring that we don our rain gear for protection. The forest was bleak and sodden from the recent effect of rain and snow; however, there was a somber beauty in the ever-changing vistas that we enjoyed as we traveled the old road. We had the trail to ourselves on this bleak day and only met one dayhiker during our afternoon walk.

Eventually, we reached the Beard Cane Trail and followed it approximately one mile to the Beard Cane Campsite, our day's destination, which we reached at 5:10 p.m. With little time to spare before dark, we immediately pitched our tent, laid out our sleeping bags and filtered water from the creek for our supper. This was followed by the preparation of a simple dehydrated meal.

We completed our final chores in the dark and were in sleeping bags by 6:30 p.m. After a period of silence, Sara told me that she was cold despite the fact that she was in a cold-weather down sleeping bag with a protection rating of five degrees. The cold she felt resulted from not removing her rain gear, which trapped moisture in her clothing. I shared extra clothing of mine with her that allowed her to warm up, and eventually she went to sleep. Before drifting off, however, Sara told me that she thought we should not

View of the main crest of the Smokies covered in rime from Cades Cove, November 29, 2003.

continue our hike the next day because of the weather. I did not protest. The thought of a warm weekend at home certainly appealed to me.

During the night, I heard the sound of sleet striking our tent. We were warm and secure, and I enjoyed listening to the patter against a backdrop of the whispers of the nearby stream. It was twenty-four degrees when we awoke, and a dusting of snow covered the ground. We packed in short order and finalized our decision to return to Cades Cove. Despite the cold, we had an enjoyable walk to our awaiting vehicle.

Upon reaching Cades Cove, we were treated to exquisite views. The previous day's storm had passed, and blue skies replaced gray. The mountains that arose from the base of the golden fields before us were covered in rime beginning at an elevation of about four thousand feet. It was as if an imaginary line had been drawn, leaving the peaks in white, made more vivid and brilliant by the reflected rays of the sun. Below the crest of white, the mountains wore their winter garb, drab in contrast to the stark white above.

This was a rewarding end to our trip. I had thoroughly enjoyed my time with Sara and respected her stamina as a walker. She regularly waited for me to catch up with her after effortlessly climbing hills that I ascended in a slow, plodding pace. Although reluctant to admit it, age may have contributed to my lack of speed.

As a postscript, I learned later that Sara had conveyed her thoughts about our cold night on Beard Cane to her mother—thoughts that she had not shared with me. Sara told her mother: "I thought that if I lived to morning, I was not going to spend another night out in the cold."

Snow

Walking in Untracked Snow

Deep Creek Trail

November 27, 1971

An early morning snow caught Bob F., Tom L., Don and me by surprise; however, we were determined to enjoy a weekend outing, and we waited out the early morning storm in Cherokee before driving to the crest of Thomas Divide and beginning our trek down Deep Creek along the Deep Creek Trail. A six-inch blanket of snow covered the ground on the crest and coated bare tree limbs, causing them to stand out vividly like a complex etching. The green of rhododendron and doghobble seemed incongruous in a world of white. Vivid blue skies and sunshine replaced the snow and fog, adding to the perfection of an exhilarating winter day.

We took turns leading our small column through pristine snow that was unmarked by any human footprint. The only signs of life were the tracks of birds and small animals that crisscrossed the trail. The most interesting tracks observed were those of a black bear that had started to cross Deep Creek on a fallen log four or five feet above the stream. These tracks led out on the log to a point where the log narrowed mid-stream. At this point, the bear decided that it was not prudent to continue along this perilous route and had reversed its course, leaving a second set of footprints back to secure footing.

We continued our walk amidst the beauty of a snow-cloaked world to the Pole Road Campsite. After chores, we built a fire for four and gathered around it for warmth, roasting one side and then the other and occasionally changing positions to escape the shifting smoke as breezes swept our camp. The smell of the smoke was a pleasant dimension to our cold camp. We enjoyed an evening of fellowship and all the elements of our fire in that remote place that had no doubt been enjoyed by humans for eons.

Random Patterns

Chestnut Branch Trail

March 23, 1981

I arose and glanced outside and was surprised to find that a trace of snow had fallen during the night. Rather than let the weather bluff me out of my trip, I resolved to drive toward the Smokies and to turn back if snow began or if the roads proved hazardous. It was a good decision. I reached the Big Creek Rangers Station without difficulty.

My chosen route was the Chestnut Branch Trail, and I followed it past former homesites and overgrown fields. Here and there I noted the ubiquitous washtub and rusting stove parts at old homeplaces, common reminders of the fact that this valley was once settled. Eventually, the trail, actually an old road, turned into a footpath that I followed upward to the Appalachian Trail.

While I climbed, a few fluffy flakes of snow began floating lazily earthward. When I reached a high bowl-shaped cove that had once been cleared for grazing but now was timbered with second-growth tulip poplar, I paused to experience the beauty of the moment. Large white snowflakes drifted down randomly, their course sometimes altered by the gentlest of breezes. I enjoyed the contrast of the multitudinous flakes against the gray sky, another pleasant dimension of the snowfall. The scene was one of serenity and stark beauty that had a spellbinding quality that enhanced the somber mood of the day.

The snow was falling heartily when I reached the junction of the Chestnut Branch Trail with the Appalachian Trail, and it was slowly cloaking the forest with a mantle of white. Because of the intensity of the snowfall, I walked rapidly down the Appalachian Trail, intent on returning home before road conditions became impassable. When I reached the Davenport Gap Shelter, where the snow had accumulated to a depth of one and a half inches, I paused to warm by the fire of backpackers there and to shake the accumulated snow from my hat and clothing before hurrying on.

It had been wise to increase my pace because the roads were becoming unfit for travel. I returned home safely, however, reflecting on the joy I had experienced on a snowy day in the Smokies. The snowfall was destined to continue. A six-inch blanket of snow cloaked the mountains that night. I had witnessed its first random flakes.

Weather

The Possibility of Snow at Higher Elevations

Laurel Gap Shelter; Balsam Mountain Trail

March 9–10, 1991

Marv and I decided to enjoy an overnight hike in the Smokies and chose Laurel Gap as our destination. We were favored at the beginning of our outing by bright blue skies, sunshine and temperatures in the upper twenties. The weather forecast called for good weather; however, the possibility of snow at the higher elevations was forecasted. As a result of recent weather, snow still lay in sheltered places at lower elevations and completely covered the slopes at higher elevations. Apparently it was waiting for more, as the old saying goes.

We walked to the Palmer Creek Trail via the Pretty Hollow Gap Trail and began our ascent to Balsam Mountain. Below us Palmer Creek seemed to etch a dark line between slopes of white. The limbs of trees were highlighted by white, and distant Shanty Mountain reflected the beautifying effects of snow. Although the day was cold, the forecast for snow seemed unlikely, and we dismissed it, substituting our own more optimistic predictions for the weather.

We reached the Balsam Mountain Road and walked in three inches of snow to Pin Oak Gap, where we embarked on the Balsam Mountain Trail segment of our walk. The snow became deeper here, and care was required to climb or descend without slipping. Walking in the snow was enjoyable, however, and we were not pressed by time, so we moved at a relaxed pace to Laurel Gap.

Our arrival at the unoccupied Laurel Gap Shelter occurred mid-afternoon, and we wasted little time before engaging in the necessary chores of the camping ritual. The weather was decidedly colder—probably in the mid-twenties—and the skies were growing overcast. The sun moved behind the ridges and left the shelter in the cold shadows of late afternoon. The front of the shelter had a chain-link fence to separate humans and bears—an unlikely threat in cold weather. Previous campers had attached a sheet of translucent plastic to one side of the fencing to block the wind, and we placed our sleeping bags on this side to take advantage of the minimal protection it offered.

We prepared a hot meal and talked over cups of steaming tea, enjoying the golden glow of a flickering candle, the only light in our dark abode. Now the temperature was in the low twenties, and the wind blew in gusts. Given the cold and the wind, we concluded that our sleeping bags were the best defense against the elements.

A cold night at Laurel Gap, March 9, 1991.

I went to sleep to the sound of wind rattling the brittle plastic and slept soundly until about midnight, when I felt small pinpricks of cold against my face. It took me a few moments to realize that these pinpricks were wind-blown ice crystals. It was snowing! In brief periods of wakefulness afterward, I continued to feel this sensation as the snow fell throughout the night. The pleasure of being warm and comfortable in weather like this is one of the special joys of backpacking.

We awoke to a world of white. The ground was covered with eight to ten inches of fresh snow. The forest around the shelter clearing was cloaked with white, and the boughs of fir trees drooped under the weight of the accumulation. And the shelter fence had been turned into a pattern of lace with the effects of the frozen snow.

Our return was along the Mount Sterling Ridge Trail to Pretty Hollow Gap and by the Pretty Hollow Gap Trail to our starting point. We trudged through snow and admired the beauty about us. The scenery through which we passed had an exquisite beauty that has to be experienced because words seem inadequate to convey the imagery.

Perhaps my favorite scene of the day, the one that is preserved in memory, was near Pretty Hollow Gap. I looked back on the path that we had followed and viewed the snow-covered trail, some eight feet wide, bordered by a growth of hardwood trees. The previous night's winds had blown the snow across the top of the ridge, coating the trunks and limbs of trees. It was a scene composed of white, with the only other apparent colors being the grays and browns of tree trunks that faced away from the wind. It seemed mystical, heightened by my recollection of a wild night of wind and snow and the inspiring scenery that Marv and I had enjoyed during the morning.

We completed our walk in Cataloochee Valley without incident. It had been an enjoyable outing, one shared with a good friend. Marv was a hearty backpacking companion who dealt with the cold, wind and snow without complaint—a trait among many that I admired in him.

Like an Ocean

Hughes Ridge Trail

January 16, 2006

Marilyn, Ron, Jerry and I planned a largely off-trail trip to explore a forgotten logging incline; however, snow-covered slopes made this infeasible, and we debated whether to abort our planned walk. Because the time for this decision arrived when we were high up on the Chasteen Creek Trail, we had to decide between turning back or continuing our walk on a much longer trip. Ultimately, the decision was made to continue and make a loop that entailed climbing to the Hughes Ridge Trail and following it to the Bradley Fork Trail, which we would then follow back to Smokemont to complete our loop.

Walking in snow has its special pleasures. The forest through which we walked was a collage of muted colors—shades of gray, brown and black—that contrasted with the white of the snow. In the shaded coves, the shadows gave another dimension to these bleak woods. The higher slopes above us reflected the sun with a brilliant white radiance. As we approached the summit, gray clouds replaced the blue skies that we had enjoyed at the beginning of our walk.

We reached the crest of Hughes Ridge at noon. The depth of the snow here was eight to ten inches, and we expected to encounter greater depths where the wind had piled drifts across the trail. The next two and a half miles provided an interesting study of snowdrifts. High winds had sculpted drifts resembling soft, undulating ocean waves. The only difference between the drifts and ocean waves is that the drifts did not move as waves do. Thus, we faced static barriers to be continuously negotiated. I was interested to

A snowy trail on the crest of Hughes Ridge, January 16, 2006.

note that while the wind had piled the snow in drifts, it had left patches of open, leaf-covered earth as if there had been no snow at all. Also, the snow was not completely white. The high winds that swept the crest to create the snowdrifts had also deposited a dusting of sandlike particles of bark, leaves and grit across the blanket, giving it a somewhat gray appearance.

The general depth of the snow increased as we moved higher, and we forced our way through drifts at least two feet deep with regularity. This was a small price to pay for the enjoyment of a beautiful winter landscape and rewarding views of familiar Smoky Mountain landmarks shared with friends. By 3:30 p.m. we reached the upper terminus of the Bradley Fork Trail and began our walk to Smokemont. We arrived there after dark, tired and with various aches and pains from our sixteen-mile walk. It had all been worth the exertion to enjoy the Smokies at the height of winter.

Epilogue

Mountain Farm Museum and Collins Creek Picnic Area
October 19, 2008

Alice and I chose an exceptional autumn day for a family outing in the Smokies, a day brushed with a brilliant palette of seasonal colors framed by the bluest sky. I felt blessed to share this special day with those I love most: daughter Sara and her husband, Scott Stewart; son Bill and his wife, Lisa, and their son, Will; and Alice, my partner for forty-eight years. Our plan was a simple one. We planned to visit the Mountain Farm Museum, followed by a picnic at the Collins Creek Picnic Area.

We began at the museum and walked along the path that led us past the handsome Davis cabin and an assemblage of farm buildings located on the site from various parts of the Smokies. These structures served to demonstrate dimensions of mountain life and farming from another era. Will, who was almost four, displayed keen interest in each structure and directed many questions to his mother and father, as well as to his grandparents, about the purpose of the meat house, chicken house, apple house and corncrib and bee gums.

When we passed through the barn with chickens scampering here and there, Will marveled at its size and craned his neck to look into the loft high above. Beyond the barn, we reached the pigpen, which proved to be the highlight of Will's day. He looked through the rails of the pen and watched two hogs jostle and push each other playfully. This entertainment produced a ready supply of smiles and laughter from Will, who was completely enthralled by their antics.

Lisa and Will Hart exploring the Mountain Farm Museum, October 19, 2008.

Ultimately, we strolled along the path beside the beautiful Oconaluftee River and watched the clear stream as fallen leaves drifted and swirled in its currents. When our visit to the museum ended, we continued to Collins Creek. Our simple picnic there was accompanied by conversation and laughter beneath trees with withered leaves that whispered when touched by the gentle breezes. Will took delight in sliding his feet in drifted leaves, creating a rhythmic cadence as he walked. When our picnic concluded, we returned home, taking with us pleasant memories of our day in the Smokies.

In the week that followed, I reflected on this time of family fellowship. We had walked along the path beside the Oconaluftee River, where Native Americans had placed their feet for eons before the arrival of the first settlers. We had briefly visited the place where pioneers first homesteaded long before the national park and the Pioneer Farm Museum were first conceived. Our picnic site was located where Robert Collins and his sons—who served as guides for such noteworthy explorers as Arnold Guyot and Thomas L. Clingman—once lived and farmed. In effect, we had immersed ourselves in elements of the history of the Great Smokies. Additionally, Alice and I enjoyed visiting places that were part of our childhood memories, places that we ultimately shared with our children during their lifetimes.

Yes, we had enjoyed the Smokies, but there was another important dimension to this occasion. Alice and I had shared our first day in the

Will enjoying the antics of the hogs at the Mountain Farm Museum, October 19, 2008.

Smokies with our grandson, Will. And in so doing, we hoped to create in him a flickering flame of interest in the Great Smokies, the same flame kindled in us as children by parents who introduced us to the park. Our prayer is that Will, as he grows to adulthood, will develop a love and appreciation for the Great Smoky Mountains National Park and experience the joy and wonder in these majestic mountains that we have. And Alice and I pray that the Smokies will exist undisturbed as a special place for the generations that follow.

POSTSCRIPT

Visitors to the Great Smoky Mountains National Park will experience many rewards. At the same time, they have an obligation to be familiar with and abide by the rules that govern park use. All who visit, especially those who hike park trails and visit the backcountry, should ensure that they are fully prepared for the conditions they will face. Mistakes can result in injury and death.

Will begins his life in the Great Smokies, October 19, 2008.

About the Author

Alice Hart photograph.

Bill Hart is a native of western North Carolina. Before retirement, he enjoyed a forty-year career largely devoted to human resource management, training and consulting. He is a student of regional history with a special interest in the Great Smoky Mountains National Park. He served as a hiker/writer for *Hiking Trails of the Smokies*, published by the Great Smoky Mountain Association, and contributed a number of trail narratives to this publication. He has written two articles about renowned Japanese photographer George Masa, whose early photographs were influential in creating a desire to preserve the Great Smokies as a national park. These appeared in the first volume of *May We All Remember Well* and in the seventy-fifth-anniversary issue of *Smokies Life* magazine. He is a life member of the Great Smoky Mountains Association and the Appalachian Trail Conservancy. In addition to hiking more than three thousand miles in the Great Smokies, Bill section-hiked the Appalachian Trail, completing it in 2002.

Visit us at
www.historypress.net

www.ingramcontent.com/pod-product-compliance
Lightning Source LLC
LaVergne TN
LVHW010942100826
845153LV00002B/123
* 9 7 8 1 5 4 0 2 2 9 3 5 9 *